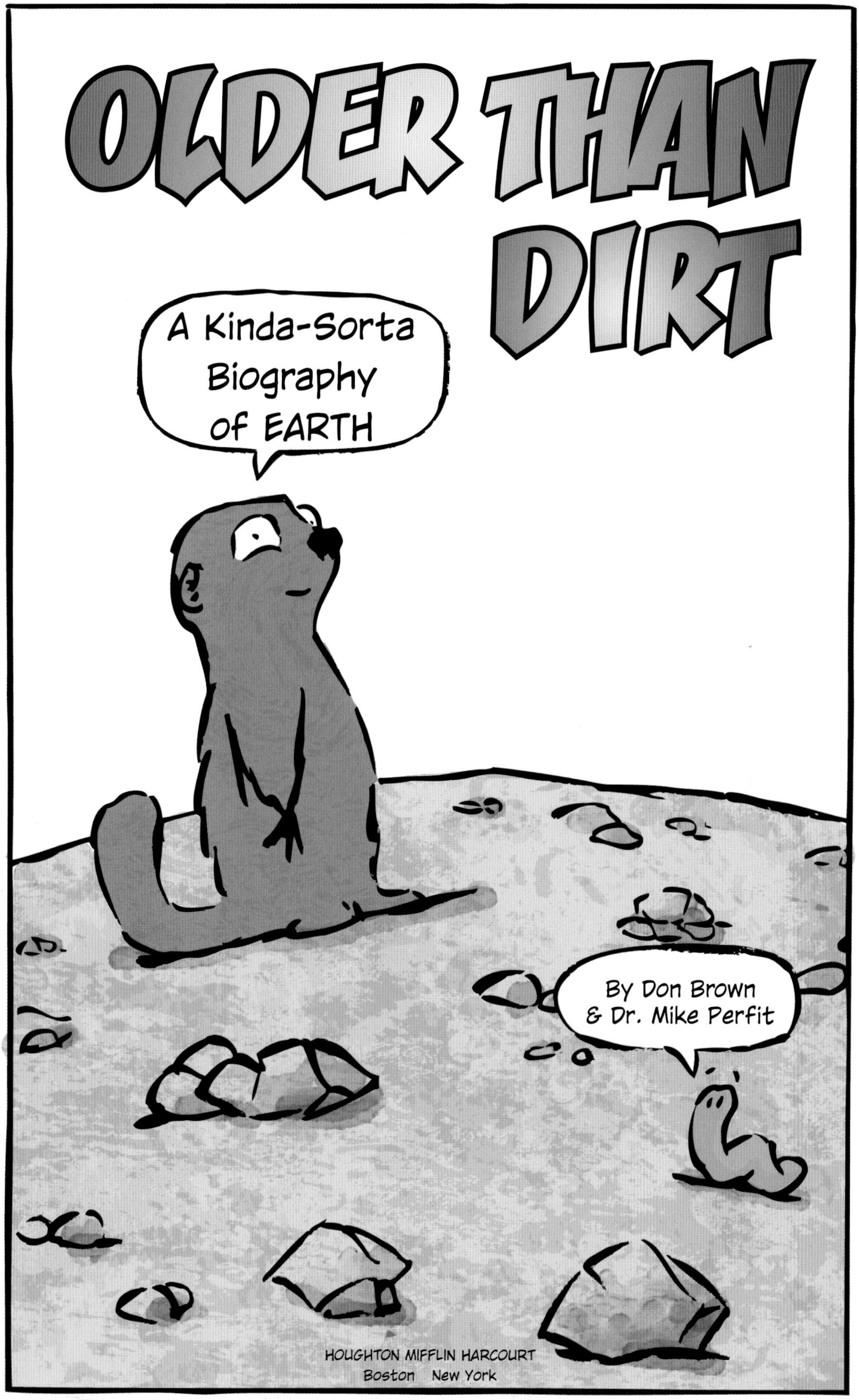
OLDER THAN DIRT
A Kinda-Sorta Biography of EARTH
By Don Brown & Dr. Mike Perfit
HOUGHTON MIFFLIN HARCOURT
Boston New York

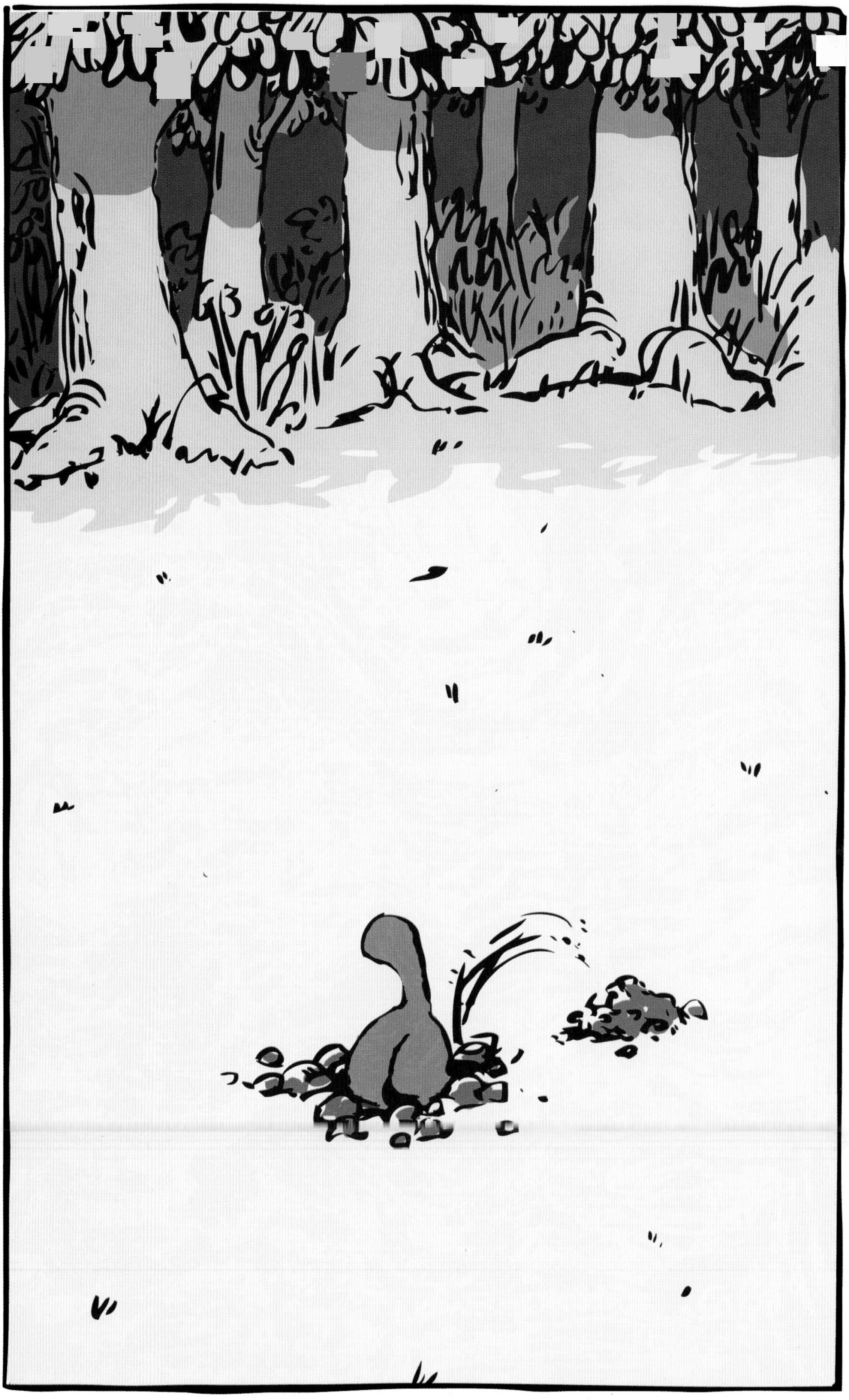

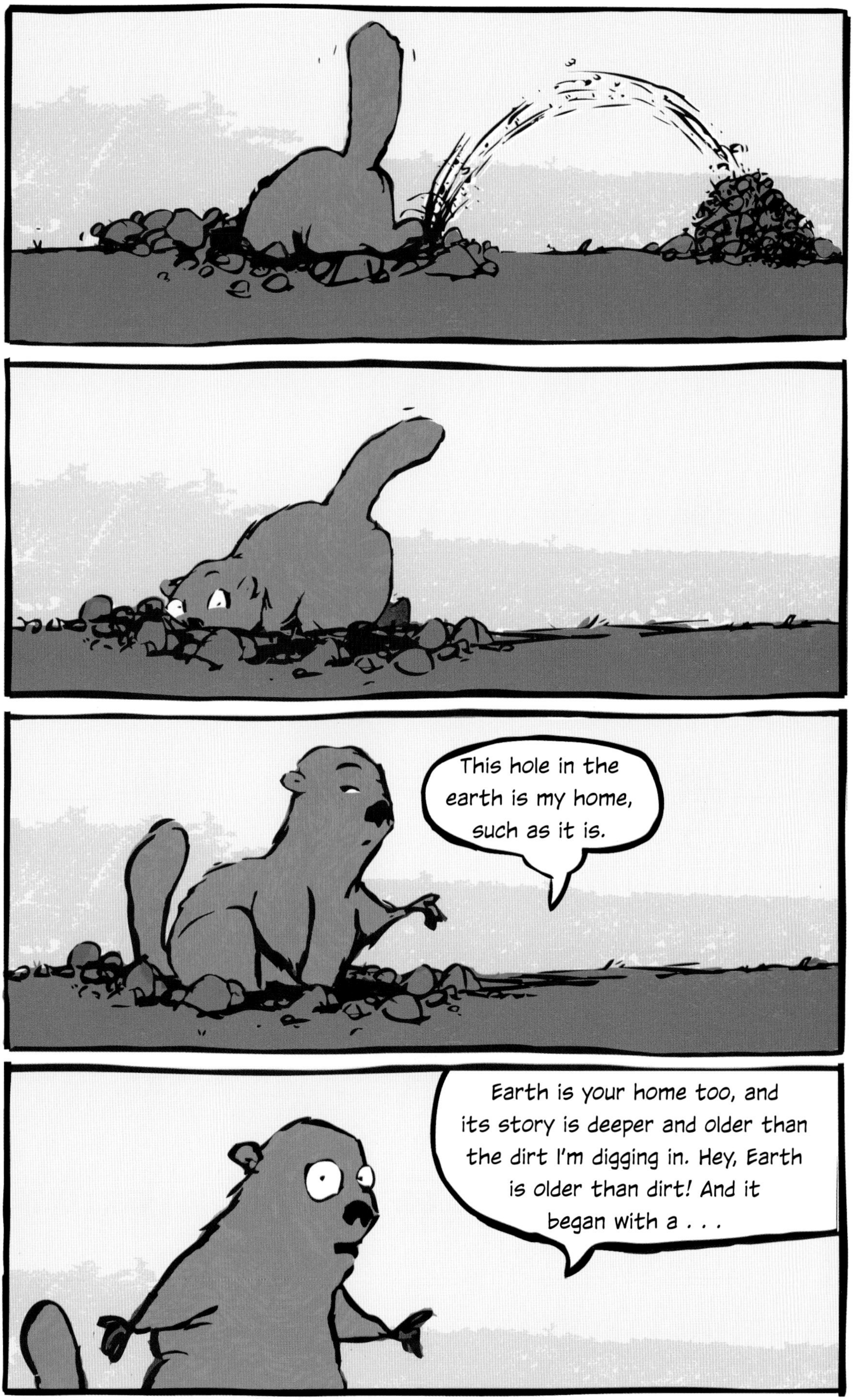
This hole in the earth is my home, such as it is.
Earth is your home too, and its story is deeper and older than the dirt I'm digging in. Hey, Earth is older than dirt! And it began with a . . .

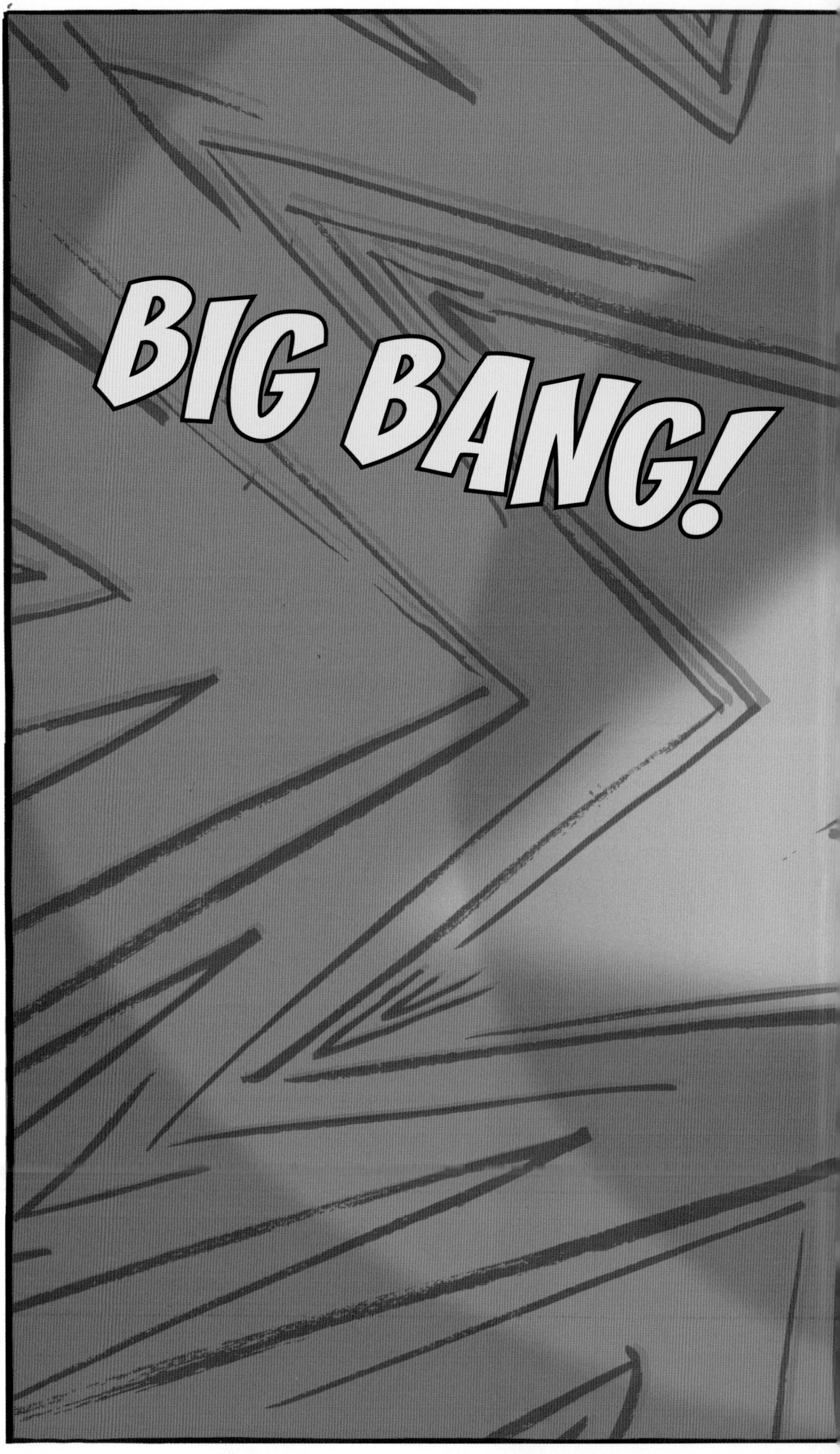
BIG BANG!

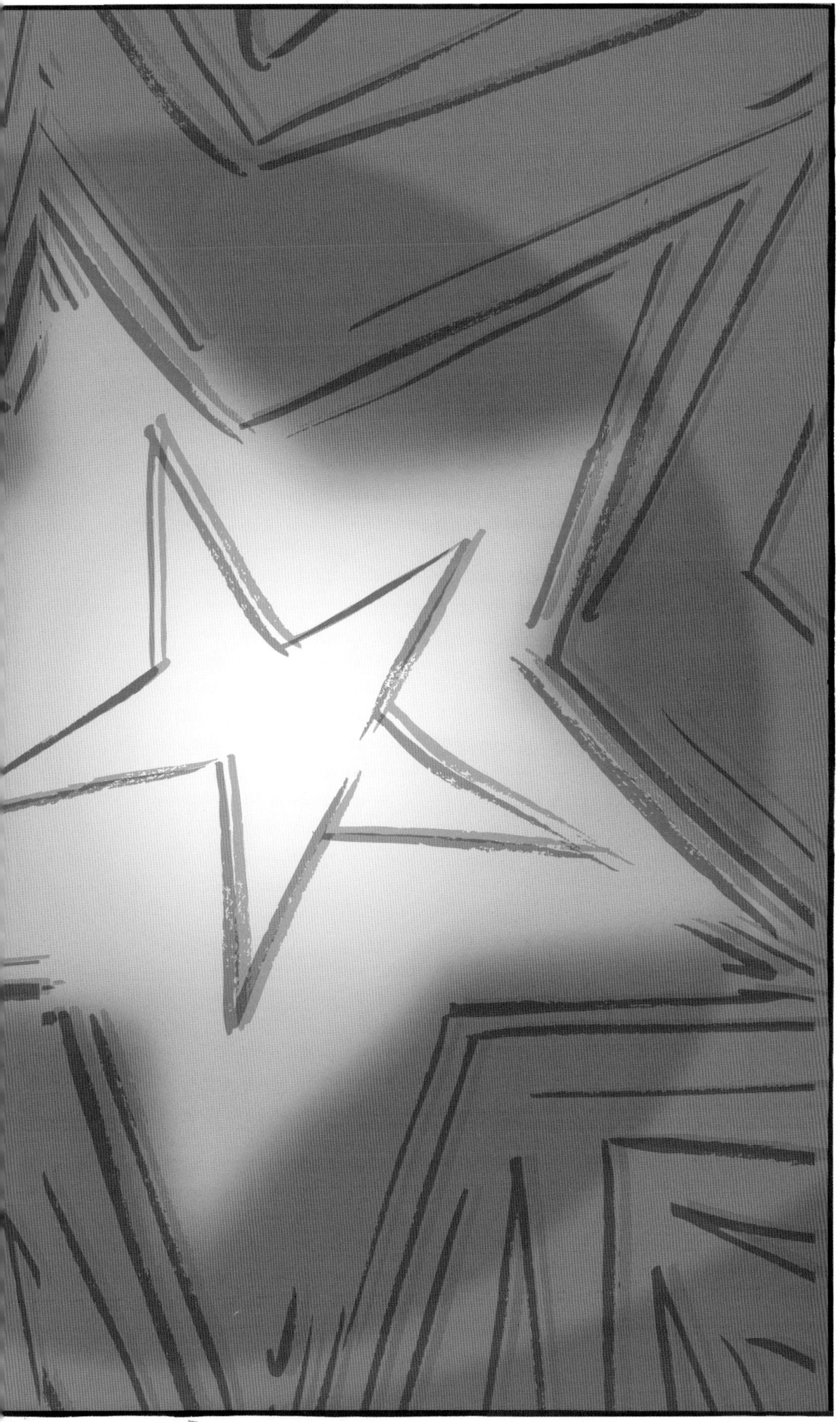

The universe exploded into existence about 14,000,000,000 years ago.
The familiar globe we call Earth wasn't there at first. Instead, there was a cloud of rock, dust, and gas. The rock and dust collided to make clumps.

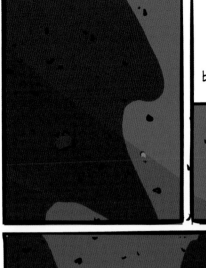

The clumps grew and grew, joined by gravity, the force that pulls objects together. Apples don't *fall* from trees but are *drawn* to the ground by gravity.

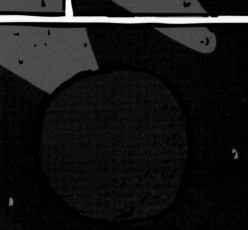

The clumps swirled around to make our solar system and sun. About 4.5 billion years ago, some of the clumps joined together to make Earth.

It was no place for a hole-digging groundhog!

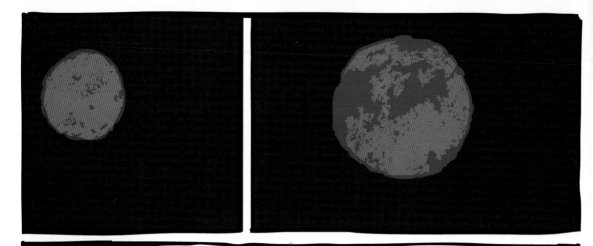

Oceans of fiery molten rock washed over the planet.

Cooled by icy outer space, a black crust formed on the outside, while inside remained red-hot magma. Earth was like a giant toasted marshmallow.

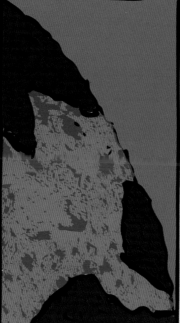

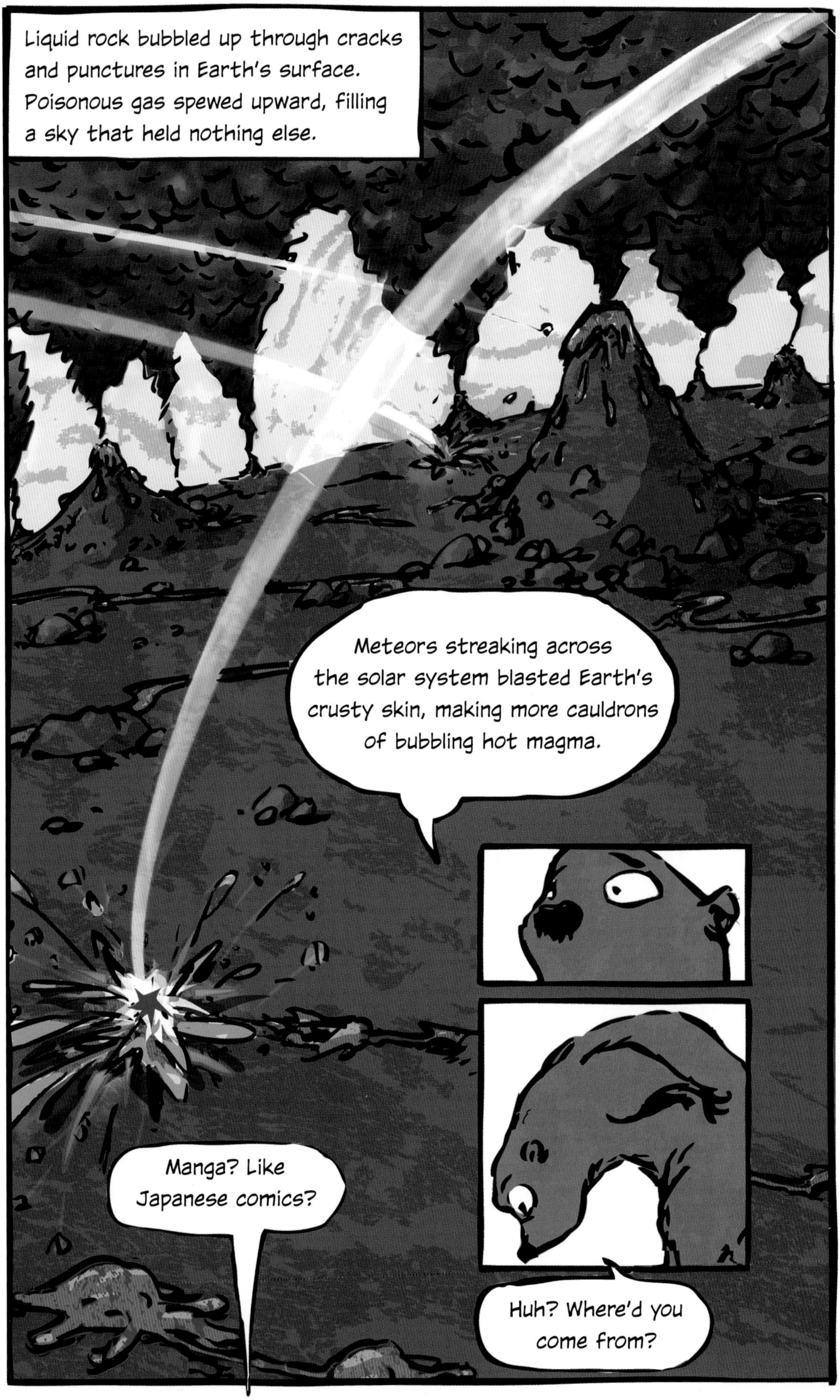
Liquid rock bubbled up through cracks and punctures in Earth's surface. Poisonous gas spewed upward, filling a sky that held nothing else.
Meteors streaking across the solar system blasted Earth's crusty skin, making more cauldrons of bubbling hot magma.
Manga? Like Japanese comics?
Huh? Where'd you come from?

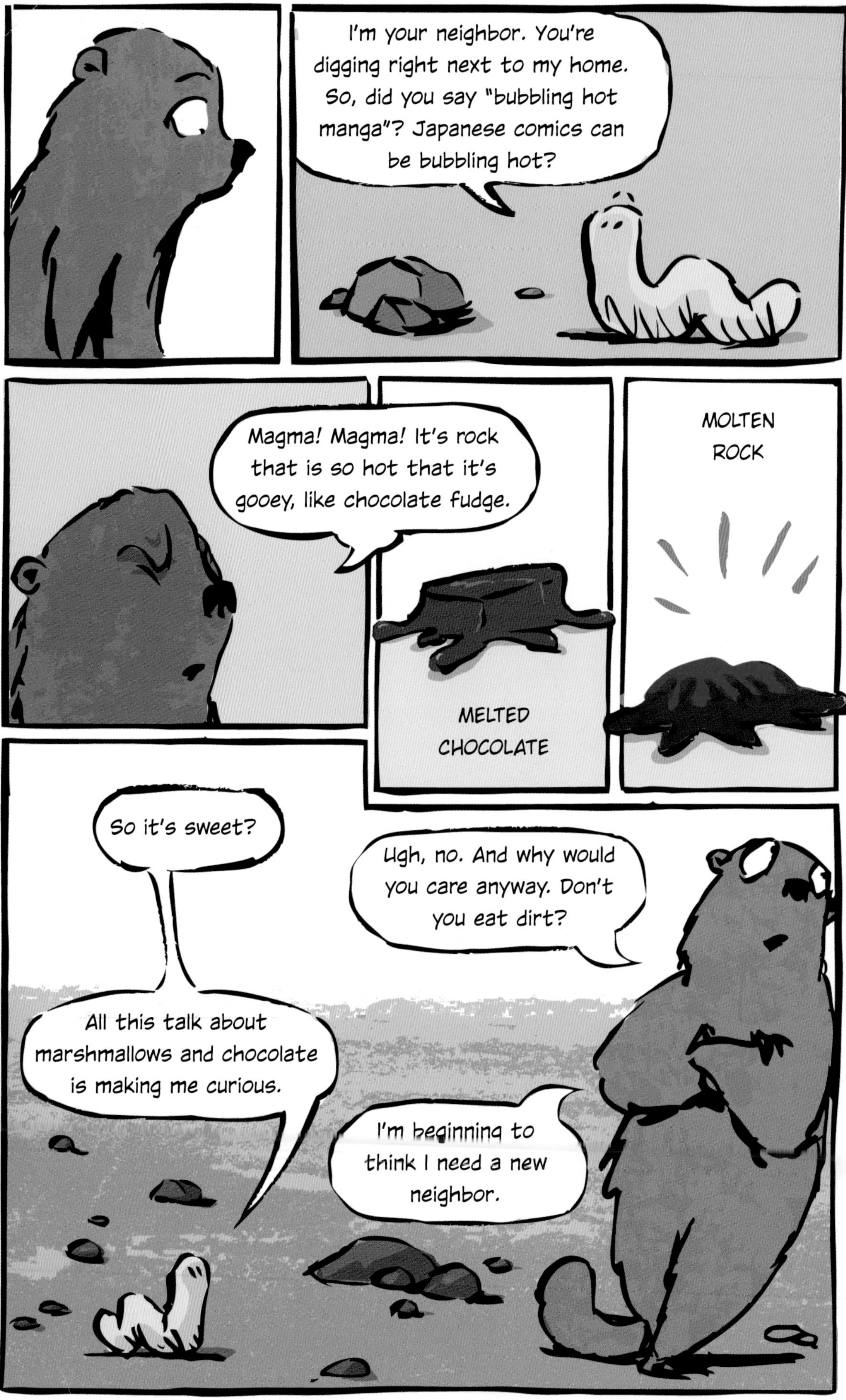

I'm your neighbor. You're digging right next to my home. So, did you say "bubbling hot manga"? Japanese comics can be bubbling hot?
Magma! Magma! It's rock that is so hot that it's gooey, like chocolate fudge.
MELTED CHOCOLATE
MOLTEN ROCK
So it's sweet?
Ugh, no. And why would you care anyway. Don't you eat dirt?
All this talk about marshmallows and chocolate is making me curious.
I'm beginning to think I need a new neighbor.

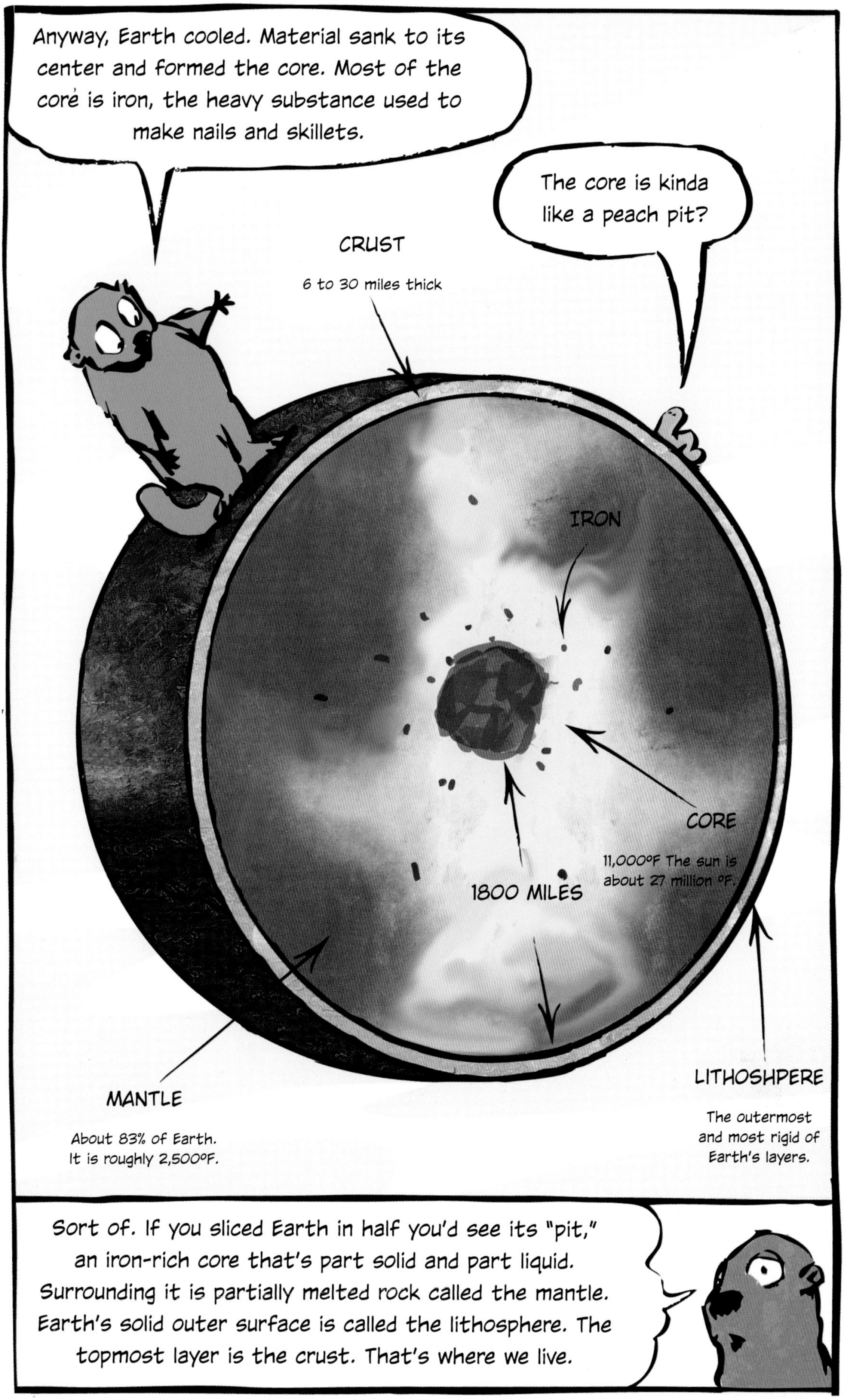

Anyway, Earth cooled. Material sank to its center and formed the core. Most of the core is iron, the heavy substance used to make nails and skillets.
The core is kinda like a peach pit?
CRUST
6 to 30 miles thick
IRON
CORE
11,000°F The sun is about 27 million °F.
1800 MILES
MANTLE
About 83% of Earth. It is roughly 2,500°F.
LITHOSHPERE
The outermost and most rigid of Earth's layers.
Sort of. If you sliced Earth in half you'd see its "pit," an iron-rich core that's part solid and part liquid. Surrounding it is partially melted rock called the mantle. Earth's solid outer surface is called the lithosphere. The topmost layer is the crust. That's where we live.

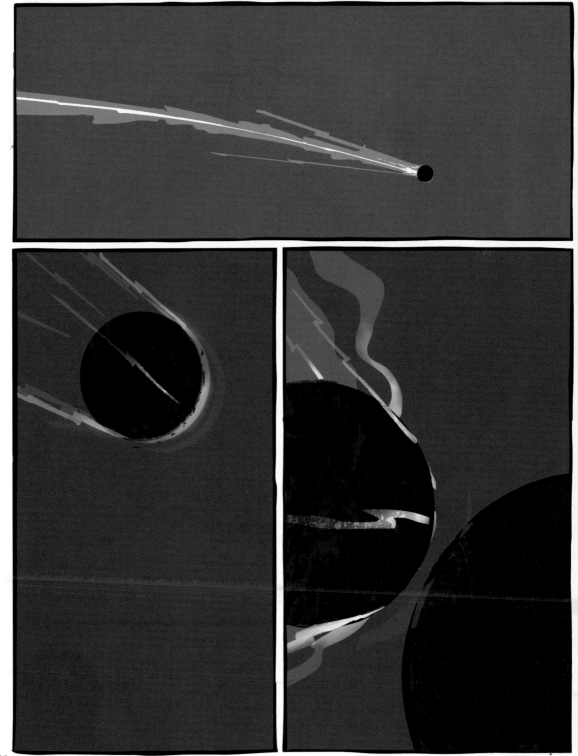

Then while young Earth was still forming, something REALLY BIG happened.

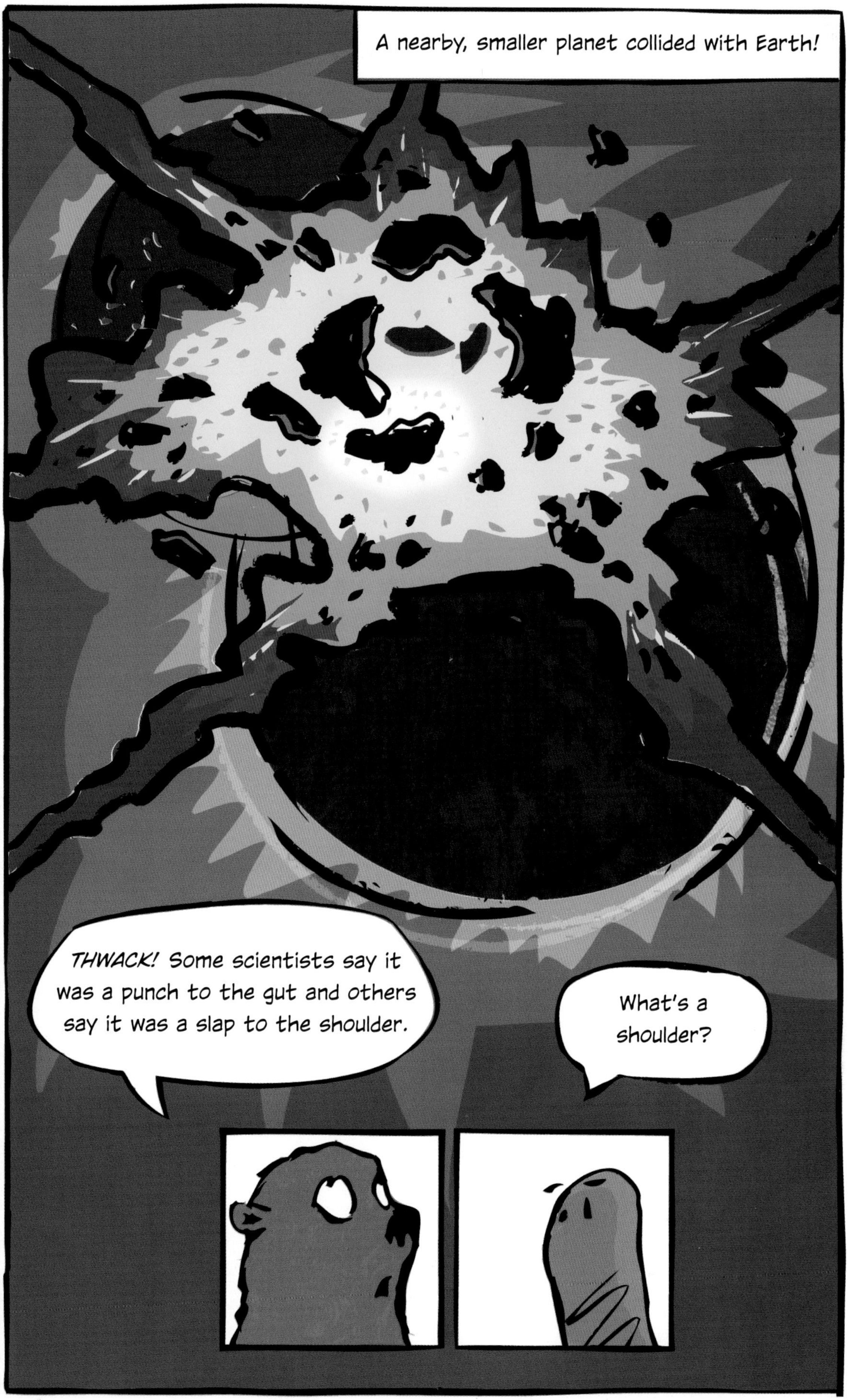
A nearby, smaller planet collided with Earth!
THWACK! Some scientists say it was a punch to the gut and others say it was a slap to the shoulder.
What's a shoulder?

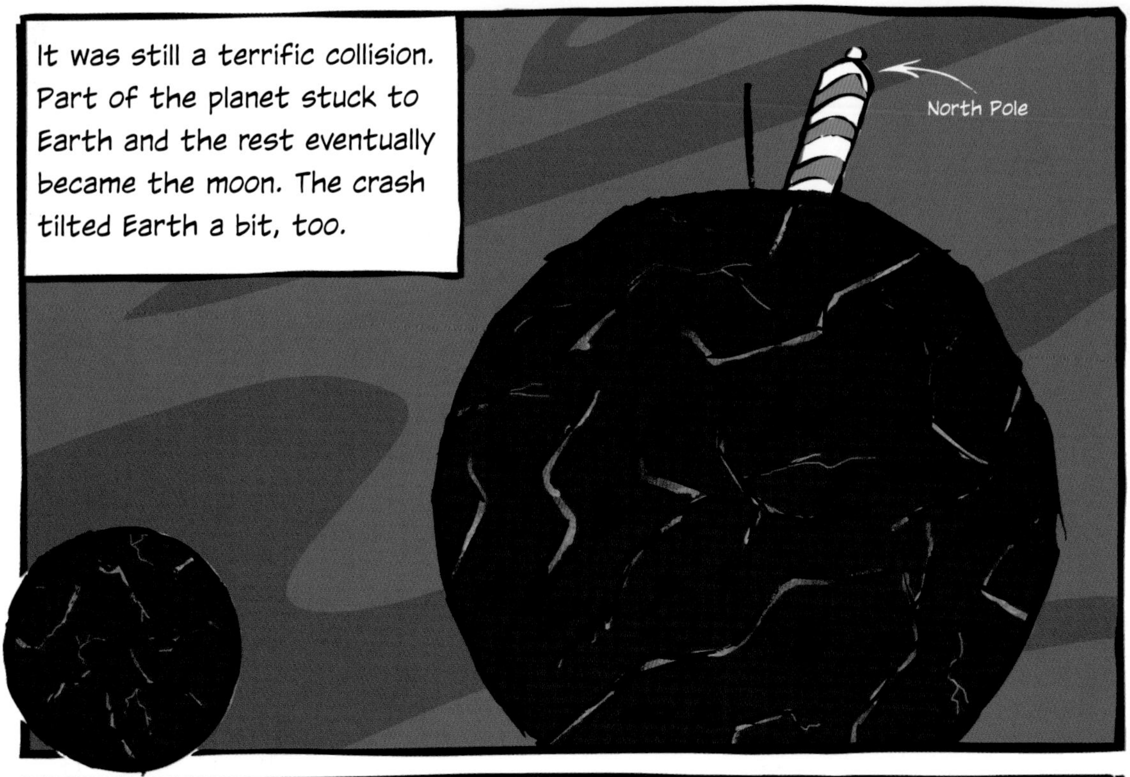
It was still a terrific collision. Part of the planet stuck to Earth and the rest eventually became the moon. The crash tilted Earth a bit, too.
North Pole

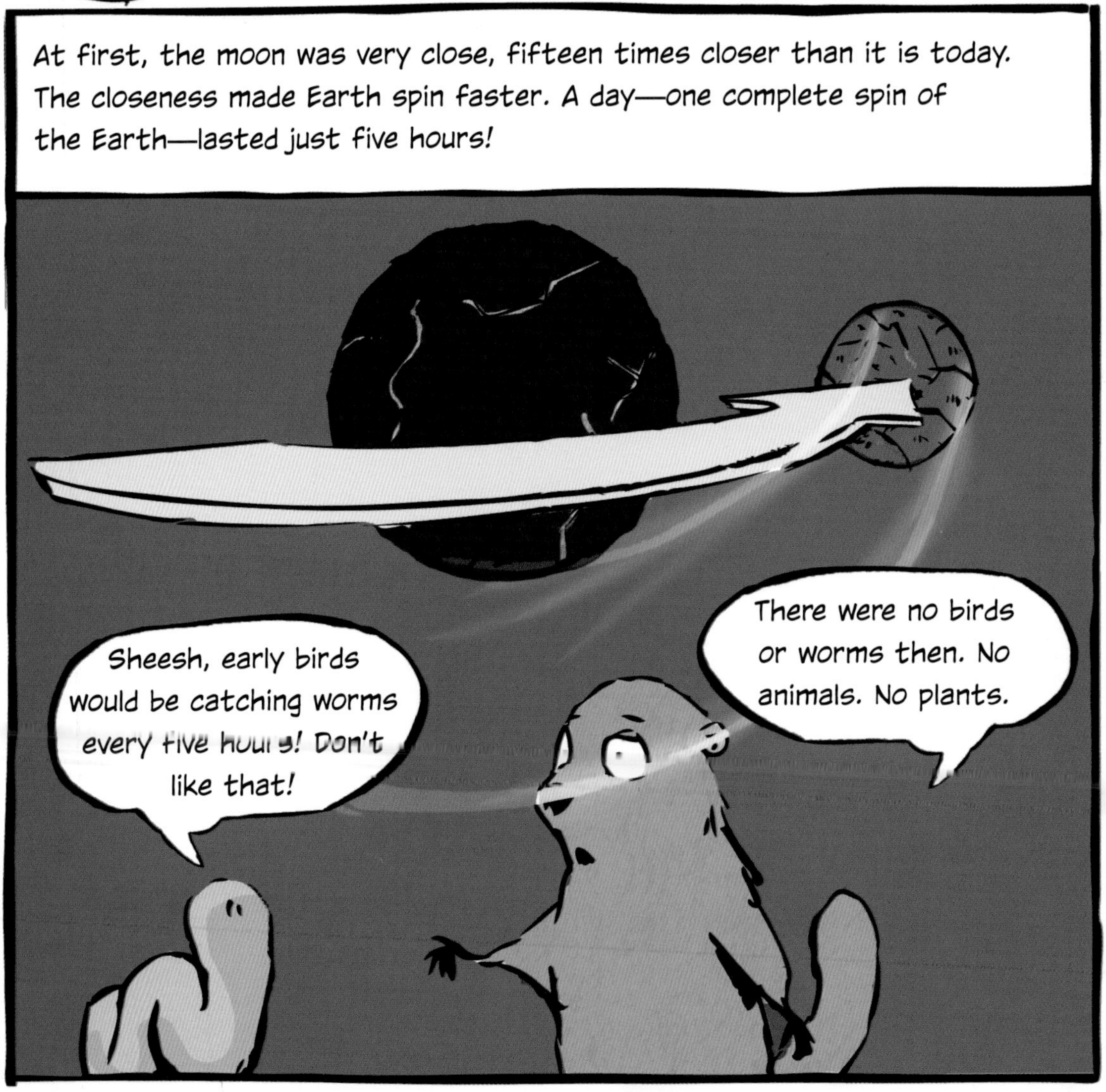
At first, the moon was very close, fifteen times closer than it is today. The closeness made Earth spin faster. A day—one complete spin of the Earth—lasted just five hours!
Sheesh, early birds would be catching worms every five hours! Don't like that!
There were no birds or worms then. No animals. No plants.

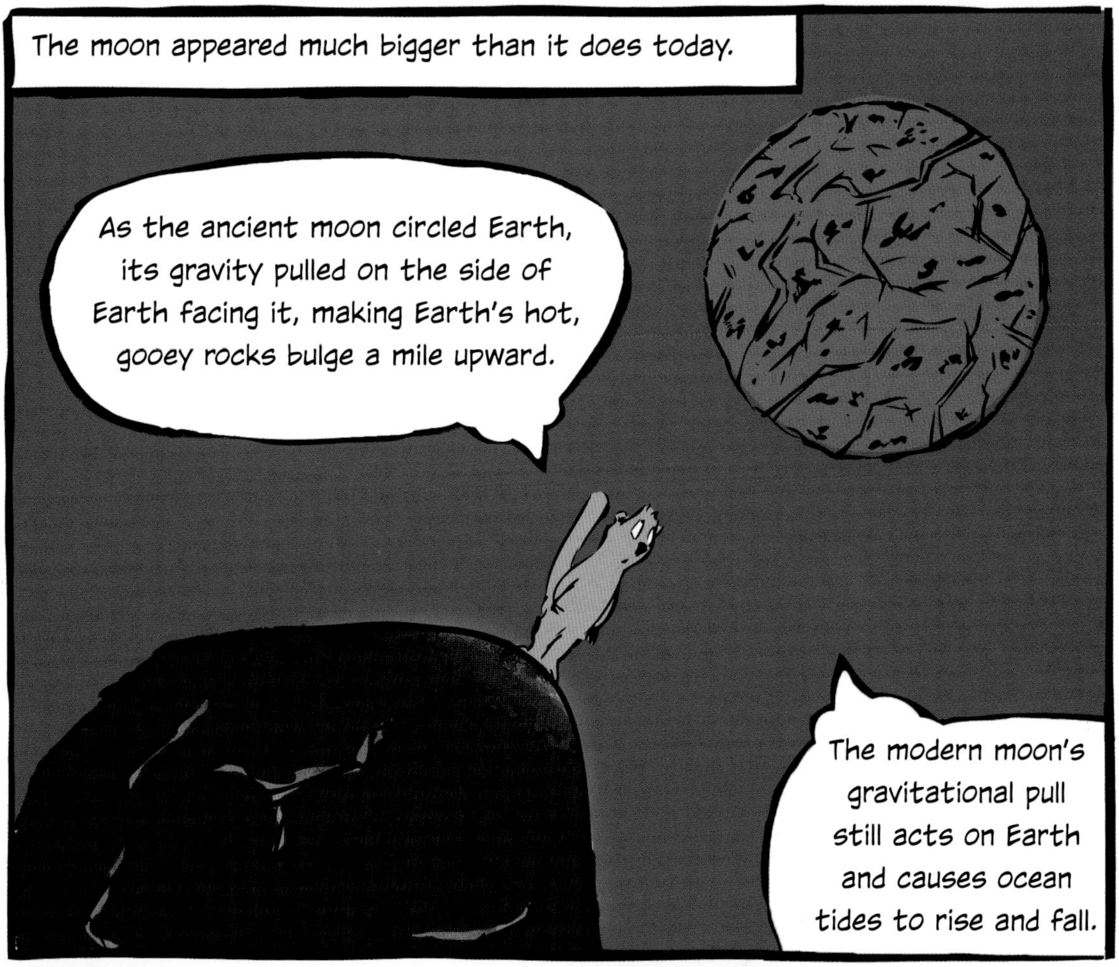
The moon appeared much bigger than it does today.
As the ancient moon circled Earth, its gravity pulled on the side of Earth facing it, making Earth's hot, gooey rocks bulge a mile upward.
The modern moon's gravitational pull still acts on Earth and causes ocean tides to rise and fall.

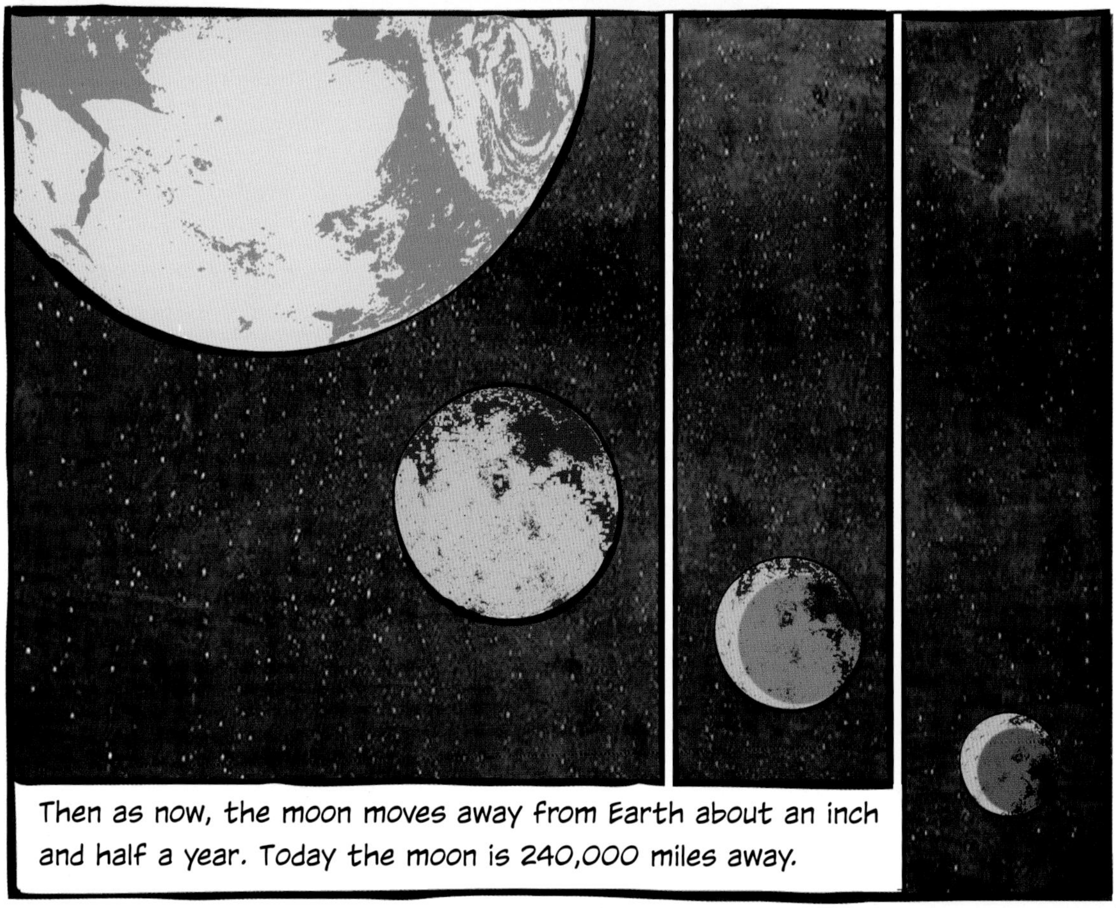
Then as now, the moon moves away from Earth about an inch and half a year. Today the moon is 240,000 miles away.

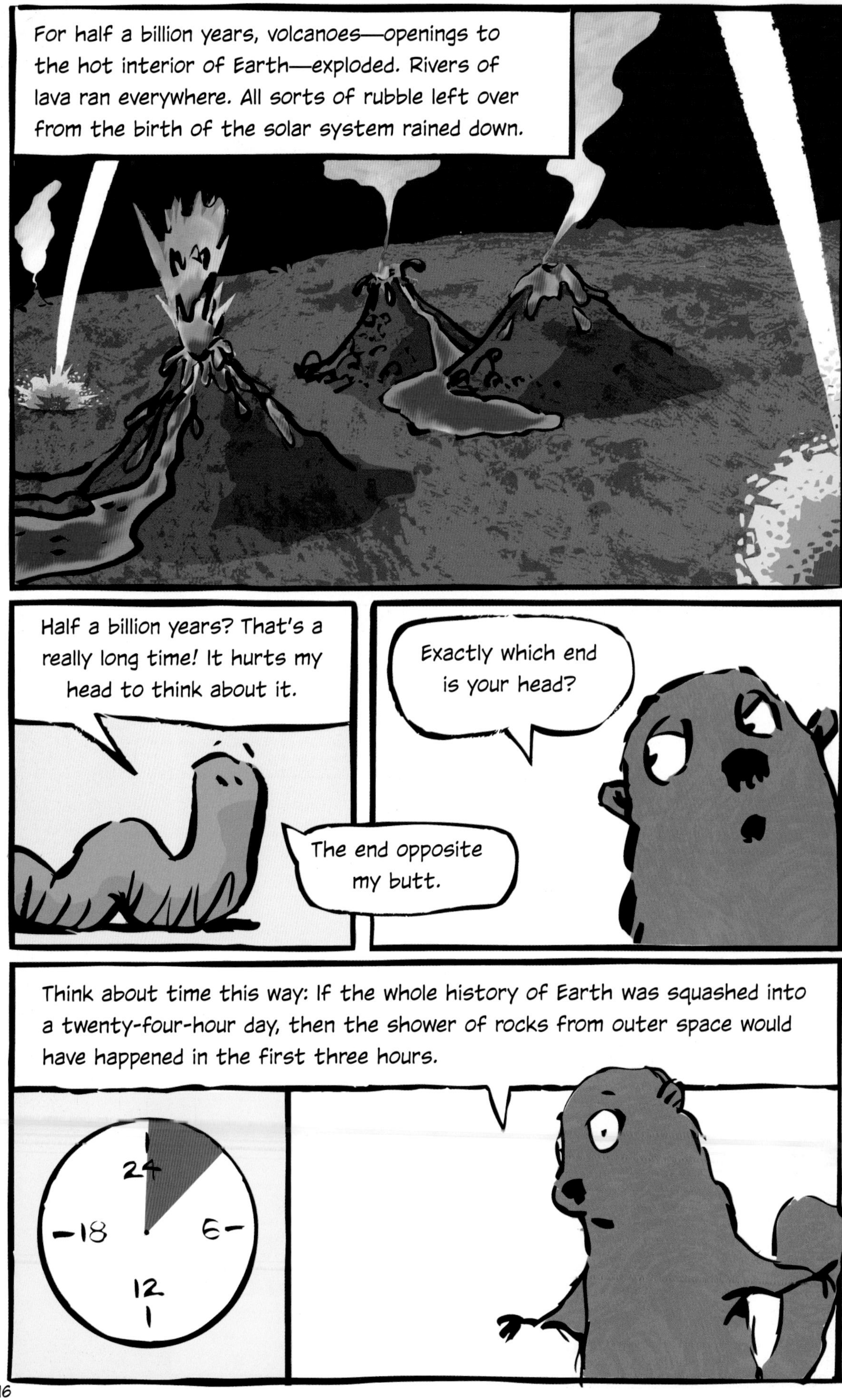
For half a billion years, volcanoes—openings to the hot interior of Earth—exploded. Rivers of lava ran everywhere. All sorts of rubble left over from the birth of the solar system rained down.
Half a billion years? That's a really long time! It hurts my head to think about it.
Exactly which end is your head?
The end opposite my butt.
Think about time this way: If the whole history of Earth was squashed into a twenty-four-hour day, then the shower of rocks from outer space would have happened in the first three hours.
24
6
12
18

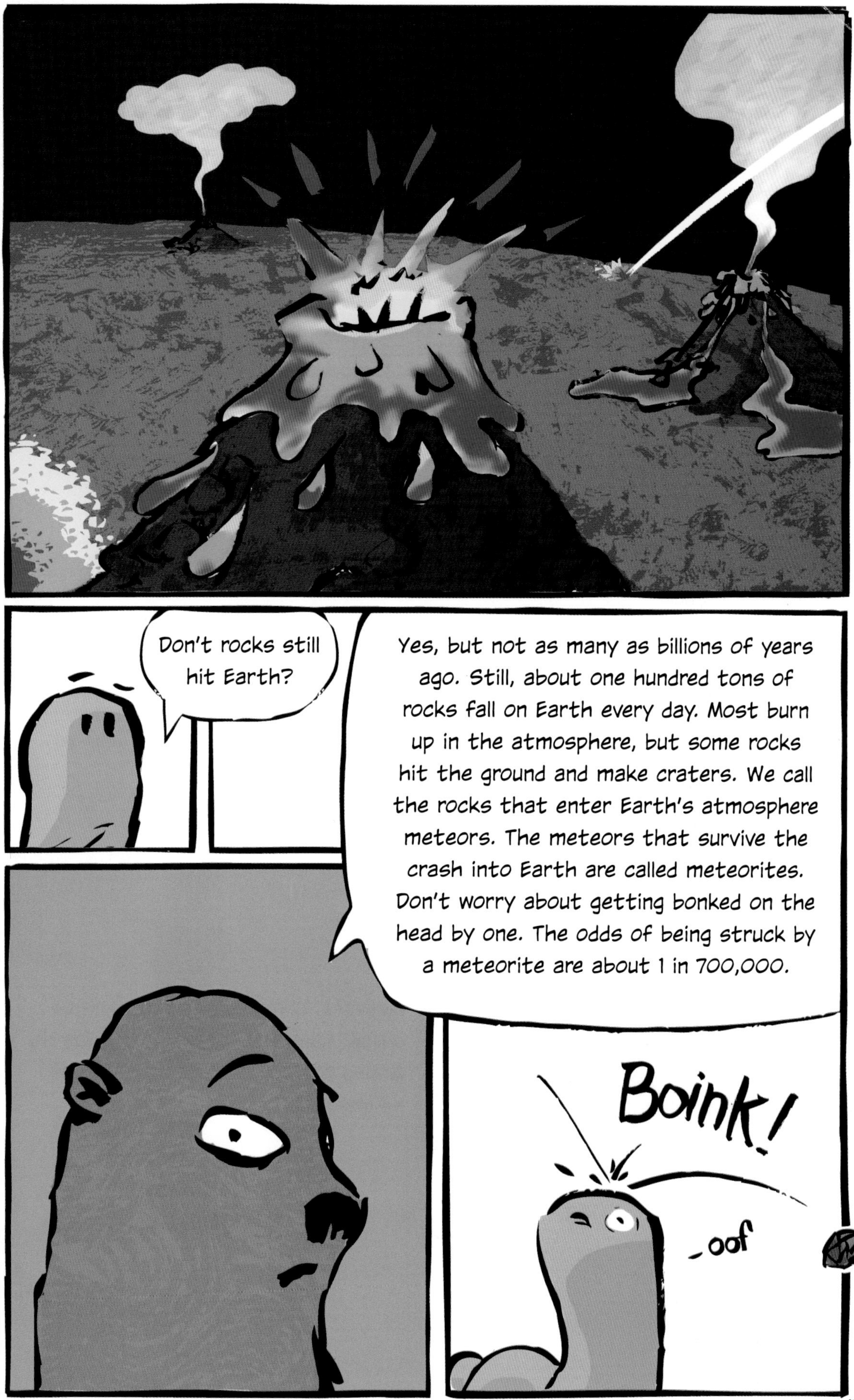
Don't rocks still hit Earth?
Yes, but not as many as billions of years ago. Still, about one hundred tons of rocks fall on Earth every day. Most burn up in the atmosphere, but some rocks hit the ground and make craters. We call the rocks that enter Earth's atmosphere meteors. The meteors that survive the crash into Earth are called meteorites. Don't worry about getting bonked on the head by one. The odds of being struck by a meteorite are about 1 in 700,000.
Boink!
-oof

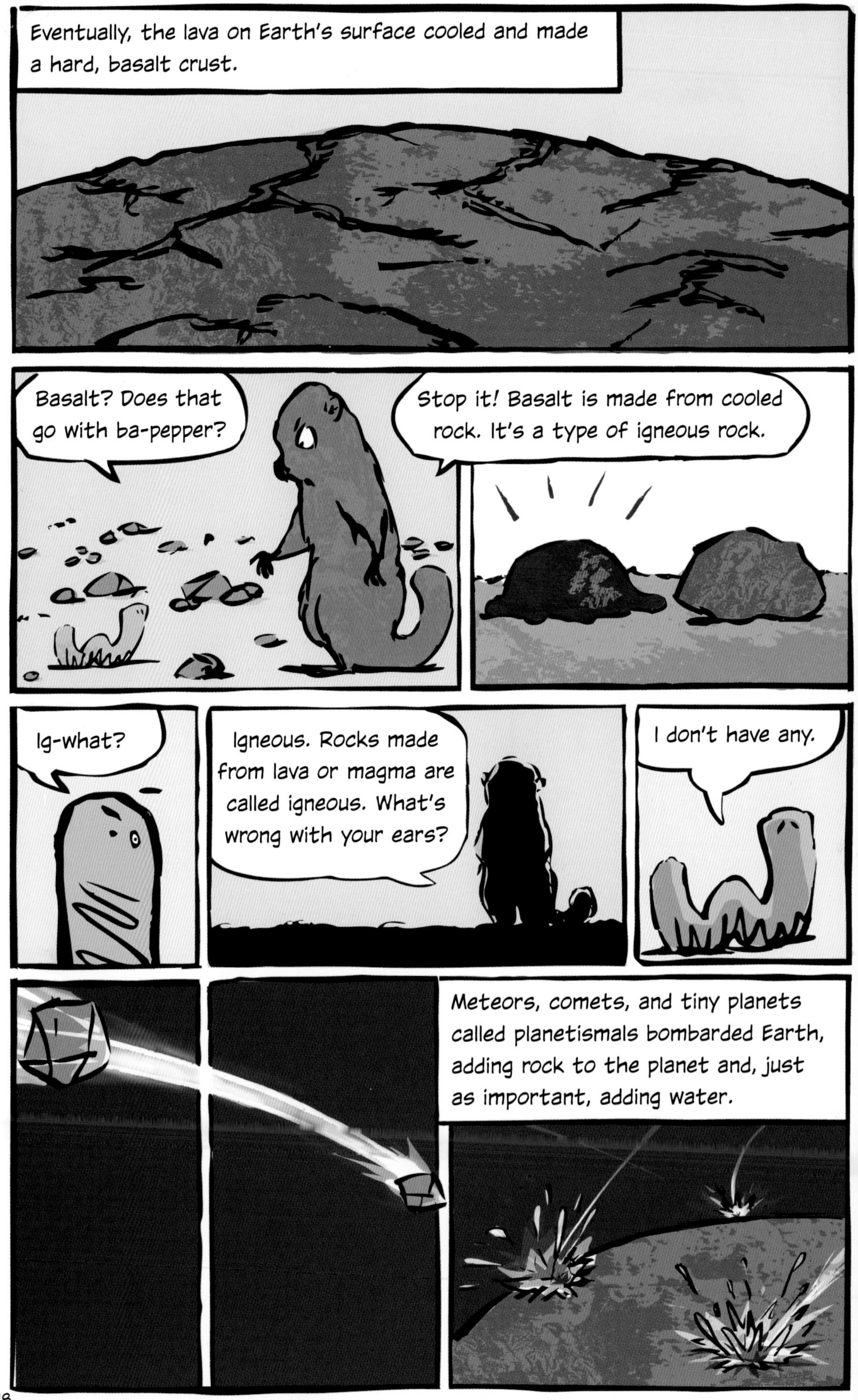
Eventually, the lava on Earth's surface cooled and made a hard, basalt crust.
Basalt? Does that go with ba-pepper?
Stop it! Basalt is made from cooled rock. It's a type of igneous rock.
Ig-what?
Igneous. Rocks made from lava or magma are called igneous. What's wrong with your ears?
I don't have any.
Meteors, comets, and tiny planets called planetismals bombarded Earth, adding rock to the planet and, just as important, adding water.

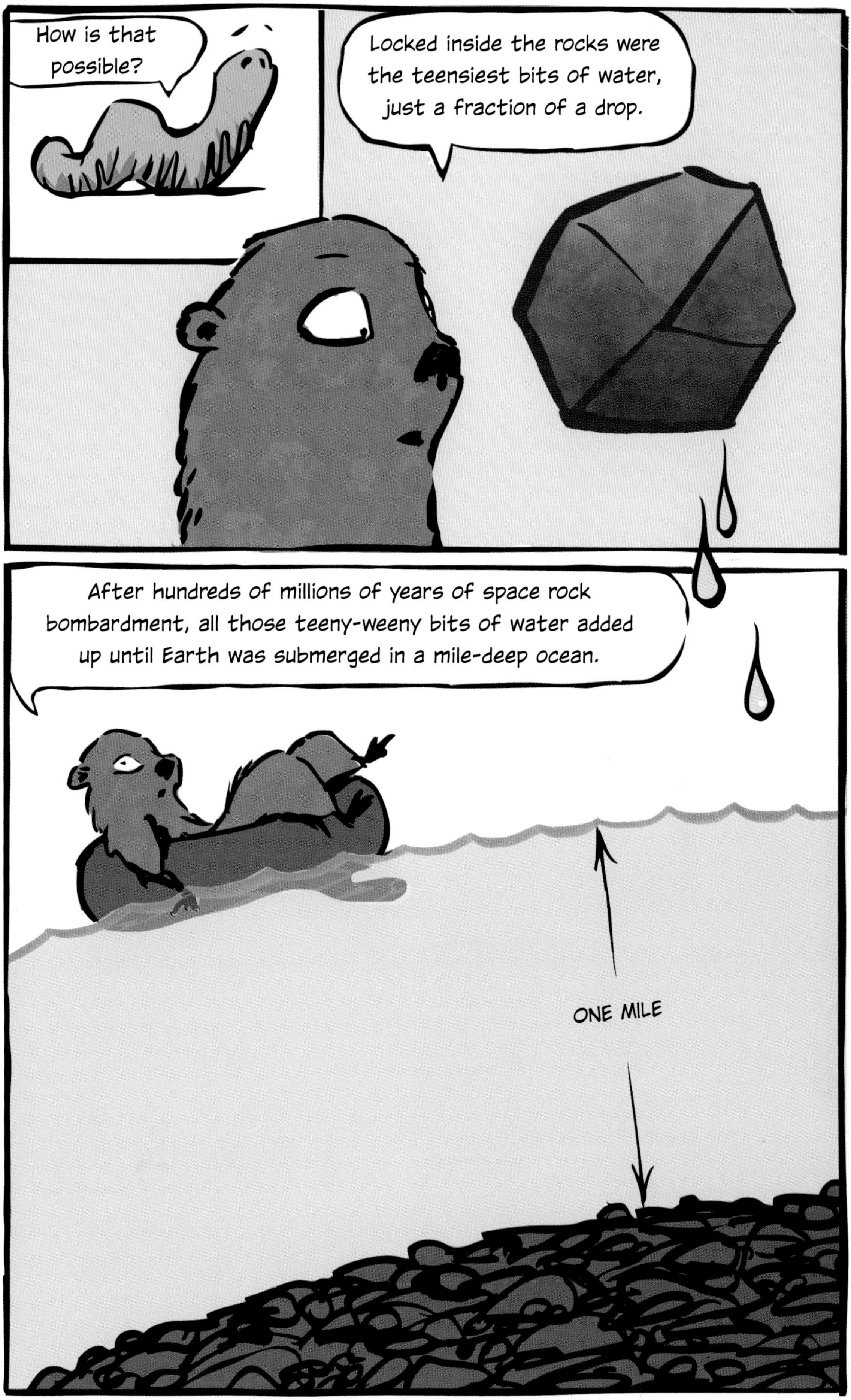
How is that possible?
Locked inside the rocks were the teensiest bits of water, just a fraction of a drop.
After hundreds of millions of years of space rock bombardment, all those teeny-weeny bits of water added up until Earth was submerged in a mile-deep ocean.
ONE MILE

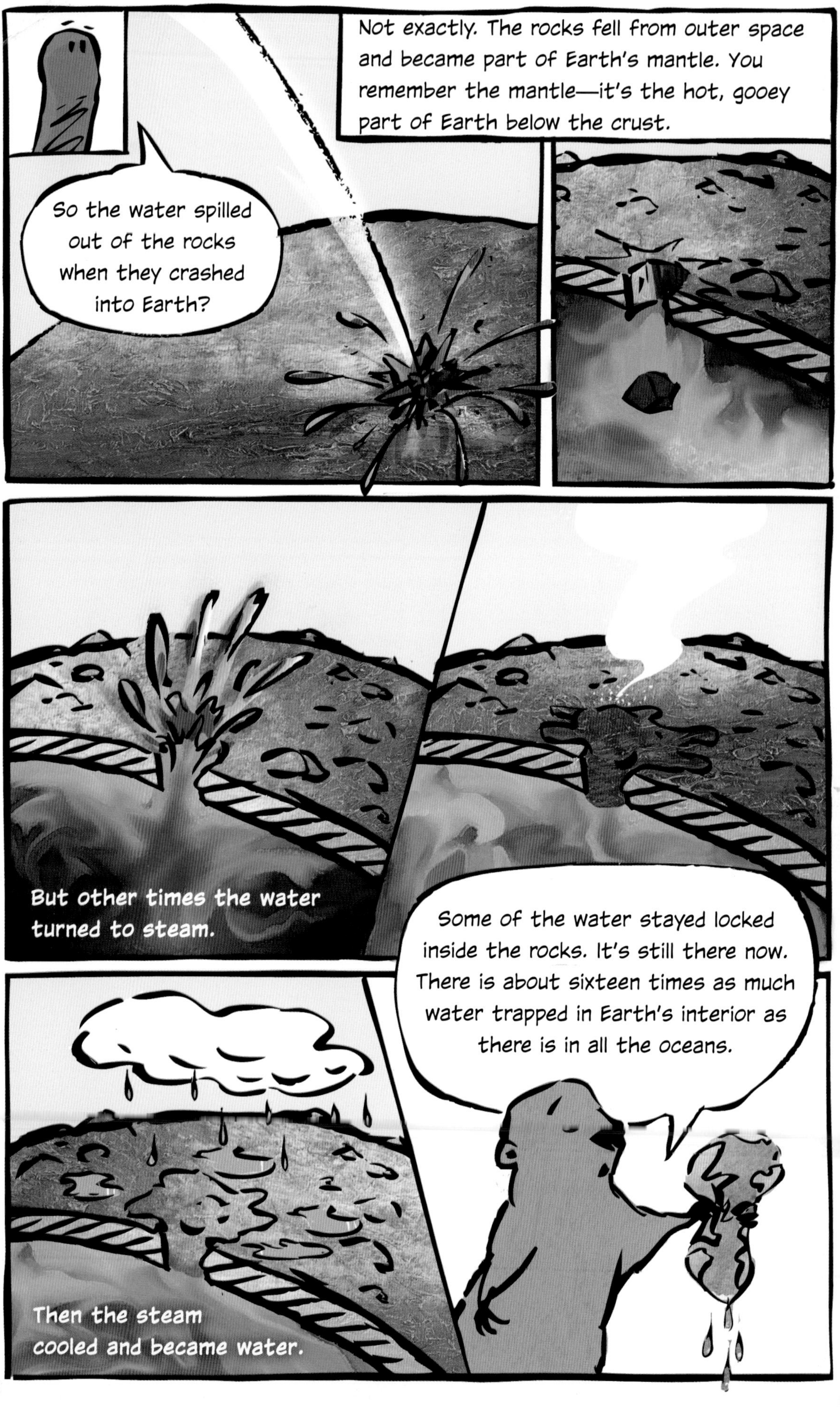
Not exactly. The rocks fell from outer space and became part of Earth's mantle. You remember the mantle—it's the hot, gooey part of Earth below the crust.
So the water spilled out of the rocks when they crashed into Earth?
But other times the water turned to steam.
Some of the water stayed locked inside the rocks. It's still there now. There is about sixteen times as much water trapped in Earth's interior as there is in all the oceans.
Then the steam cooled and became water.

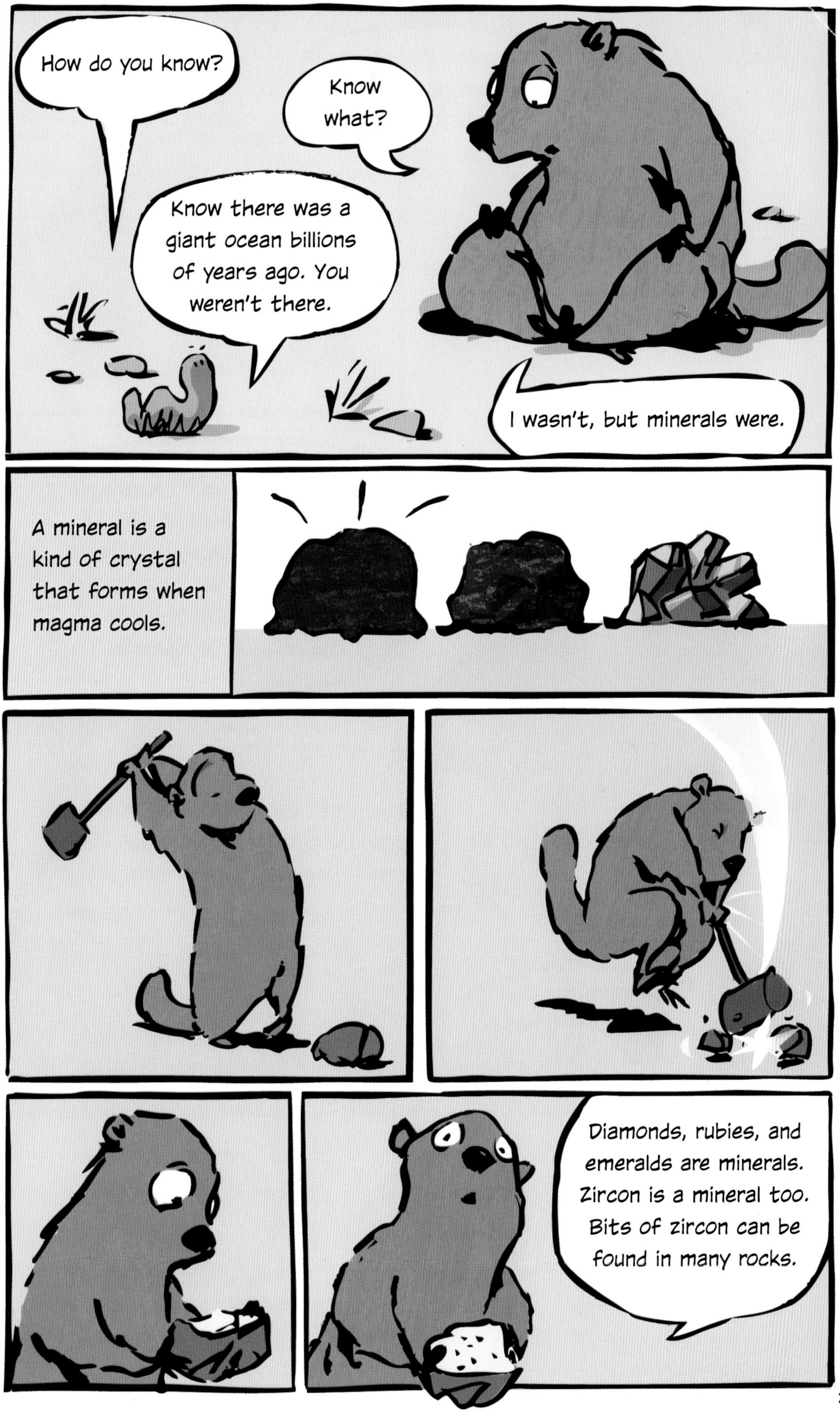
How do you know?
Know what?
Know there was a giant ocean billions of years ago. You weren't there.
I wasn't, but minerals were.
A mineral is a kind of crystal that forms when magma cools.
Diamonds, rubies, and emeralds are minerals. Zircon is a mineral too. Bits of zircon can be found in many rocks.

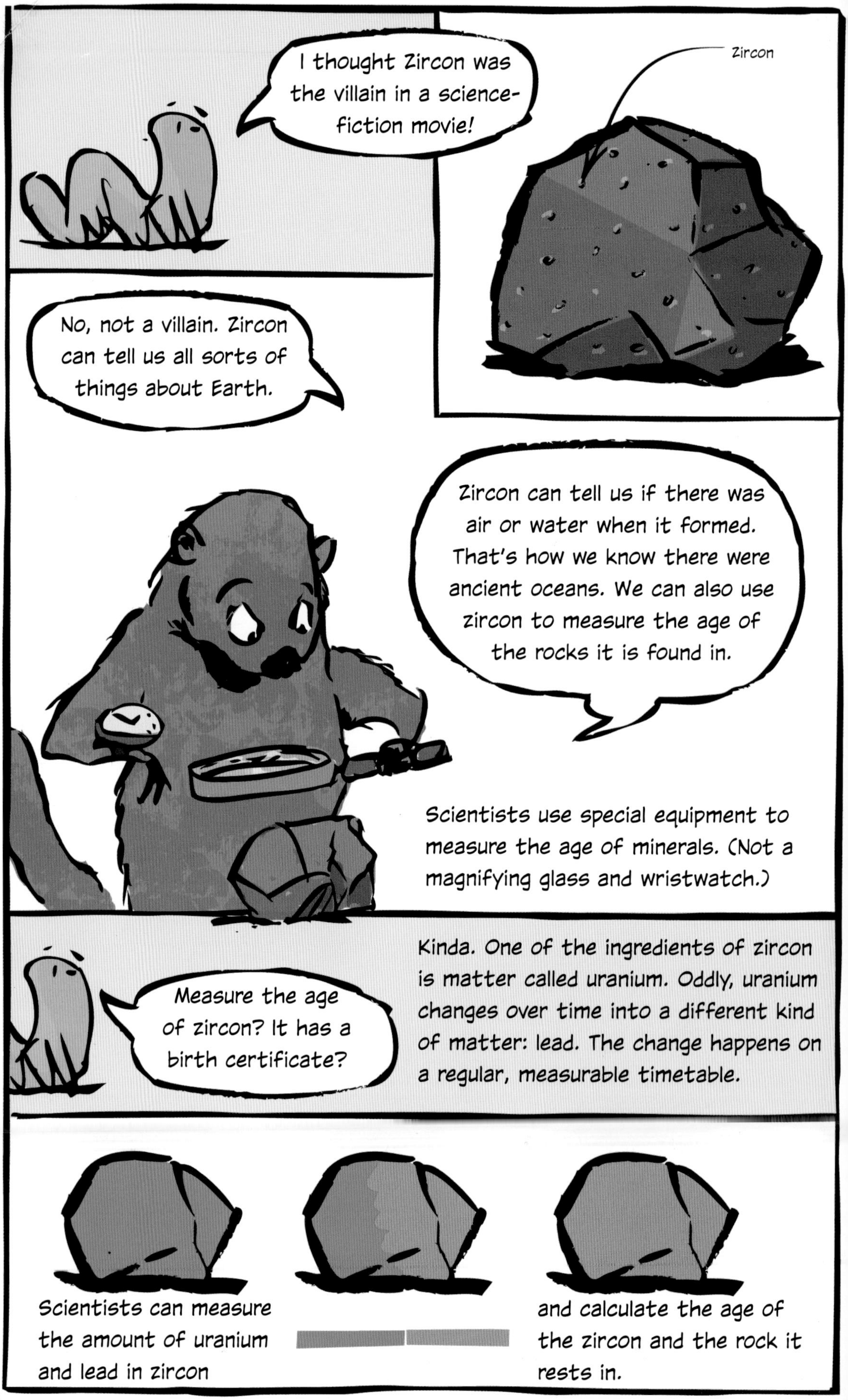
I thought Zircon was the villain in a science-fiction movie!
Zircon
No, not a villain. Zircon can tell us all sorts of things about Earth.
Zircon can tell us if there was air or water when it formed. That's how we know there were ancient oceans. We can also use zircon to measure the age of the rocks it is found in.
Scientists use special equipment to measure the age of minerals. (Not a magnifying glass and wristwatch.)
Measure the age of zircon? It has a birth certificate?
Kinda. One of the ingredients of zircon is matter called uranium. Oddly, uranium changes over time into a different kind of matter: lead. The change happens on a regular, measurable timetable.
Scientists can measure the amount of uranium and lead in zircon
and calculate the age of the zircon and the rock it rests in.

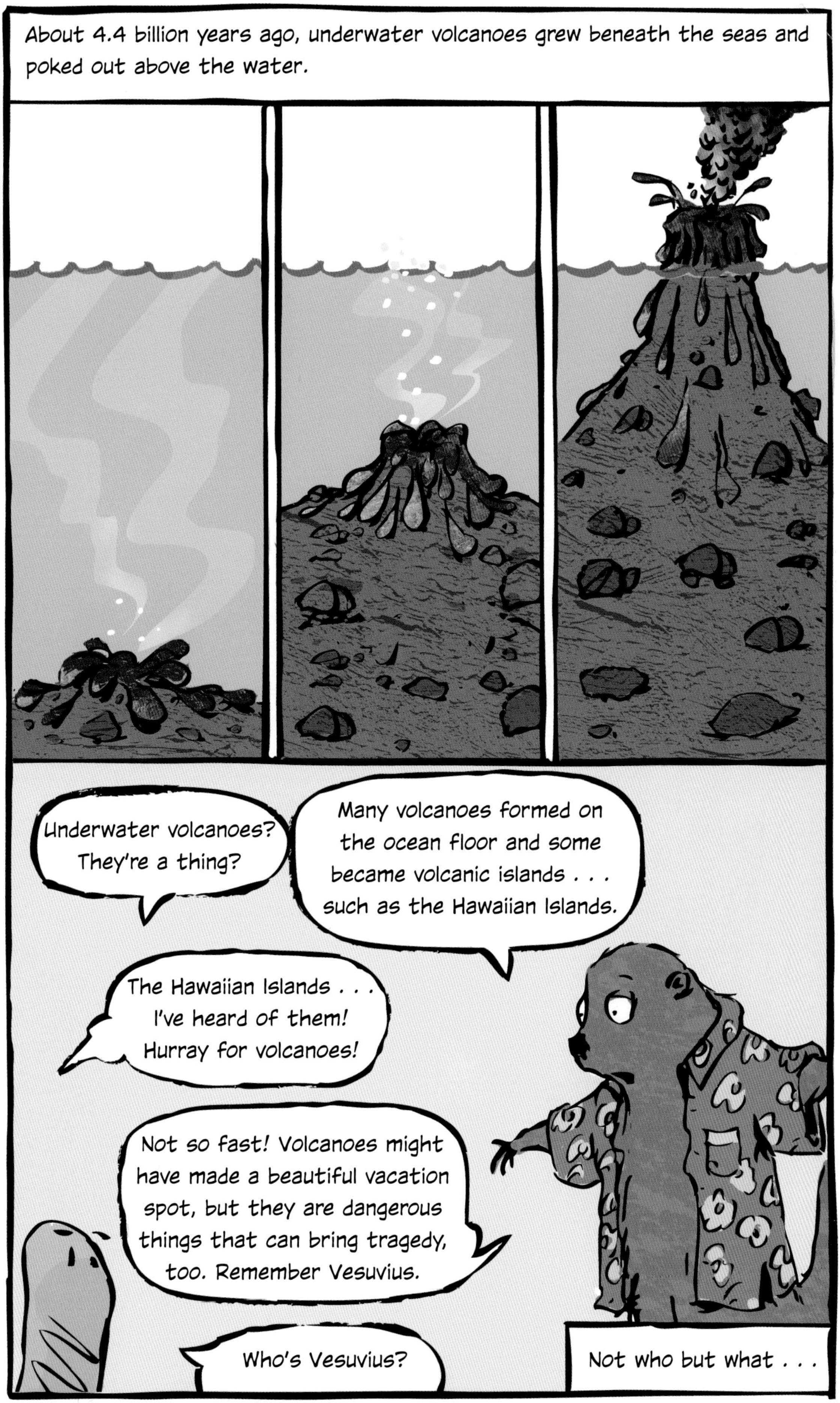
About 4.4 billion years ago, underwater volcanoes grew beneath the seas and poked out above the water.
Underwater volcanoes? They're a thing?
Many volcanoes formed on the ocean floor and some became volcanic islands . . . such as the Hawaiian Islands.
The Hawaiian Islands . . . I've heard of them! Hurray for volcanoes!
Not so fast! Volcanoes might have made a beautiful vacation spot, but they are dangerous things that can bring tragedy, too. Remember Vesuvius.
Who's Vesuvius?
Not who but what . . .

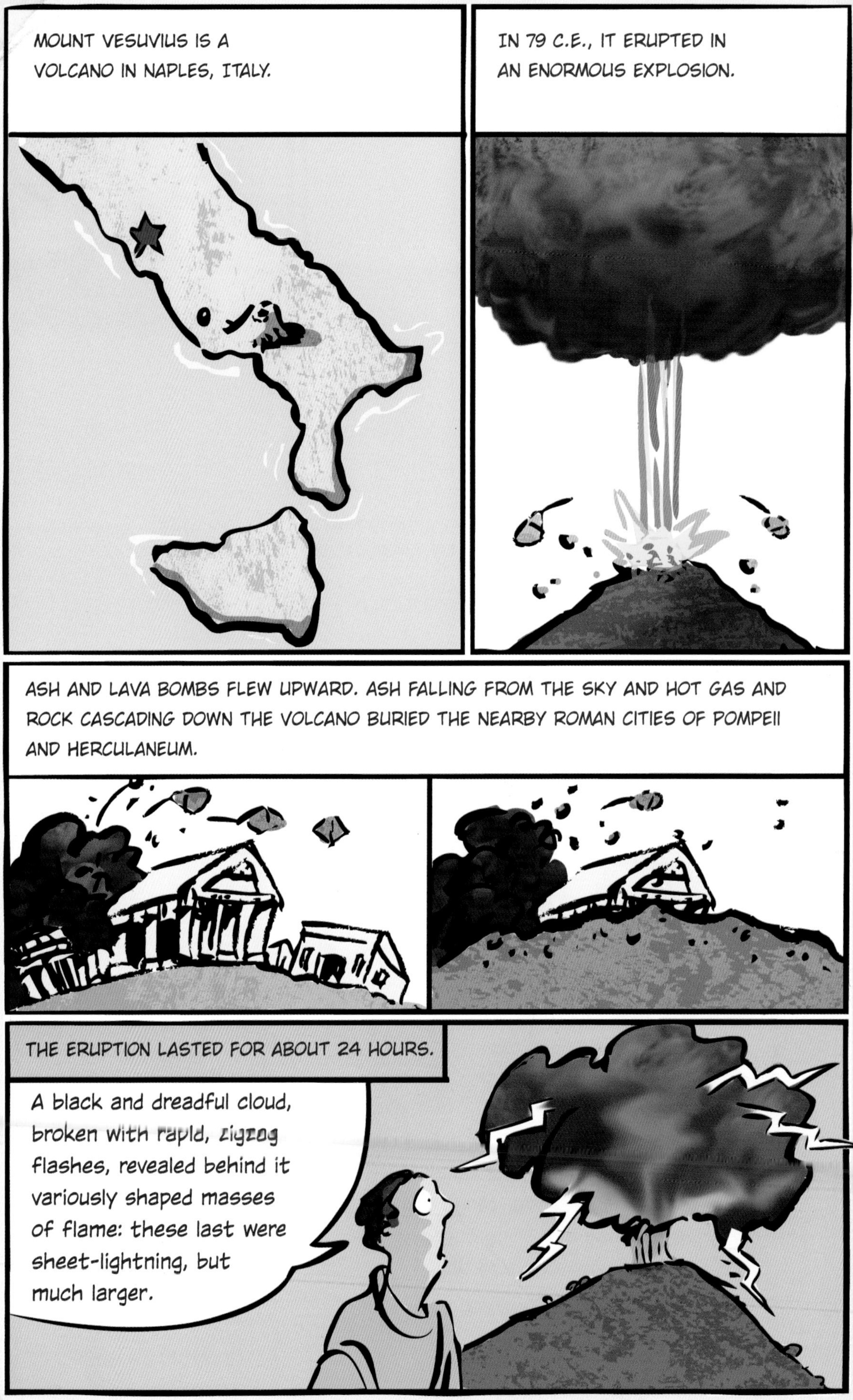
MOUNT VESUVIUS IS A VOLCANO IN NAPLES, ITALY.
IN 79 C.E., IT ERUPTED IN AN ENORMOUS EXPLOSION.
ASH AND LAVA BOMBS FLEW UPWARD. ASH FALLING FROM THE SKY AND HOT GAS AND ROCK CASCADING DOWN THE VOLCANO BURIED THE NEARBY ROMAN CITIES OF POMPEII AND HERCULANEUM.
THE ERUPTION LASTED FOR ABOUT 24 HOURS.
A black and dreadful cloud, broken with rapid, zigzag flashes, revealed behind it variously shaped masses of flame: these last were sheet-lightning, but much larger.

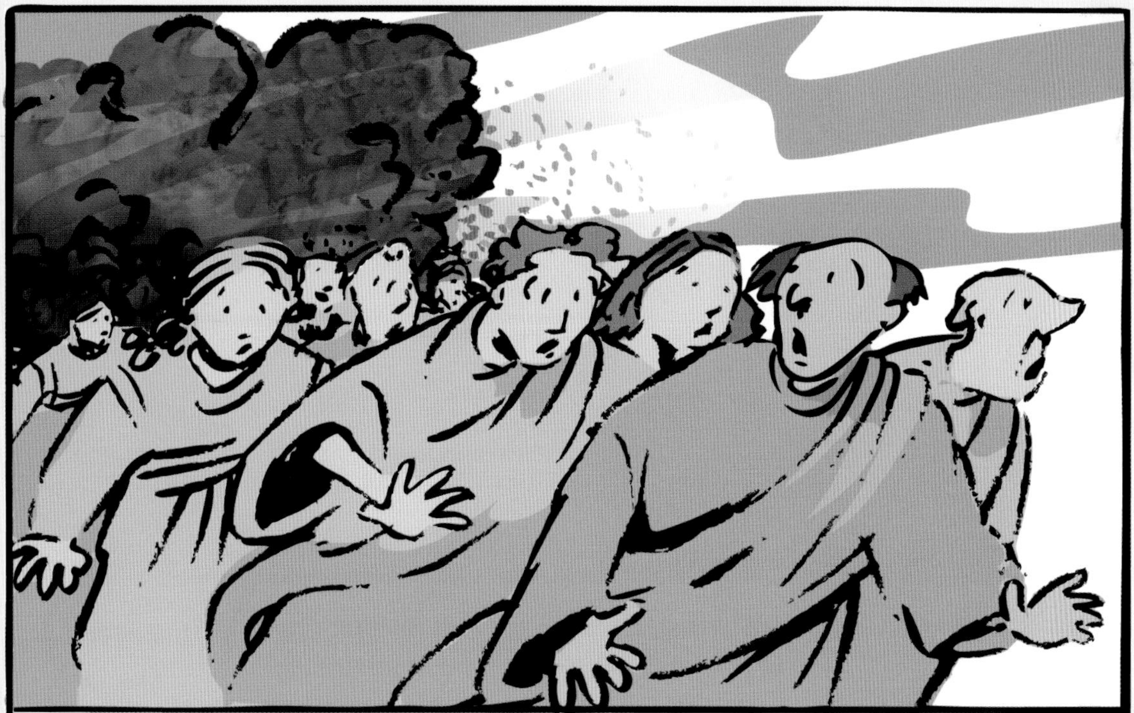

FLEEING RESIDENTS WERE BURIED IN BURNING AND CHOKING ASH. THAT AND INTENSE HEAT KILLED AN UNTOLD AMOUNT. ABOUT 3,000 PEOPLE DIED.

LOST BENEATH TEN FEET OF ASH, THE CITIES WERE FORGOTTEN BY NEARLY EVERYONE EXCEPT LOOTERS WHO TUNNELED THROUGH THE ASH AND INTO BUILDINGS IN SEARCH OF VALUABLES.

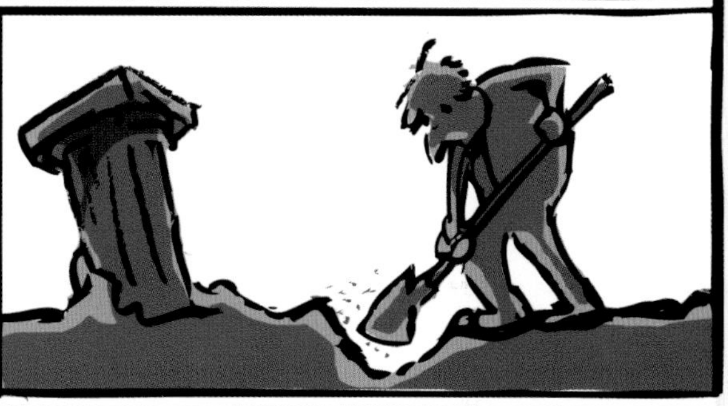

THEN IN THE EIGHTEENTH CENTURY, THE STORY OF THE VESUVIUS ERUPTION EXCITED PEOPLE'S IMAGINATION. IN 1748, SCIENTIFIC EXCAVATION STARTED. IN THE 1800S, HOLLOWS WITHIN THE ASH WERE RECOGNIZED AS A KIND OF A CASTING MOLD. THEY WERE FILLED WITH PLASTER, REVEALING IN DETAIL THE SHAPE OF THE PERSON OR ANIMAL THAT HAD PERISHED THERE.

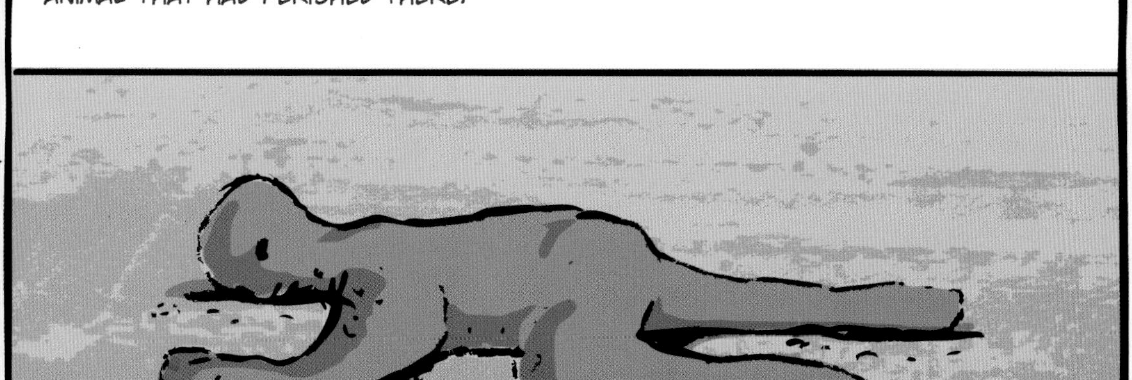

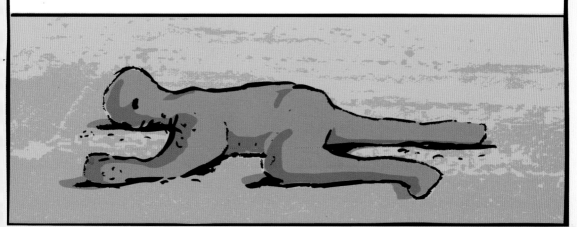

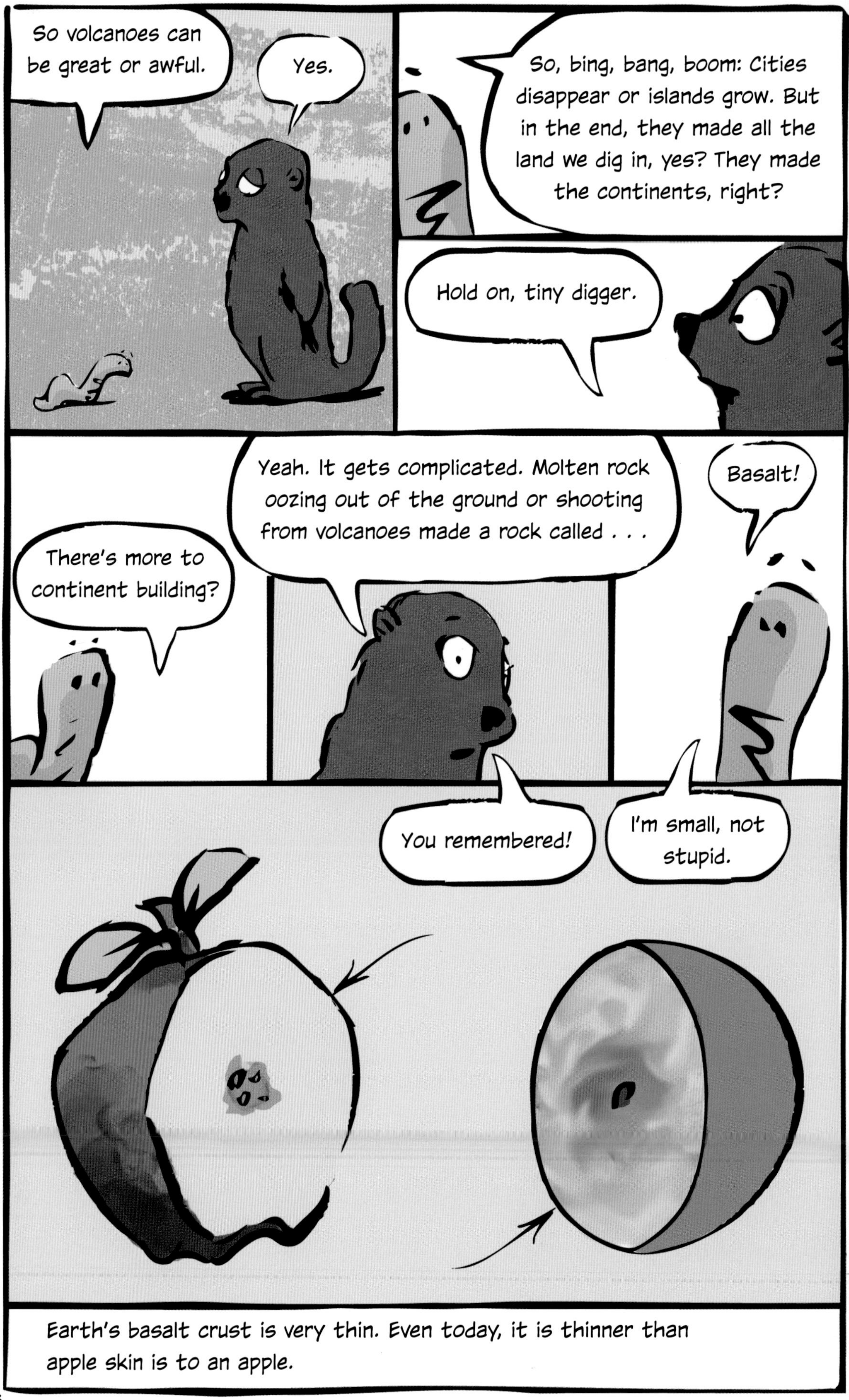
So volcanoes can be great or awful.
Yes.
So, bing, bang, boom: Cities disappear or islands grow. But in the end, they made all the land we dig in, yes? They made the continents, right?
Hold on, tiny digger.
There's more to continent building?
Yeah. It gets complicated. Molten rock oozing out of the ground or shooting from volcanoes made a rock called . . .
Basalt!
You remembered!
I'm small, not stupid.
Earth's basalt crust is very thin. Even today, it is thinner than apple skin is to an apple.

Around three billion years ago, some basalt rocks under the ocean sank into the mantle, bringing seawater with it.

The seawater and basalt heated up and melted with the mantle to make a new type of molten rock.

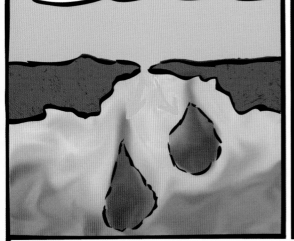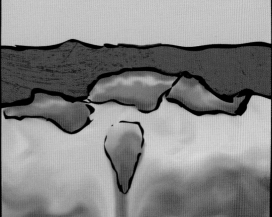

For millions of years, it cooled beneath the surface of the crust until it became solid rock such as granite. For the next billion years the plutonic rock, as it's named, collected.

In time, it made its way to the surface, sometimes pushed upward by forces within Earth or revealed when wind and rain eroded the less durable basalt rock.

Great clumps of plutonic rock made mountains.

Like an iceberg, most of a mountain lies beneath the surface and hidden from view.

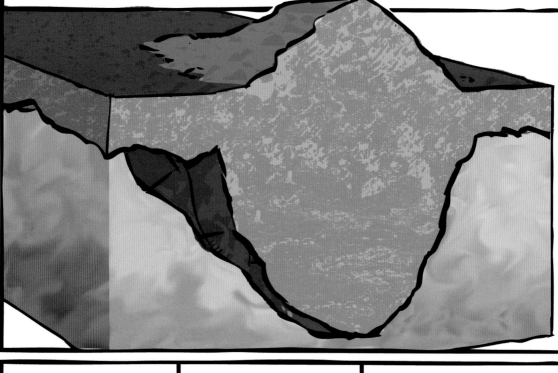

Why didn't granite and the other plutonic rock sink into the mantle?

The mantle is only partly molten and flows something like peanut butter. The plutonic rock floats on it.

Huh? A big, heavy rock like granite floats? You're pulling my leg. Okay, maybe not the right expression for me to use . . . but a floating rock? Come on!

Plutons float because they are less dense than the mantle.

Worms, apparently.

What's "dense"?

No, really.

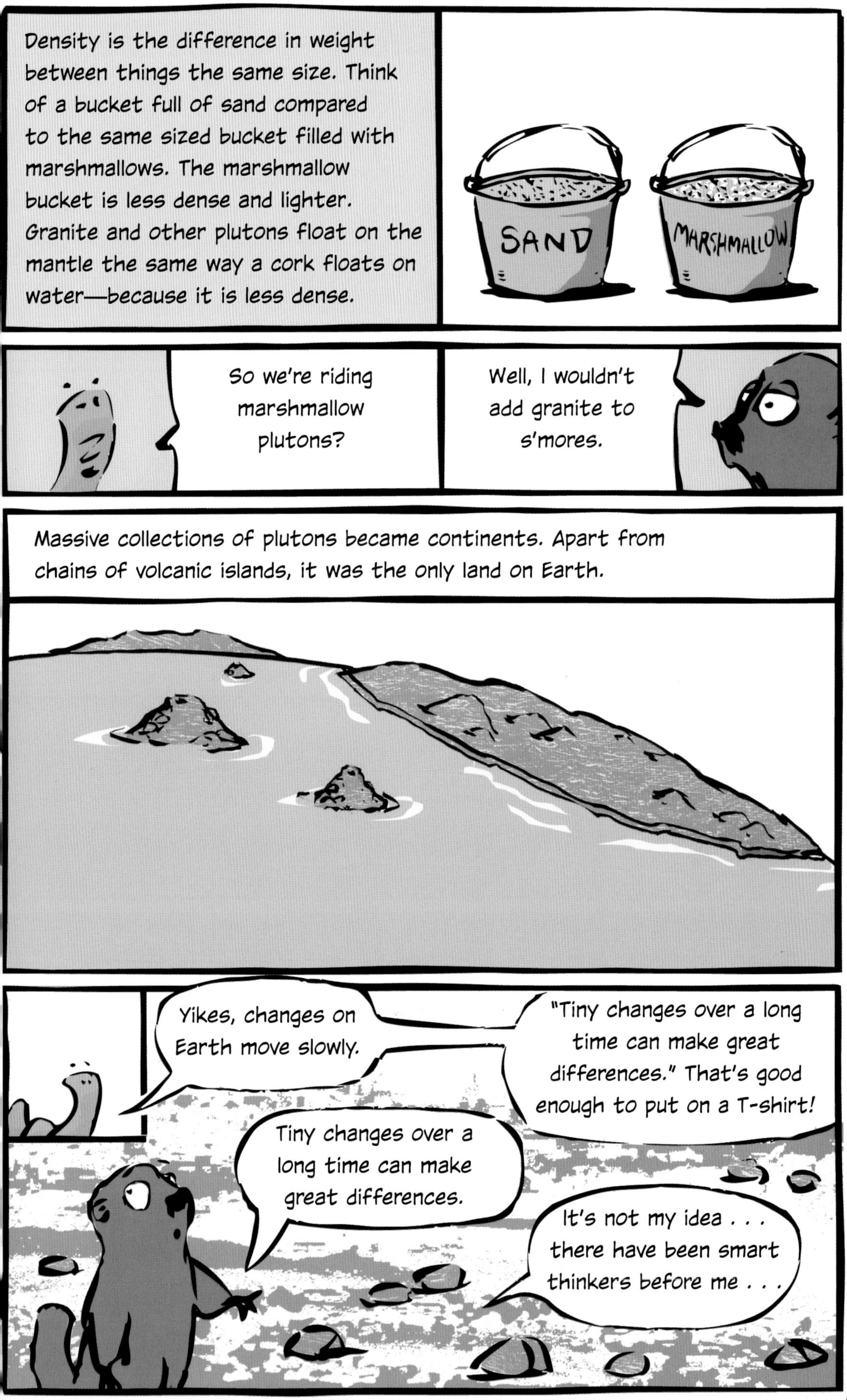
Density is the difference in weight between things the same size. Think of a bucket full of sand compared to the same sized bucket filled with marshmallows. The marshmallow bucket is less dense and lighter. Granite and other plutons float on the mantle the same way a cork floats on water—because it is less dense.
SAND
MARSHMALLOW
So we're riding marshmallow plutons?
Well, I wouldn't add granite to s'mores.
Massive collections of plutons became continents. Apart from chains of volcanic islands, it was the only land on Earth.
Yikes, changes on Earth move slowly.
Tiny changes over a long time can make great differences.
"Tiny changes over a long time can make great differences." That's good enough to put on a T-shirt!
It's not my idea . . . there have been smart thinkers before me . . .

DEEP TIME COMIX

JAMES HUTTON: FATHER OF GEOLOGY

JAMES HUTTON WAS BORN IN SCOTLAND IN 1726. HE WAS A DOCTOR AND A FARMER. HE GAVE UP BOTH TO STUDY EARTH.

IN 1753 HE BECAME "VERY FOND OF STUDYING THE SURFACE OF THE EARTH AND WAS LOOKING WITH ANXIOUS CURIOSITY INTO EVERY PIT OR DITCH OR BED OF A RIVER THAT FELL HIS WAY."

IT STRUCK HUTTON THAT EROSION WILL CARRY AWAY ALL THE LAND, EVEN THE GREATEST MOUNTAIN. HE BELIEVED RIVERS AND STREAMS CARRIED DIRT, PEBBLES, AND SAND—THE PRODUCTS OF EROSION—TO THE SEA, WHERE THEY COVERED THE OCEAN FLOOR. THE CARPET OF MATERIAL IS CALLED SEDIMENT. PRESSURE FROM THE COLLECTED DIRT, PEBBLES, AND SAND COMPRESS THE LAYERS INTO SEDIMENTARY ROCK. FORCES AND HEAT DEEP WITHIN EARTH LIFTED THE NEW ROCK UPWARD AND MADE NEW LAND AND MOUNTAINS, BEGINNING ANEW THE CIRCLE OF DESTRUCTION AND BIRTH.

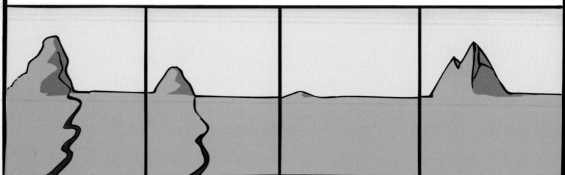

WHILE BOBBING ON A SMALL BOAT ALONG THE SCOTTISH COAST AT SICCAR POINT, HE DISCOVERED A LAYER OF FLAT-LYING ROCKS ATOP VERTICAL ROCKS. IT DEMONSTRATED HIS IDEAS OF EROSION, DEPOSITION, UPLIFT, AND TILT.

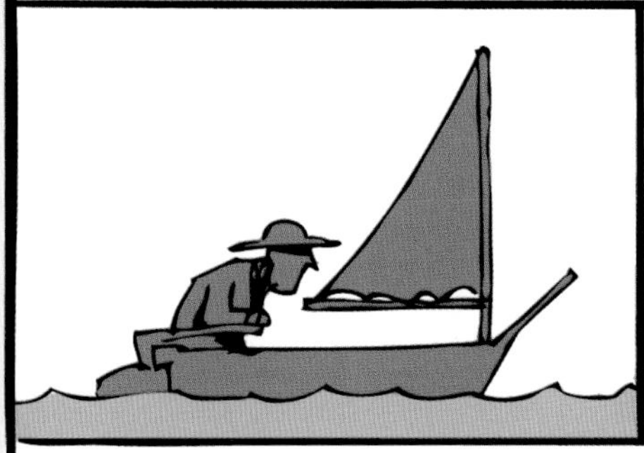

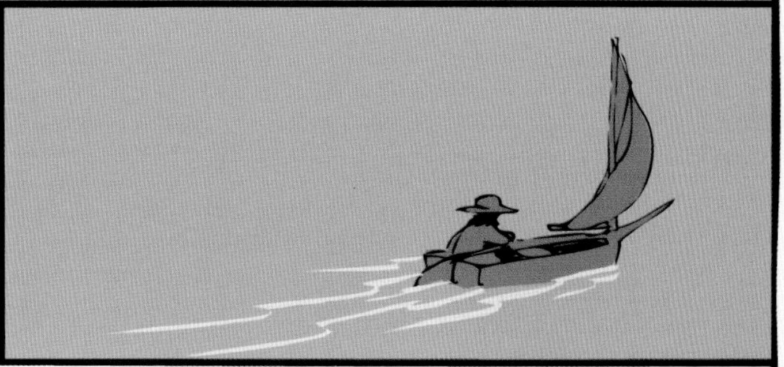

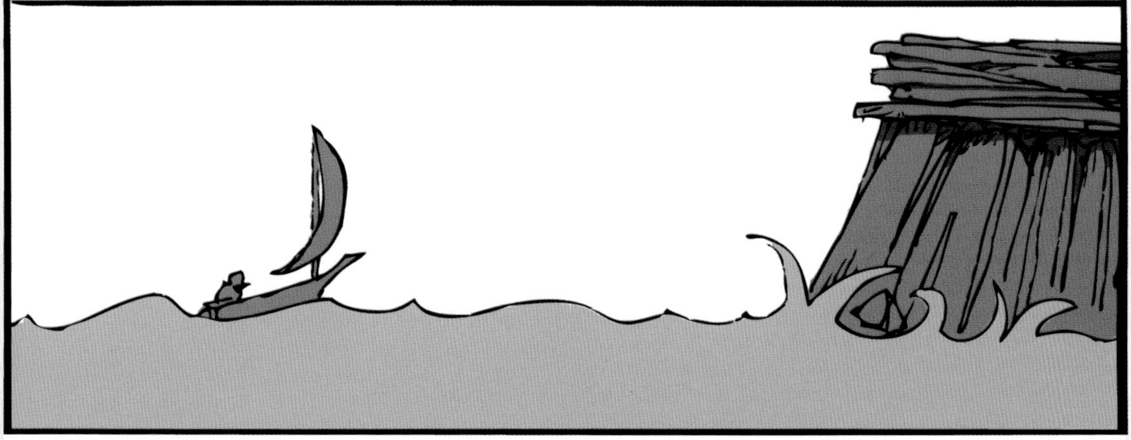

IN 1705, HUTTON OUTLINED HIS IDEAS IN A BOOK, *THE THEORY OF EARTH.* HUTTON'S THEORIES OF ROCK DESTRUCTION AND CREATION SUGGESTED AN IMMENSE SPAN OF TIME THAT WAS UNNERVING TO A WORLD THAT BELIEVED EARTH WAS ONLY SIX THOUSAND YEARS OLD.

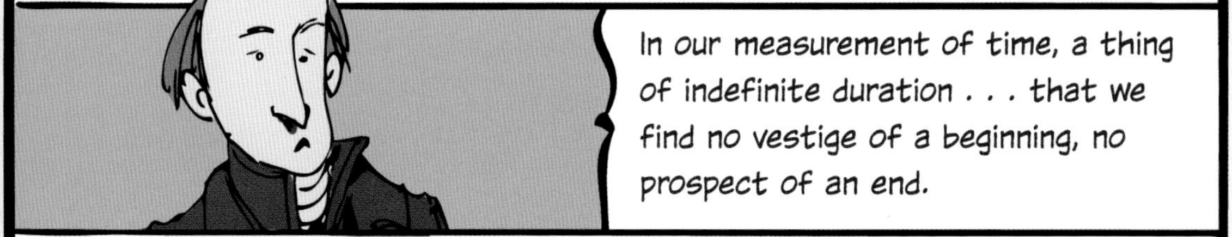
In our measurement of time, a thing of indefinite duration . . . that we find no vestige of a beginning, no prospect of an end.

TO BE TRUTHFUL, HUTTON WAS AN AWFUL WRITER AND HIS IDEAS WERE BETTER SERVED BY OTHERS SUCH AS CHARLES LYELL AND HIS 1830 BOOK, *PRINCIPLES OF GEOLOGY.* LYELL'S WRITINGS POPULARIZED THE IDEA OF A VERY OLD EARTH. SCIENTISTS EVENTUALLY CALLED IT DEEP TIME. CHARLES DARWIN'S THEORY OF EVOLUTION OWES MUCH TO LYELL, HIS FRIEND.

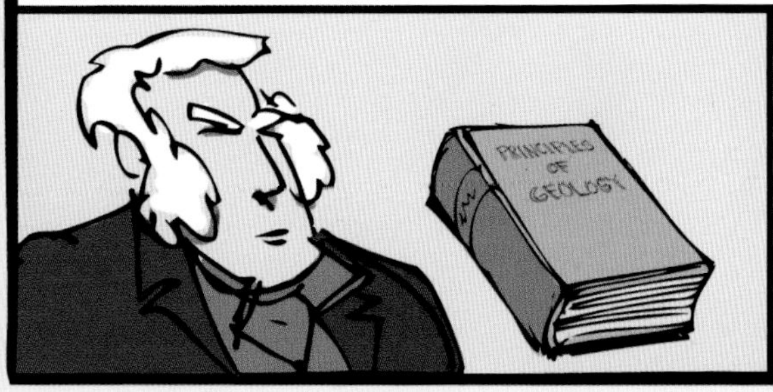
PRINCIPLES OF GEOLOGY

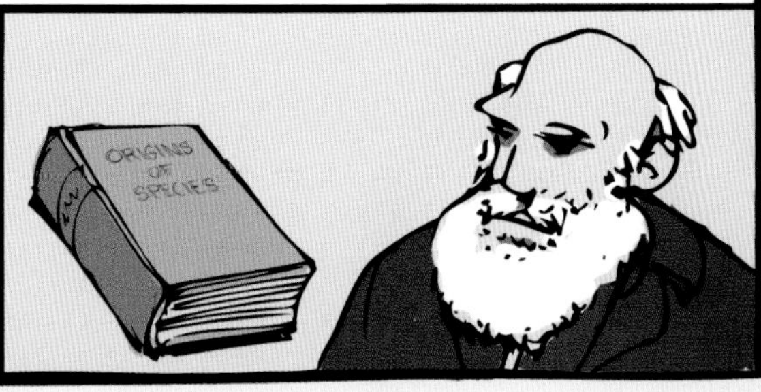
ORIGINS OF SPECIES

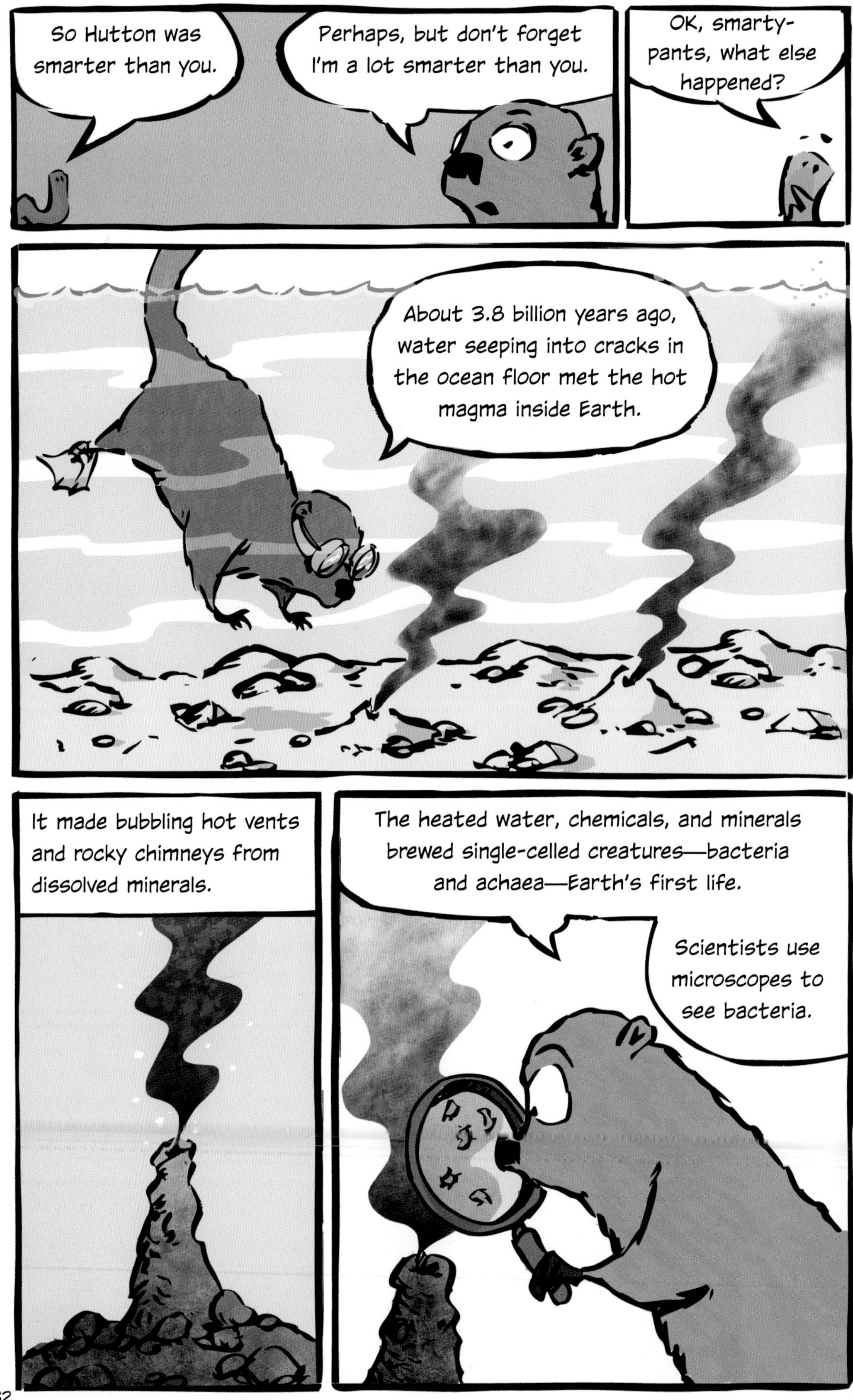
So Hutton was smarter than you.
Perhaps, but don't forget I'm a lot smarter than you.
OK, smarty-pants, what else happened?
About 3.8 billion years ago, water seeping into cracks in the ocean floor met the hot magma inside Earth.
It made bubbling hot vents and rocky chimneys from dissolved minerals.
The heated water, chemicals, and minerals brewed single-celled creatures—bacteria and achaea—Earth's first life.
Scientists use microscopes to see bacteria.

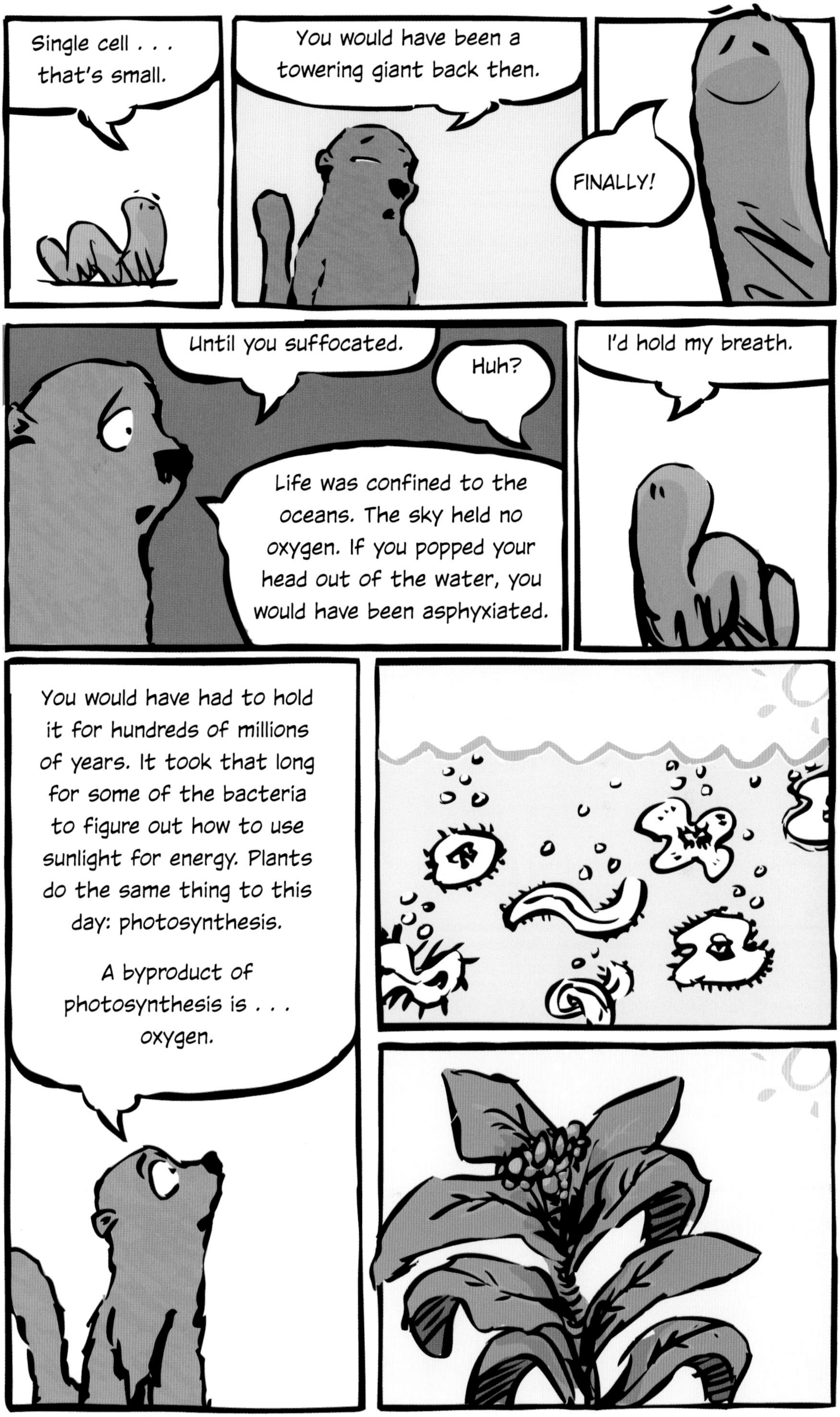
Single cell . . . that's small.
You would have been a towering giant back then.
FINALLY!
Until you suffocated.
Huh?
Life was confined to the oceans. The sky held no oxygen. If you popped your head out of the water, you would have been asphyxiated.
I'd hold my breath.
You would have had to hold it for hundreds of millions of years. It took that long for some of the bacteria to figure out how to use sunlight for energy. Plants do the same thing to this day: photosynthesis.
A byproduct of photosynthesis is . . . oxygen.

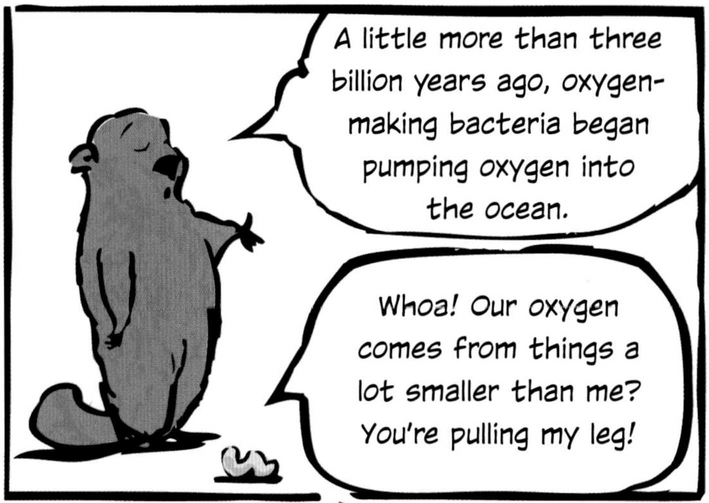
A little more than three billion years ago, oxygen-making bacteria began pumping oxygen into the ocean.
Whoa! Our oxygen comes from things a lot smaller than me? You're pulling my leg!

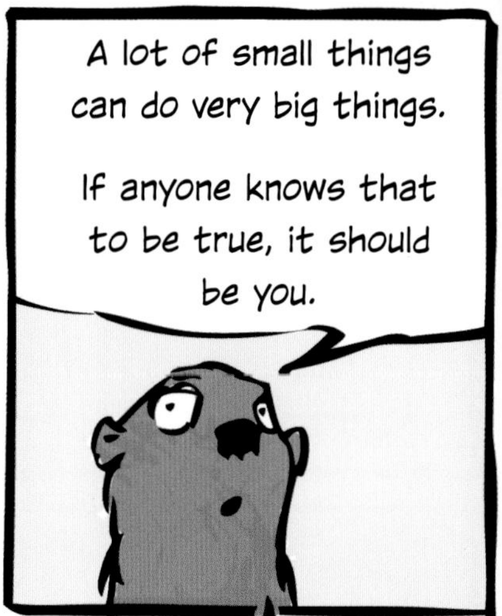
A lot of small things can do very big things.
If anyone knows that to be true, it should be you.

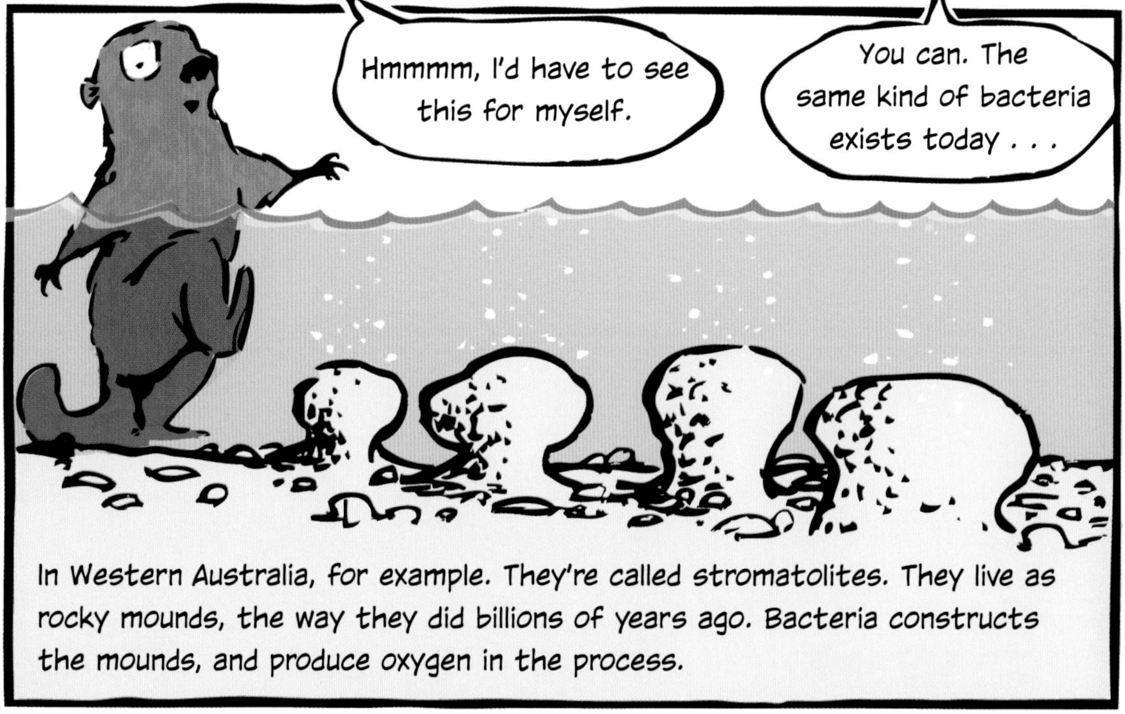
Hmmmm, I'd have to see this for myself.
You can. The same kind of bacteria exists today . . .
In Western Australia, for example. They're called stromatolites. They live as rocky mounds, the way they did billions of years ago. Bacteria constructs the mounds, and produce oxygen in the process.

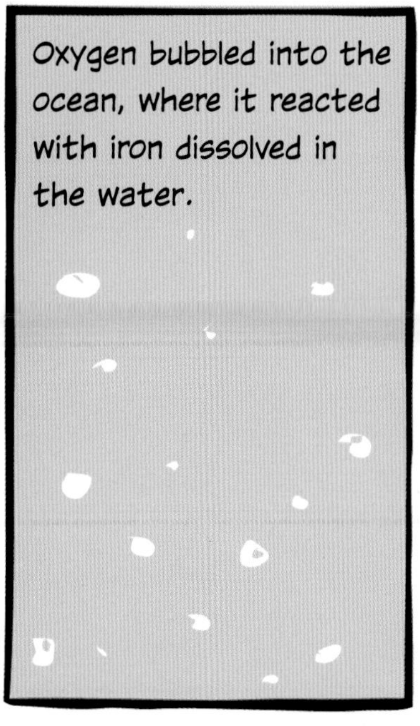
Oxygen bubbled into the ocean, where it reacted with iron dissolved in the water.

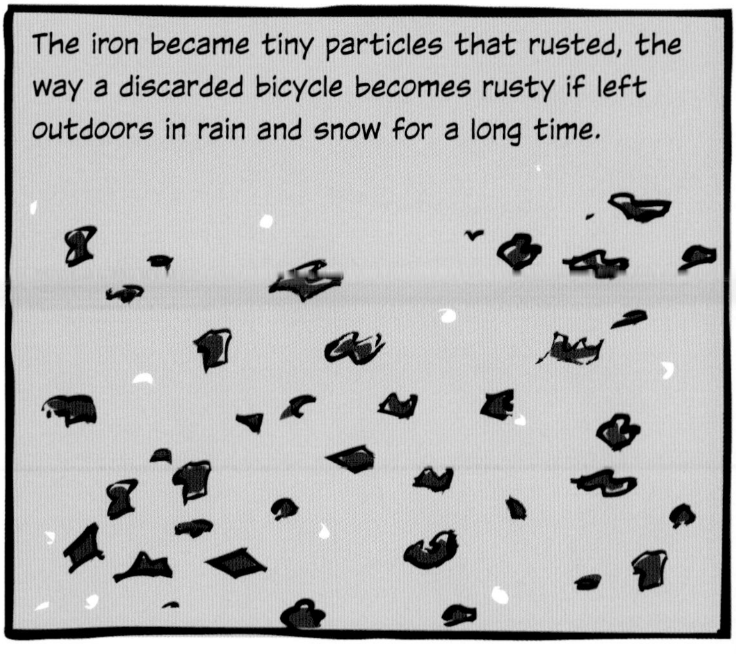
The iron became tiny particles that rusted, the way a discarded bicycle becomes rusty if left outdoors in rain and snow for a long time.

The rust settled to the bottom of the ocean. Layer after layer of rust collected.

The iron-rich sediment resembled the dirt we dig in ground. The collected sediment grew extraordinarily heavy. After pressing down for a long time, sedimentary iron rocks were made.

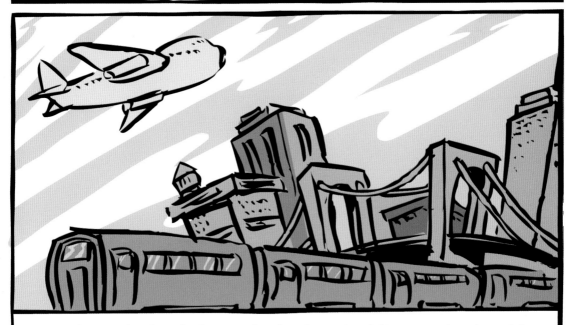

Iron rocks can be found all over. They're dug out of the ground and used to make steel. Steel bridges, buildings, automobiles, and airplanes owe a part of their existence to the tiny bacteria that added extra oxygen to the ocean.

Oxygen, whether it was made first by bacteria or later, by algae—plants living in the sea—was a great thing. Without it, you, me, nobody around now could breathe. But it took nearly a billion years before oxygen made up one-fifth of the air we know today.

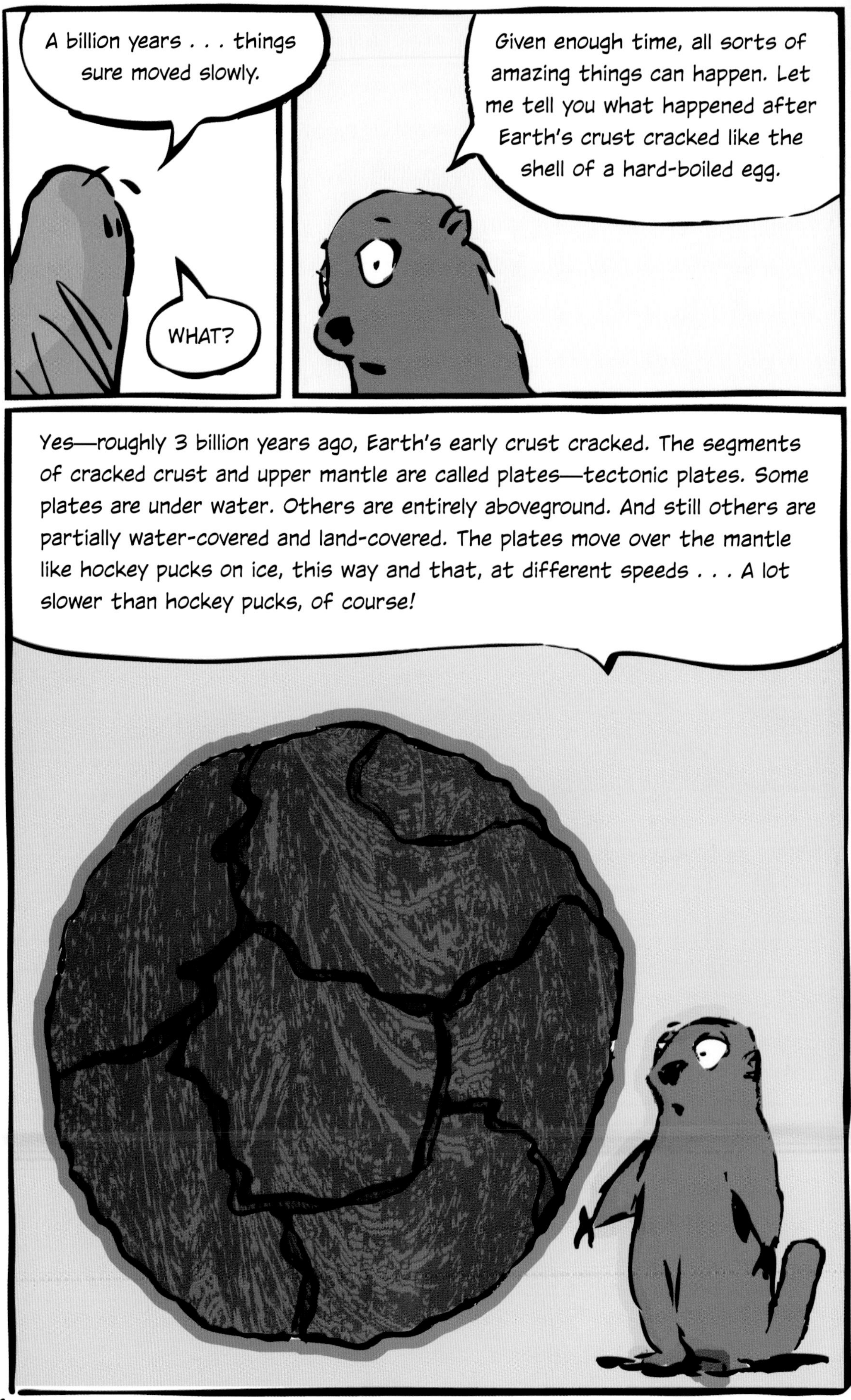
A billion years . . . things sure moved slowly.
WHAT?
Given enough time, all sorts of amazing things can happen. Let me tell you what happened after Earth's crust cracked like the shell of a hard-boiled egg.
Yes—roughly 3 billion years ago, Earth's early crust cracked. The segments of cracked crust and upper mantle are called plates—tectonic plates. Some plates are under water. Others are entirely aboveground. And still others are partially water-covered and land-covered. The plates move over the mantle like hockey pucks on ice, this way and that, at different speeds . . . A lot slower than hockey pucks, of course!

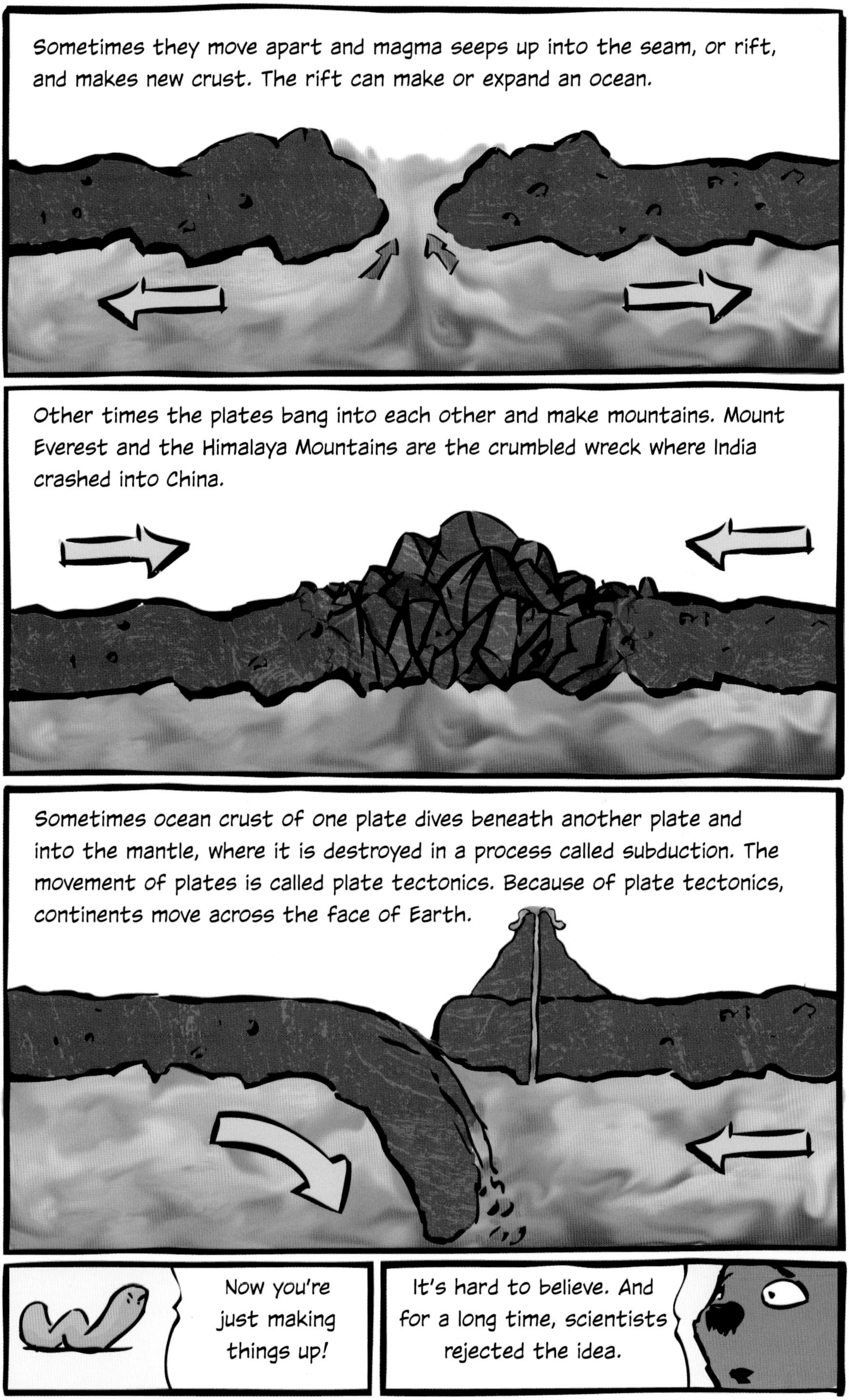

Sometimes they move apart and magma seeps up into the seam, or rift, and makes new crust. The rift can make or expand an ocean.

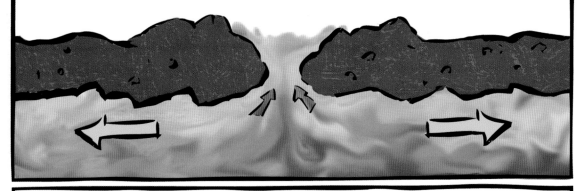

Other times the plates bang into each other and make mountains. Mount Everest and the Himalaya Mountains are the crumbled wreck where India crashed into China.

Sometimes ocean crust of one plate dives beneath another plate and into the mantle, where it is destroyed in a process called subduction. The movement of plates is called plate tectonics. Because of plate tectonics, continents move across the face of Earth.

Now you're just making things up!

It's hard to believe. And for a long time, scientists rejected the idea.

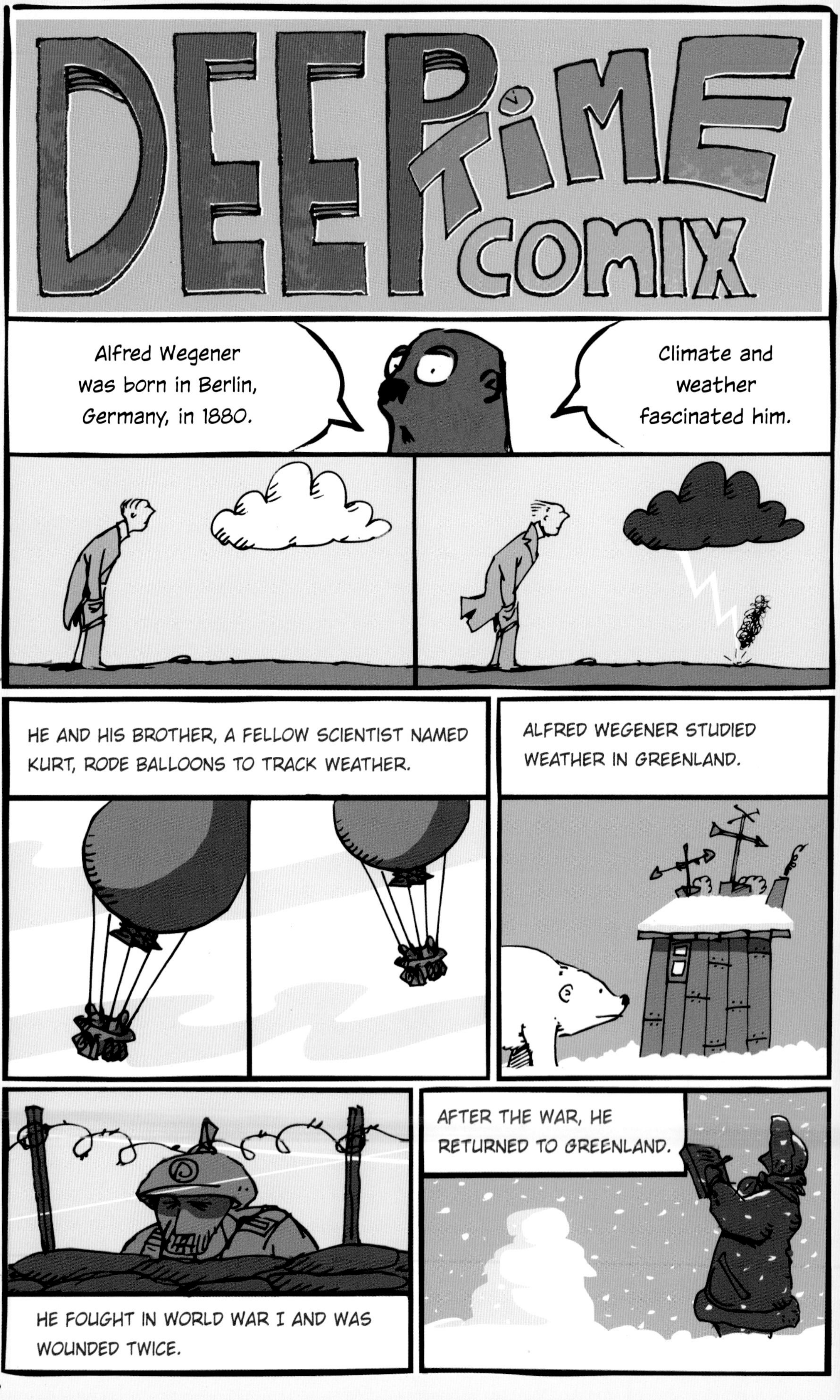
DEEP TIME COMIX
Alfred Wegener was born in Berlin, Germany, in 1880.
Climate and weather fascinated him.
HE AND HIS BROTHER, A FELLOW SCIENTIST NAMED KURT, RODE BALLOONS TO TRACK WEATHER.
ALFRED WEGENER STUDIED WEATHER IN GREENLAND.
HE FOUGHT IN WORLD WAR I AND WAS WOUNDED TWICE.
AFTER THE WAR, HE RETURNED TO GREENLAND.

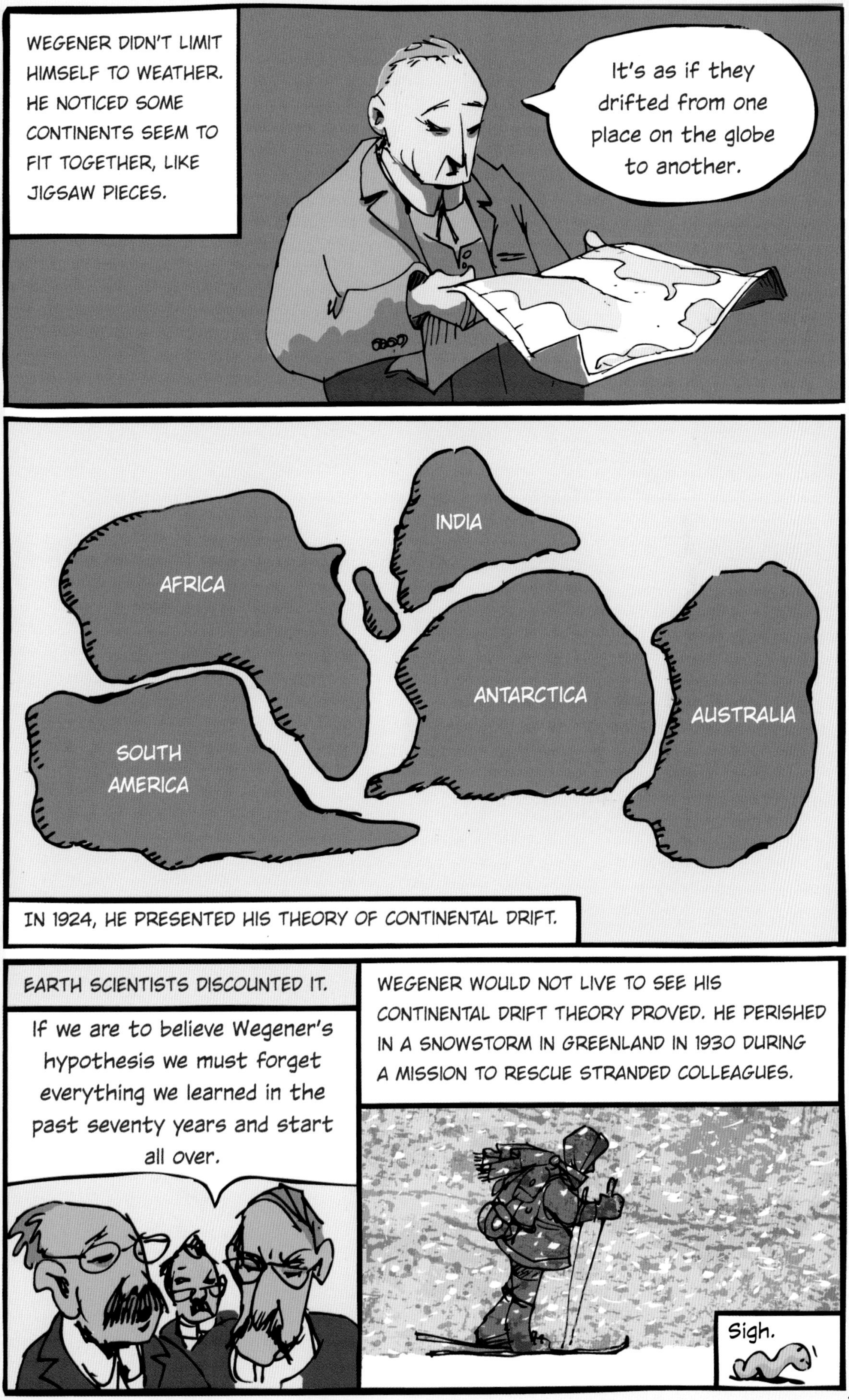
WEGENER DIDN'T LIMIT HIMSELF TO WEATHER. HE NOTICED SOME CONTINENTS SEEM TO FIT TOGETHER, LIKE JIGSAW PIECES.
It's as if they drifted from one place on the globe to another.
INDIA
AFRICA
ANTARCTICA
AUSTRALIA
SOUTH AMERICA
IN 1924, HE PRESENTED HIS THEORY OF CONTINENTAL DRIFT.
EARTH SCIENTISTS DISCOUNTED IT.
If we are to believe Wegener's hypothesis we must forget everything we learned in the past seventy years and start all over.
WEGENER WOULD NOT LIVE TO SEE HIS CONTINENTAL DRIFT THEORY PROVED. HE PERISHED IN A SNOWSTORM IN GREENLAND IN 1930 DURING A MISSION TO RESCUE STRANDED COLLEAGUES.
Sigh.

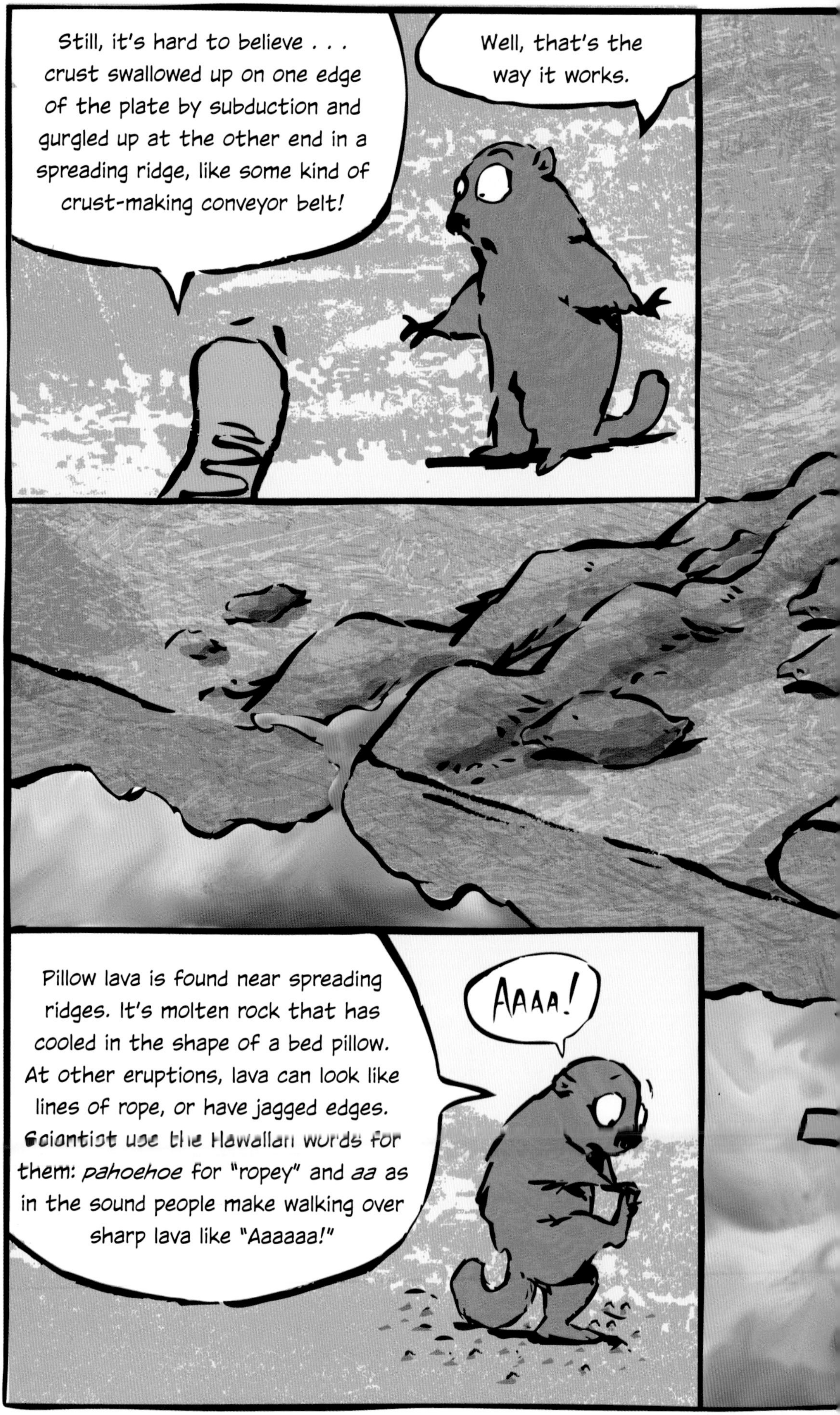
Still, it's hard to believe . . . crust swallowed up on one edge of the plate by subduction and gurgled up at the other end in a spreading ridge, like some kind of crust-making conveyor belt!
Well, that's the way it works.
Pillow lava is found near spreading ridges. It's molten rock that has cooled in the shape of a bed pillow. At other eruptions, lava can look like lines of rope, or have jagged edges. Scientist use the Hawaiian words for them: *pahoehoe* for "ropey" and *aa* as in the sound people make walking over sharp lava like "Aaaaaa!"
AAAA!

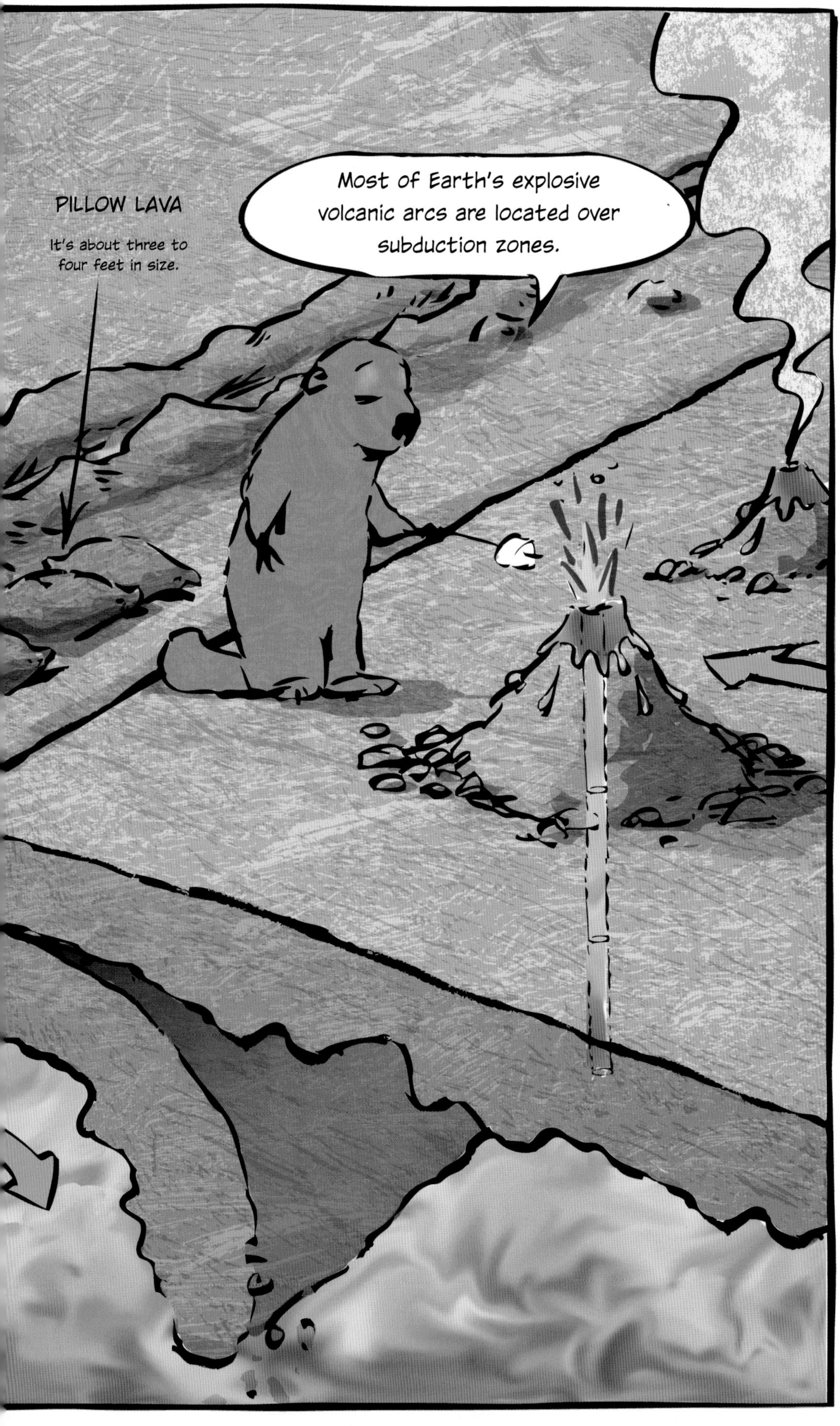
PILLOW LAVA
It's about three to four feet in size.
Most of Earth's explosive volcanic arcs are located over subduction zones.

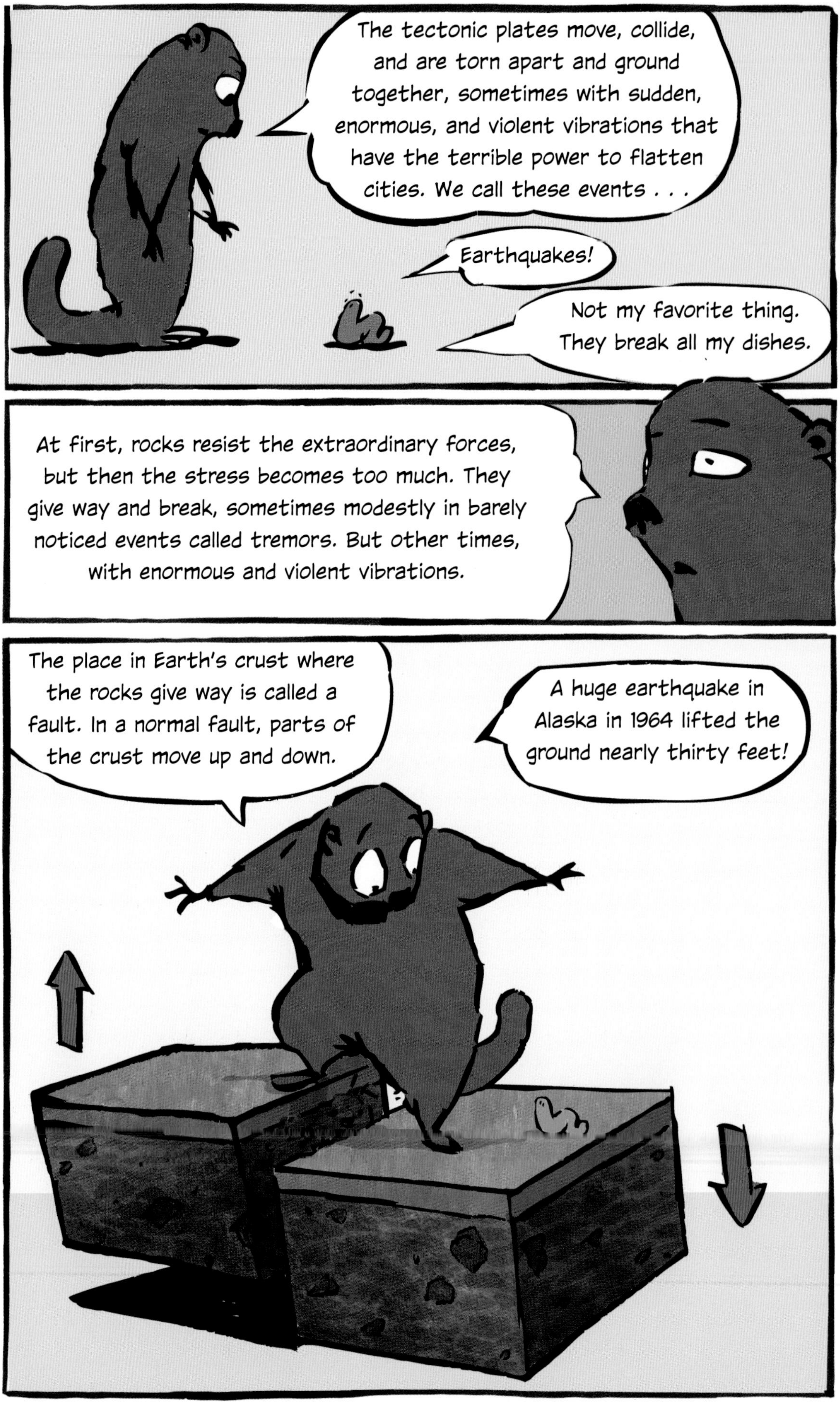
The tectonic plates move, collide, and are torn apart and ground together, sometimes with sudden, enormous, and violent vibrations that have the terrible power to flatten cities. We call these events . . .
Earthquakes!
Not my favorite thing. They break all my dishes.
At first, rocks resist the extraordinary forces, but then the stress becomes too much. They give way and break, sometimes modestly in barely noticed events called tremors. But other times, with enormous and violent vibrations.
The place in Earth's crust where the rocks give way is called a fault. In a normal fault, parts of the crust move up and down.
A huge earthquake in Alaska in 1964 lifted the ground nearly thirty feet!

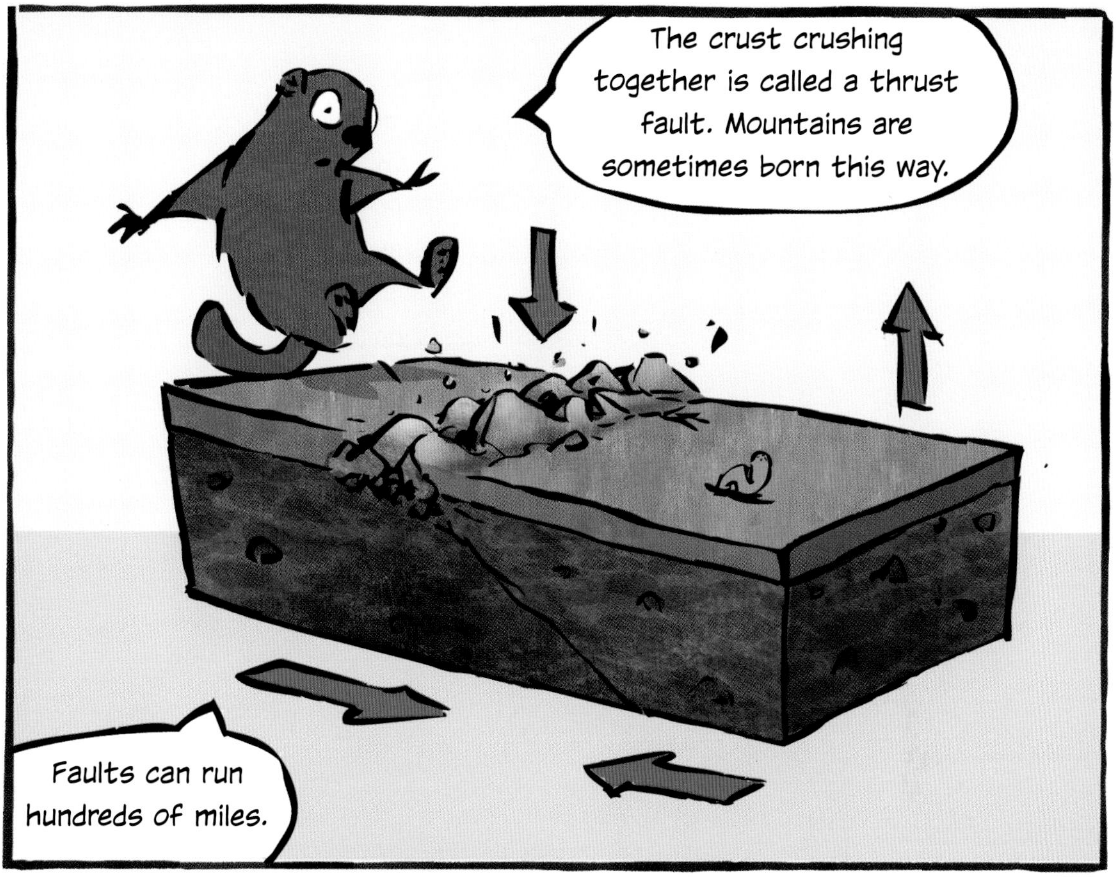
The crust crushing together is called a thrust fault. Mountains are sometimes born this way.
Faults can run hundreds of miles.

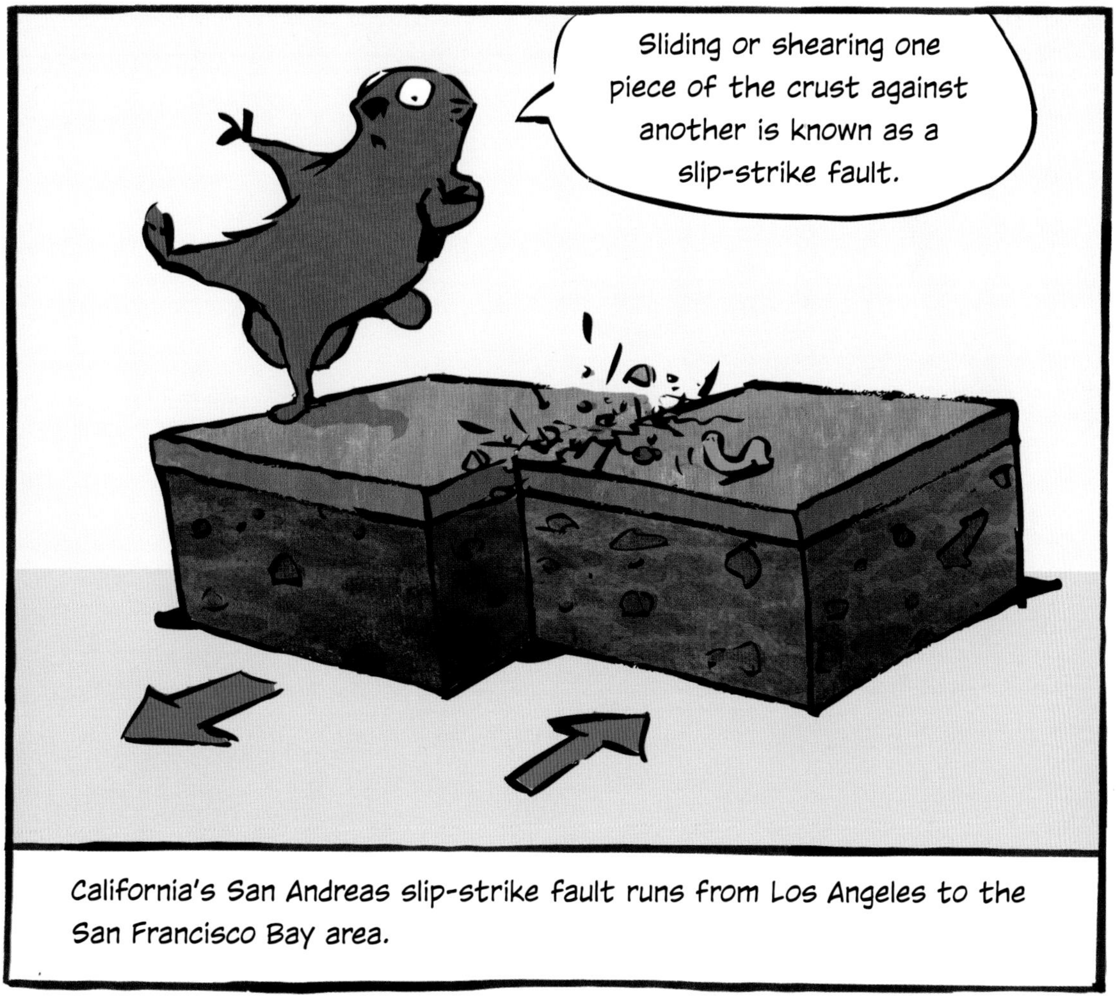
Sliding or shearing one piece of the crust against another is known as a slip-strike fault.
California's San Andreas slip-strike fault runs from Los Angeles to the San Francisco Bay area.

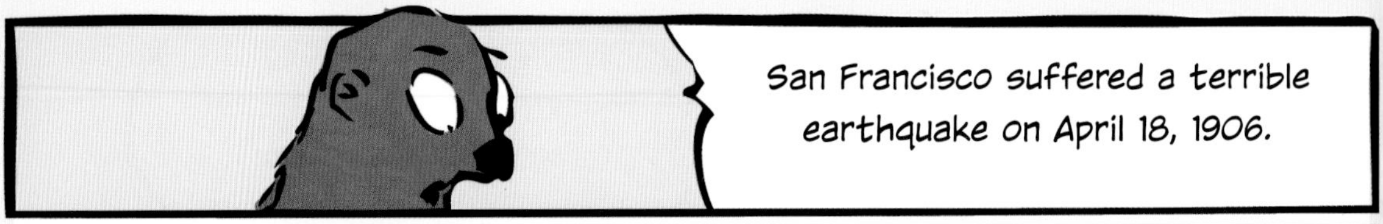
San Francisco suffered a terrible earthquake on April 18, 1906.

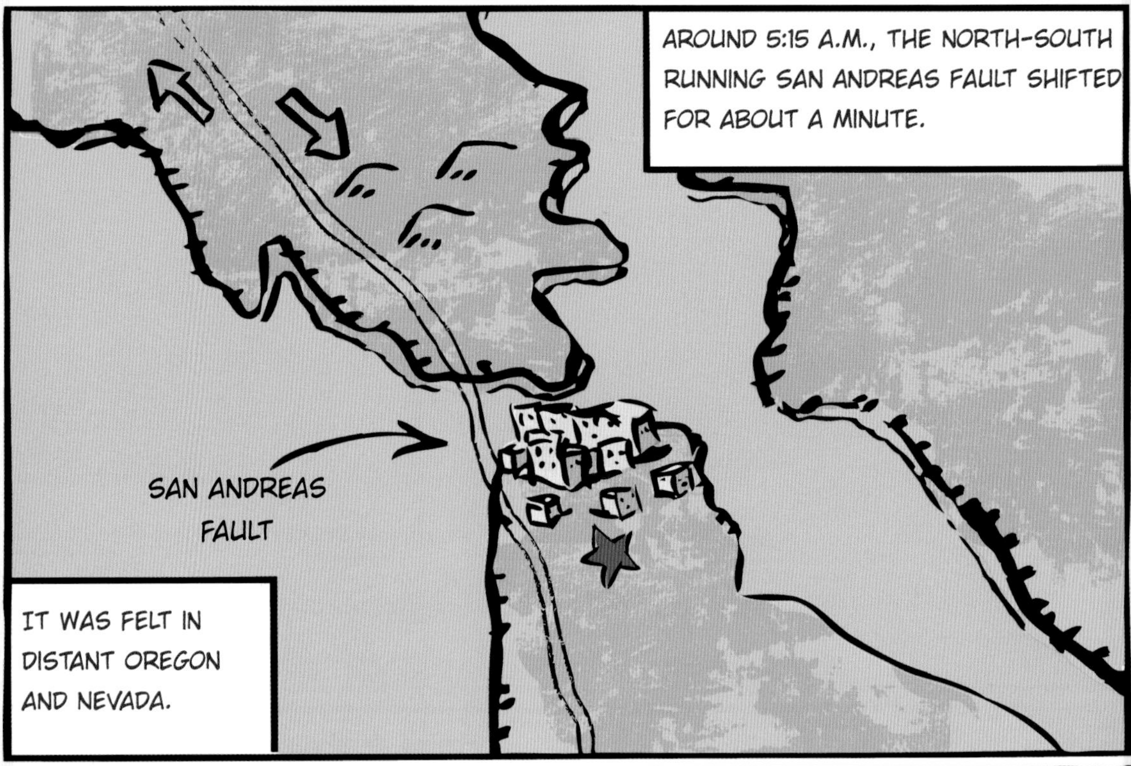
AROUND 5:15 A.M., THE NORTH-SOUTH RUNNING SAN ANDREAS FAULT SHIFTED FOR ABOUT A MINUTE.
SAN ANDREAS FAULT
IT WAS FELT IN DISTANT OREGON AND NEVADA.

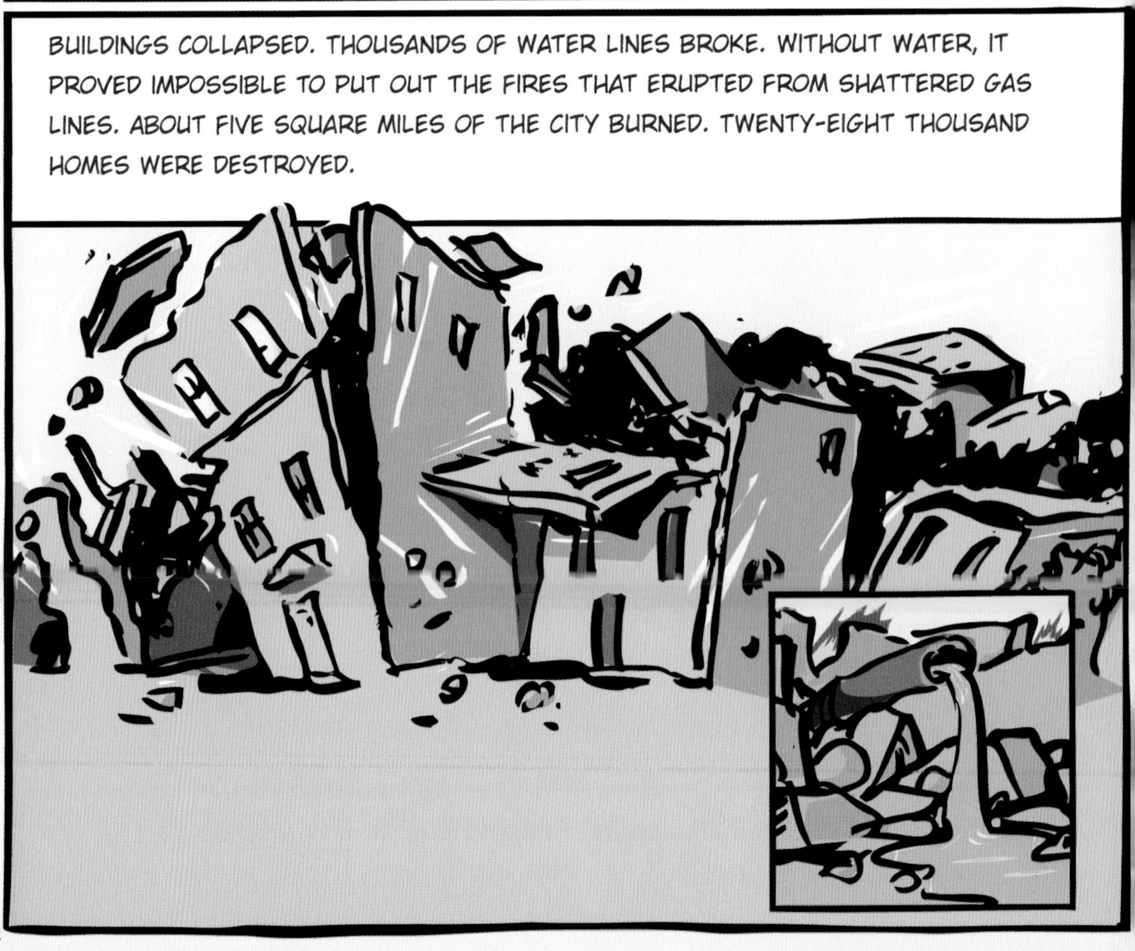
BUILDINGS COLLAPSED. THOUSANDS OF WATER LINES BROKE. WITHOUT WATER, IT PROVED IMPOSSIBLE TO PUT OUT THE FIRES THAT ERUPTED FROM SHATTERED GAS LINES. ABOUT FIVE SQUARE MILES OF THE CITY BURNED. TWENTY-EIGHT THOUSAND HOMES WERE DESTROYED.

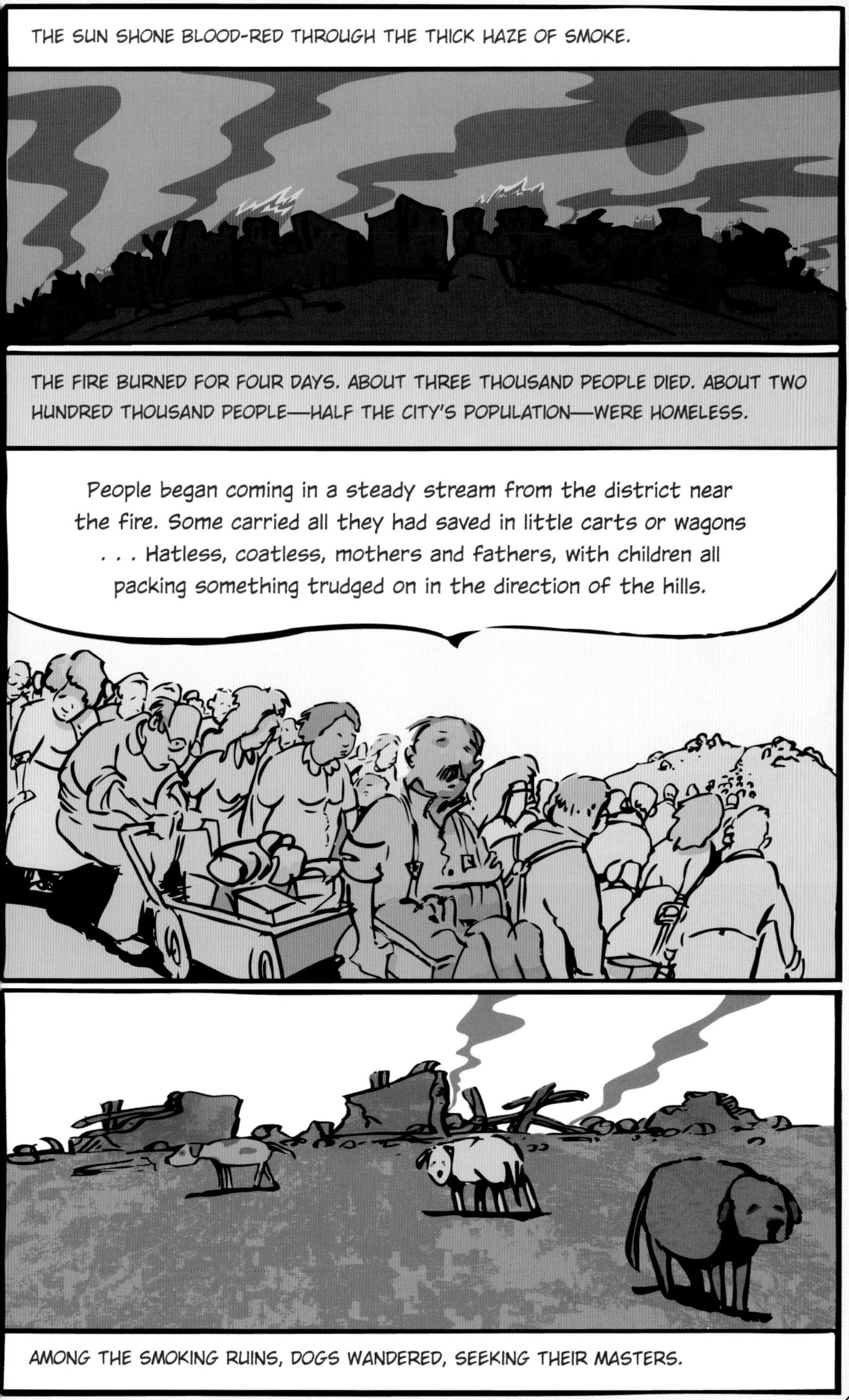
THE SUN SHONE BLOOD-RED THROUGH THE THICK HAZE OF SMOKE.
THE FIRE BURNED FOR FOUR DAYS. ABOUT THREE THOUSAND PEOPLE DIED. ABOUT TWO HUNDRED THOUSAND PEOPLE—HALF THE CITY'S POPULATION—WERE HOMELESS.
People began coming in a steady stream from the district near the fire. Some carried all they had saved in little carts or wagons . . . Hatless, coatless, mothers and fathers, with children all packing something trudged on in the direction of the hills.
AMONG THE SMOKING RUINS, DOGS WANDERED, SEEKING THEIR MASTERS.

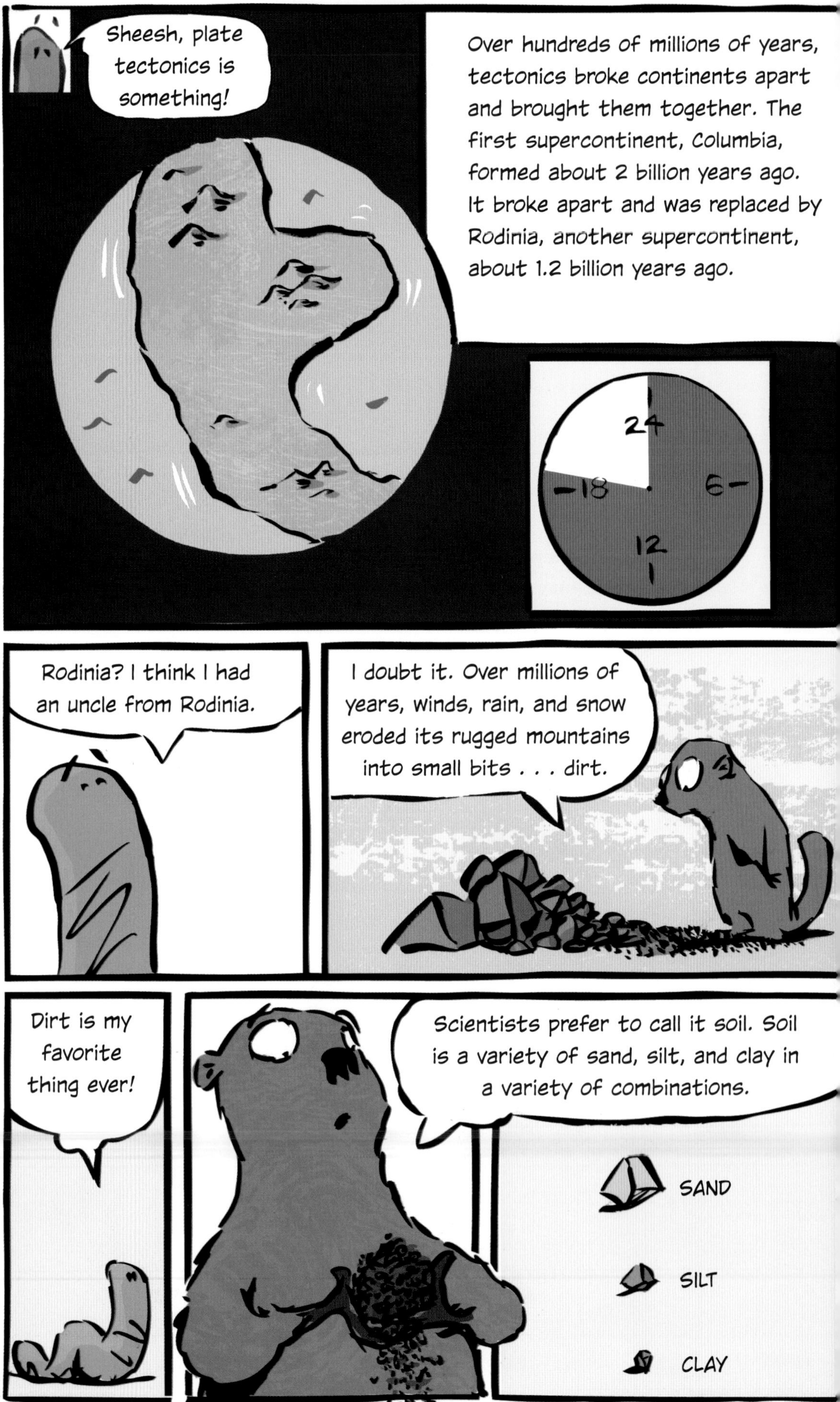
Sheesh, plate tectonics is something!
Over hundreds of millions of years, tectonics broke continents apart and brought them together. The first supercontinent, Columbia, formed about 2 billion years ago. It broke apart and was replaced by Rodinia, another supercontinent, about 1.2 billion years ago.
24
6
12
18
Rodinia? I think I had an uncle from Rodinia.
I doubt it. Over millions of years, winds, rain, and snow eroded its rugged mountains into small bits . . . dirt.
Dirt is my favorite thing ever!
Scientists prefer to call it soil. Soil is a variety of sand, silt, and clay in a variety of combinations.
SAND
SILT
CLAY

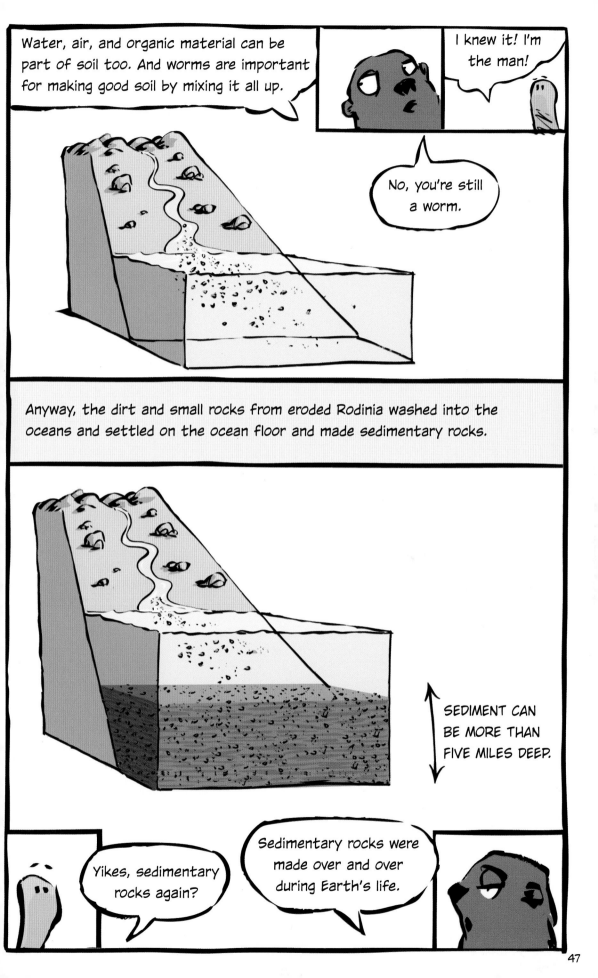

Water, air, and organic material can be part of soil too. And worms are important for making good soil by mixing it all up.

I knew it! I'm the man!

No, you're still a worm.

Anyway, the dirt and small rocks from eroded Rodinia washed into the oceans and settled on the ocean floor and made sedimentary rocks.

SEDIMENT CAN BE MORE THAN FIVE MILES DEEP.

Yikes, sedimentary rocks again?

Sedimentary rocks were made over and over during Earth's life.

47

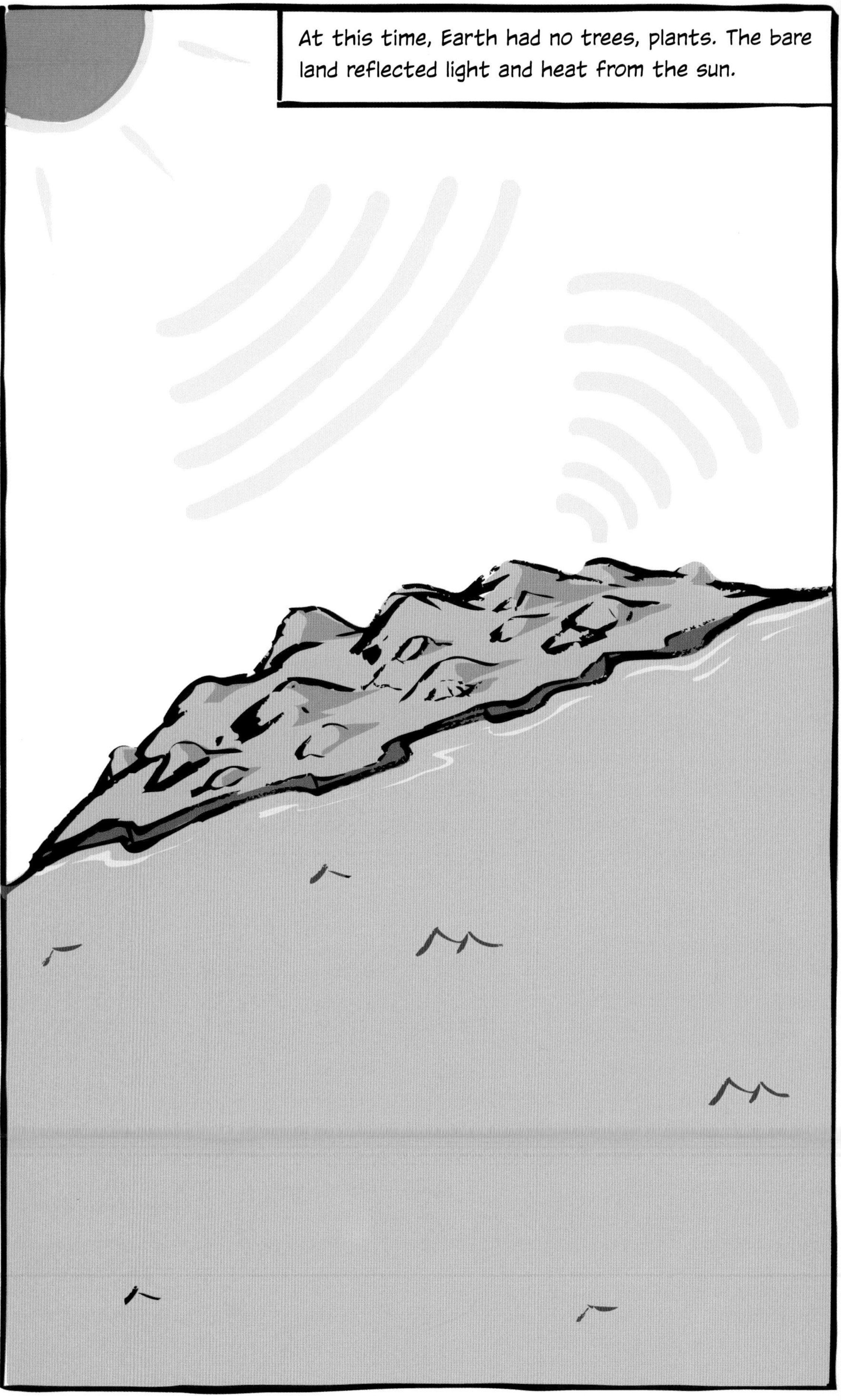
At this time, Earth had no trees, plants. The bare land reflected light and heat from the sun.

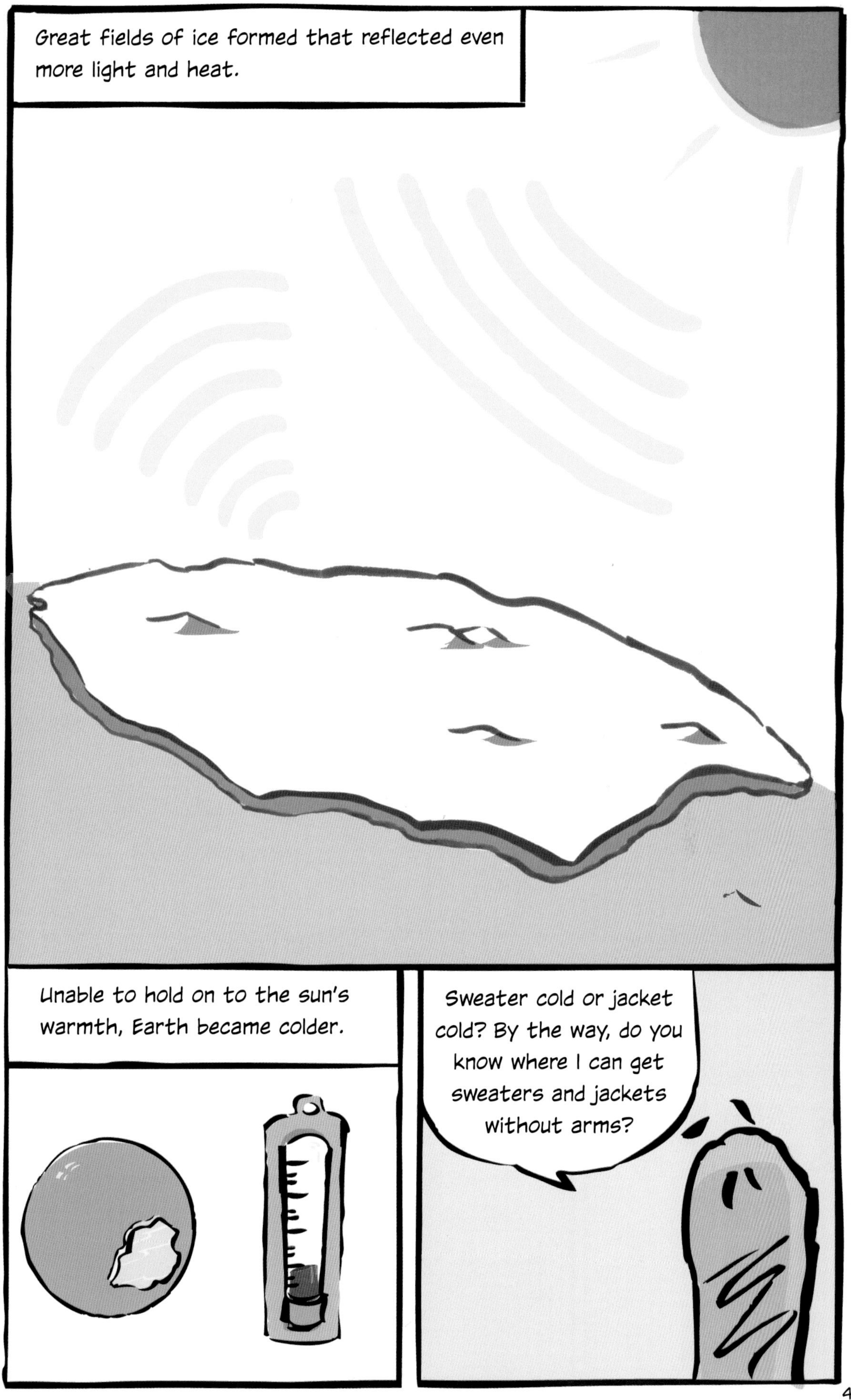

Great fields of ice formed that reflected even more light and heat.
Unable to hold on to the sun's warmth, Earth became colder.
Sweater cold or jacket cold? By the way, do you know where I can get sweaters and jackets without arms?

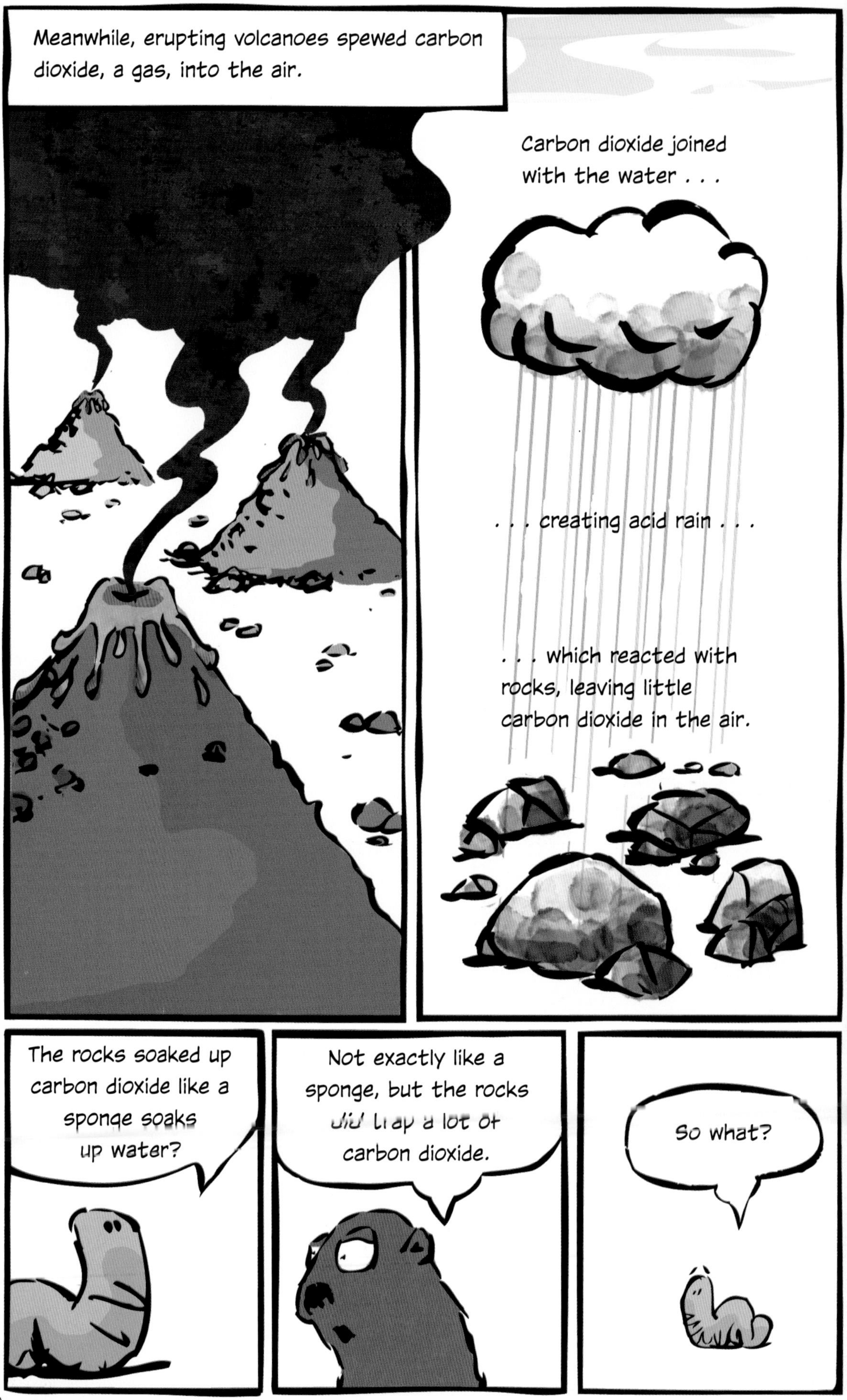
Meanwhile, erupting volcanoes spewed carbon dioxide, a gas, into the air.
Carbon dioxide joined with the water . . .
. . . creating acid rain . . .
. . . which reacted with rocks, leaving little carbon dioxide in the air.
The rocks soaked up carbon dioxide like a sponge soaks up water?
Not exactly like a sponge, but the rocks did trap a lot of carbon dioxide.
So what?

Like a blanket, carbon dioxide traps Earth's heat and doesn't let it escape into space.

Too little and Earth gets colder.

Too much carbon dioxide makes Earth warm.

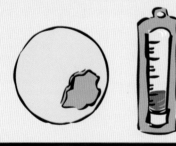

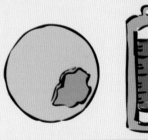

With most of the carbon dioxide trapped in rock, Earth became cold, cold. Ice and snow nearly blanketed the whole planet. It looked like a giant snowball.

You want gloves? I've got extra. No use for 'em.

It happened three times. The last episode of Snowball Earth happened about 580 million years ago.

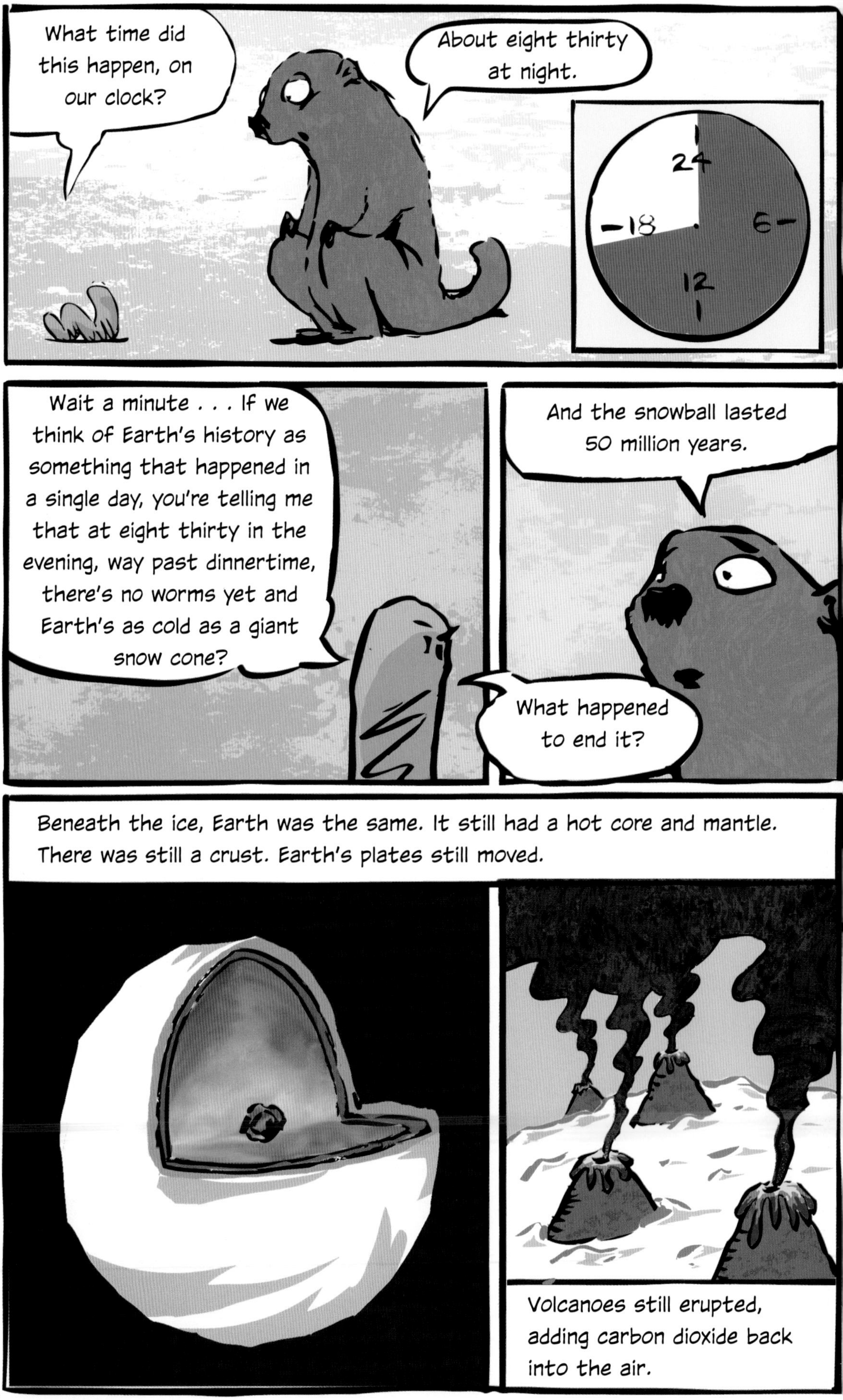
What time did this happen, on our clock?
About eight thirty at night.
24
6
12
18
Wait a minute . . . If we think of Earth's history as something that happened in a single day, you're telling me that at eight thirty in the evening, way past dinnertime, there's no worms yet and Earth's as cold as a giant snow cone?
And the snowball lasted 50 million years.
What happened to end it?
Beneath the ice, Earth was the same. It still had a hot core and mantle. There was still a crust. Earth's plates still moved.
Volcanoes still erupted, adding carbon dioxide back into the air.

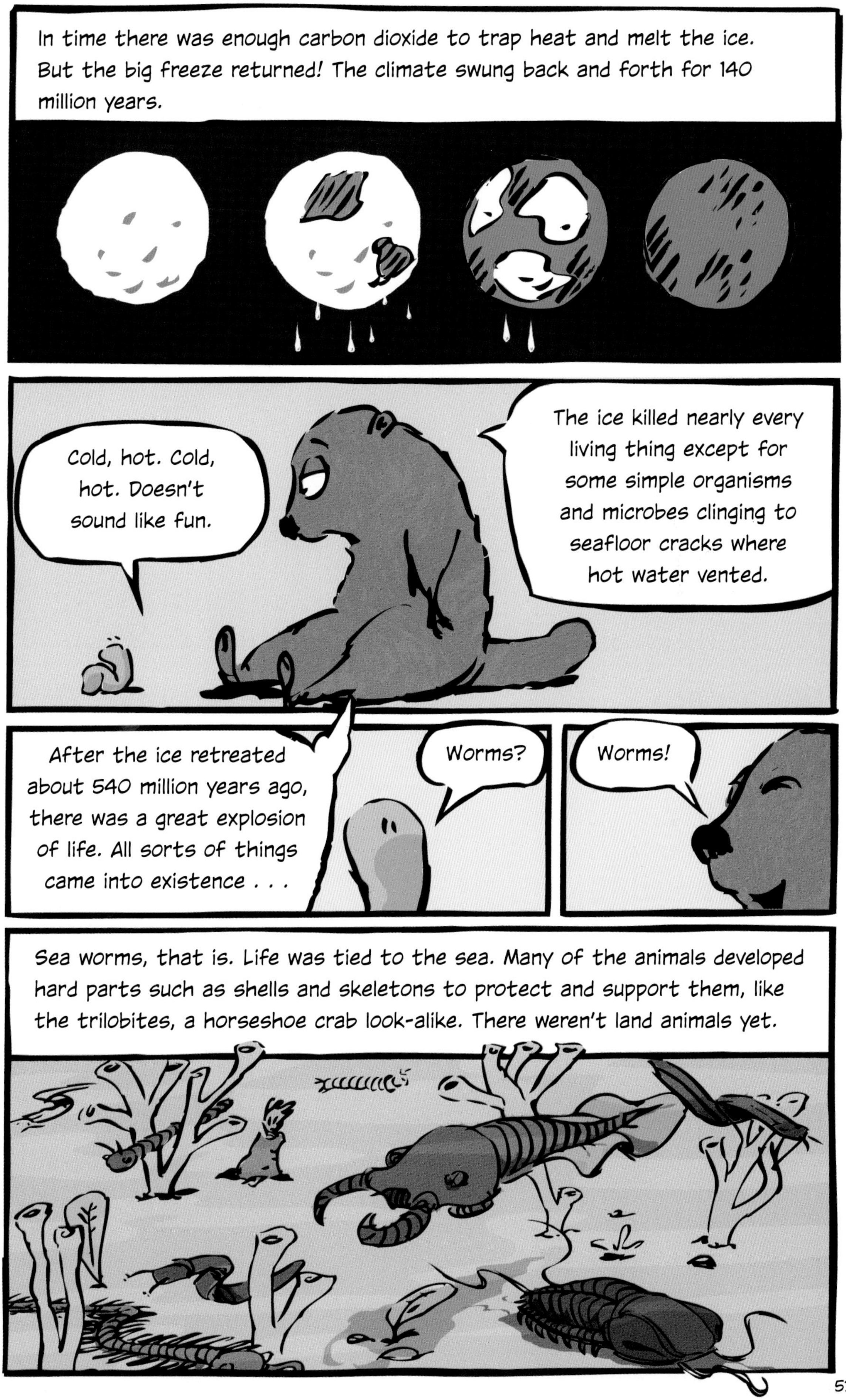
In time there was enough carbon dioxide to trap heat and melt the ice. But the big freeze returned! The climate swung back and forth for 140 million years.
Cold, hot. Cold, hot. Doesn't sound like fun.
The ice killed nearly every living thing except for some simple organisms and microbes clinging to seafloor cracks where hot water vented.
After the ice retreated about 540 million years ago, there was a great explosion of life. All sorts of things came into existence . . .
Worms?
Worms!
Sea worms, that is. Life was tied to the sea. Many of the animals developed hard parts such as shells and skeletons to protect and support them, like the trilobites, a horseshoe crab look-alike. There weren't land animals yet.

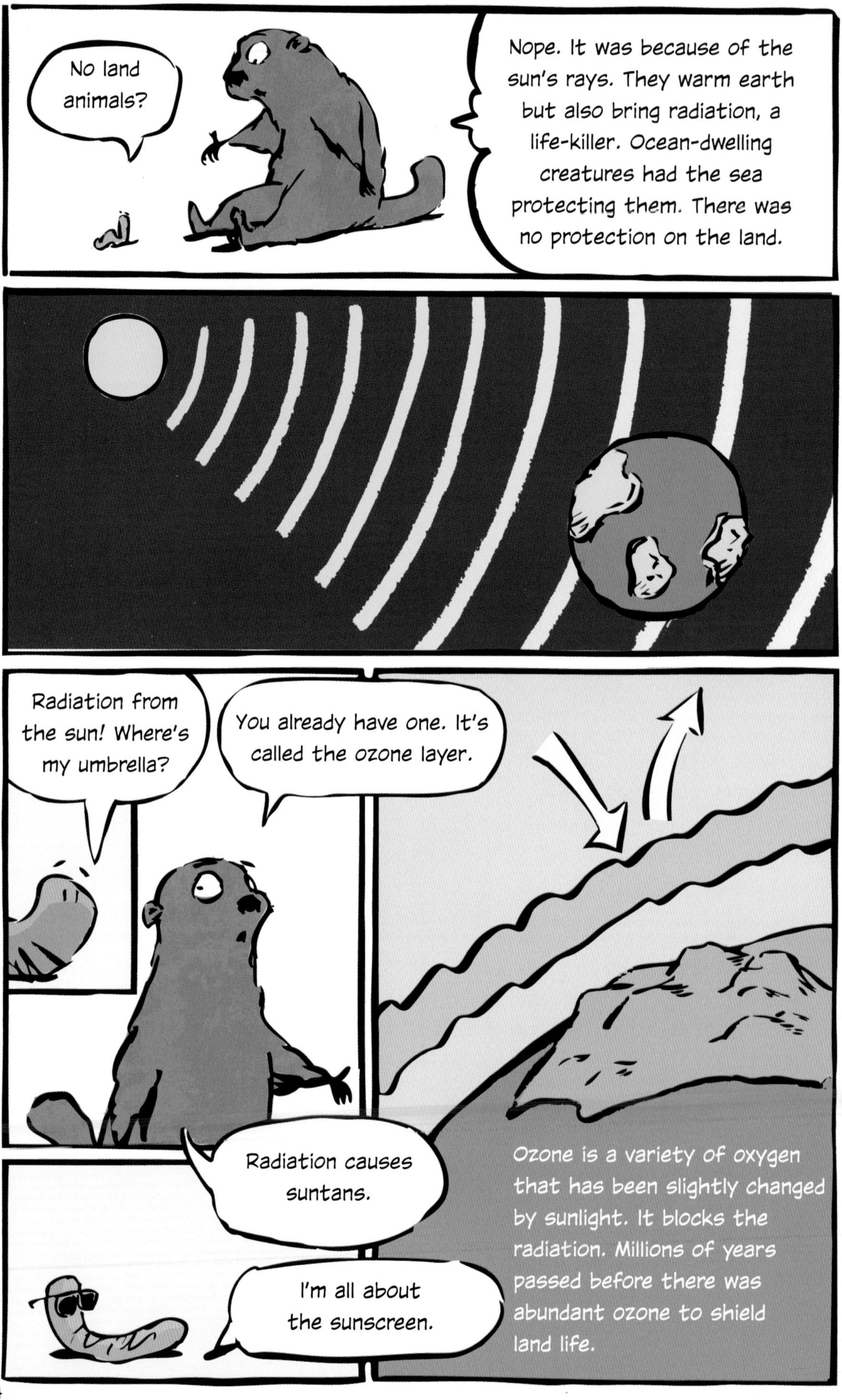

No land animals?
Nope. It was because of the sun's rays. They warm earth but also bring radiation, a life-killer. Ocean-dwelling creatures had the sea protecting them. There was no protection on the land.
Radiation from the sun! Where's my umbrella?
You already have one. It's called the ozone layer.
Ozone is a variety of oxygen that has been slightly changed by sunlight. It blocks the radiation. Millions of years passed before there was abundant ozone to shield land life.
Radiation causes suntans.
I'm all about the sunscreen.

About 395 million years ago, sea creatures crawled onto the land and evolved into tetrapods, the first four-limbed creatures . . .

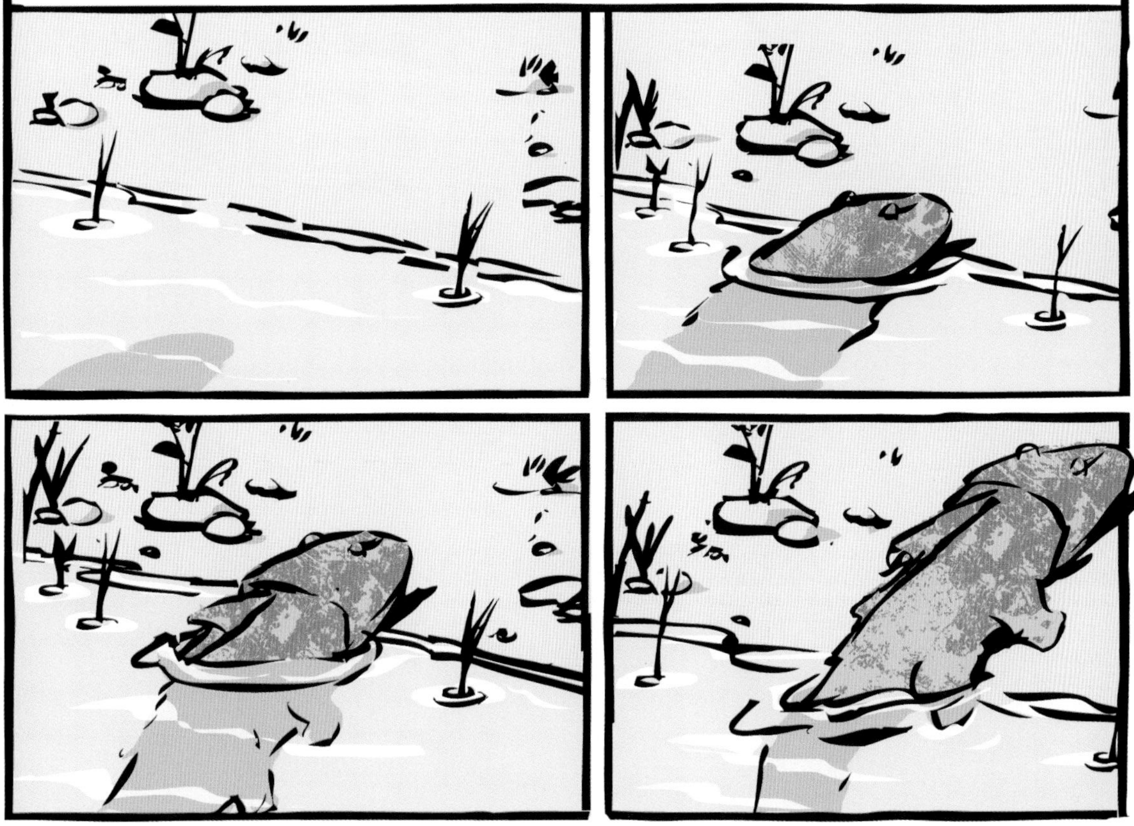

Tetrapods are the great-great-grandparents to present-day amphibians, reptiles, birds, and mammals.

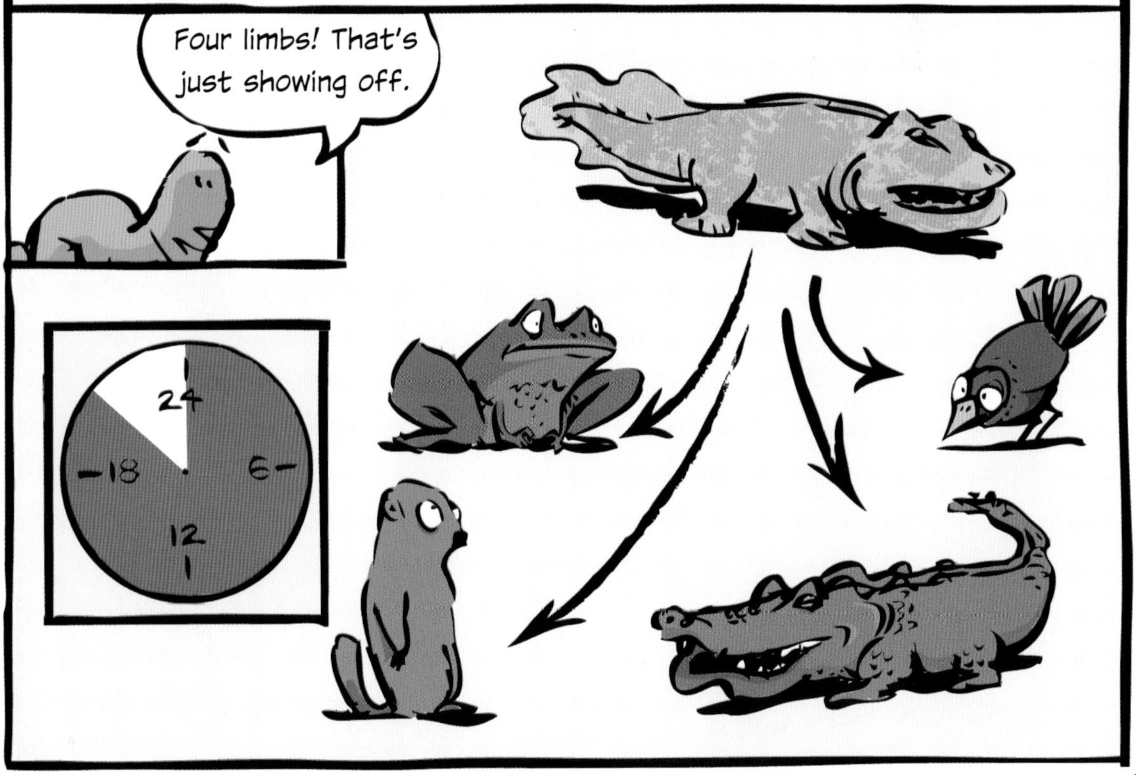
Four limbs! That's just showing off.
24
6
12
18

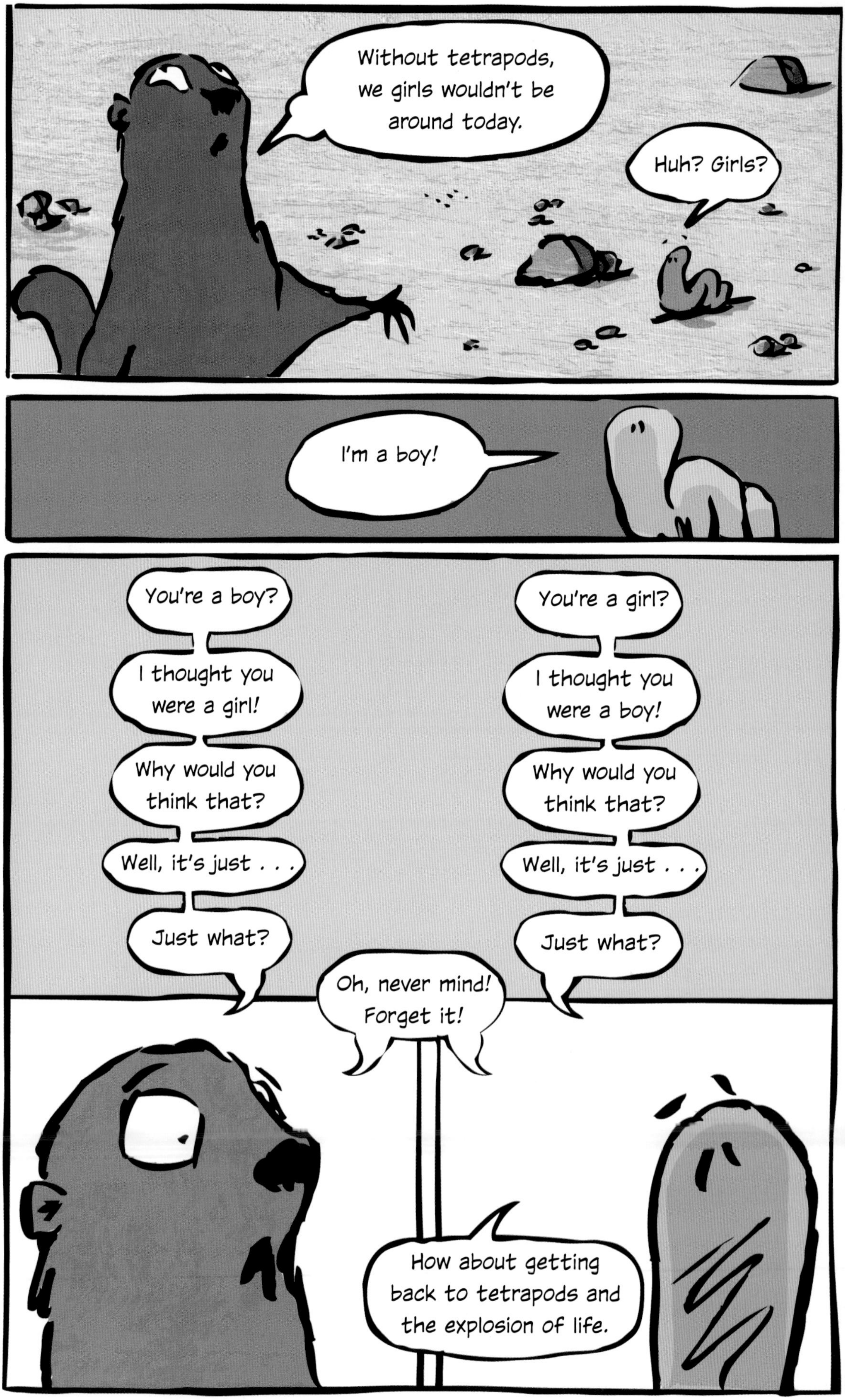
Without tetrapods, we girls wouldn't be around today.
Huh? Girls?
I'm a boy!
You're a boy?
I thought you were a girl!
Why would you think that?
Well, it's just . . .
Just what?
You're a girl?
I thought you were a boy!
Why would you think that?
Well, it's just . . .
Just what?
Oh, never mind! Forget it!
How about getting back to tetrapods and the explosion of life.

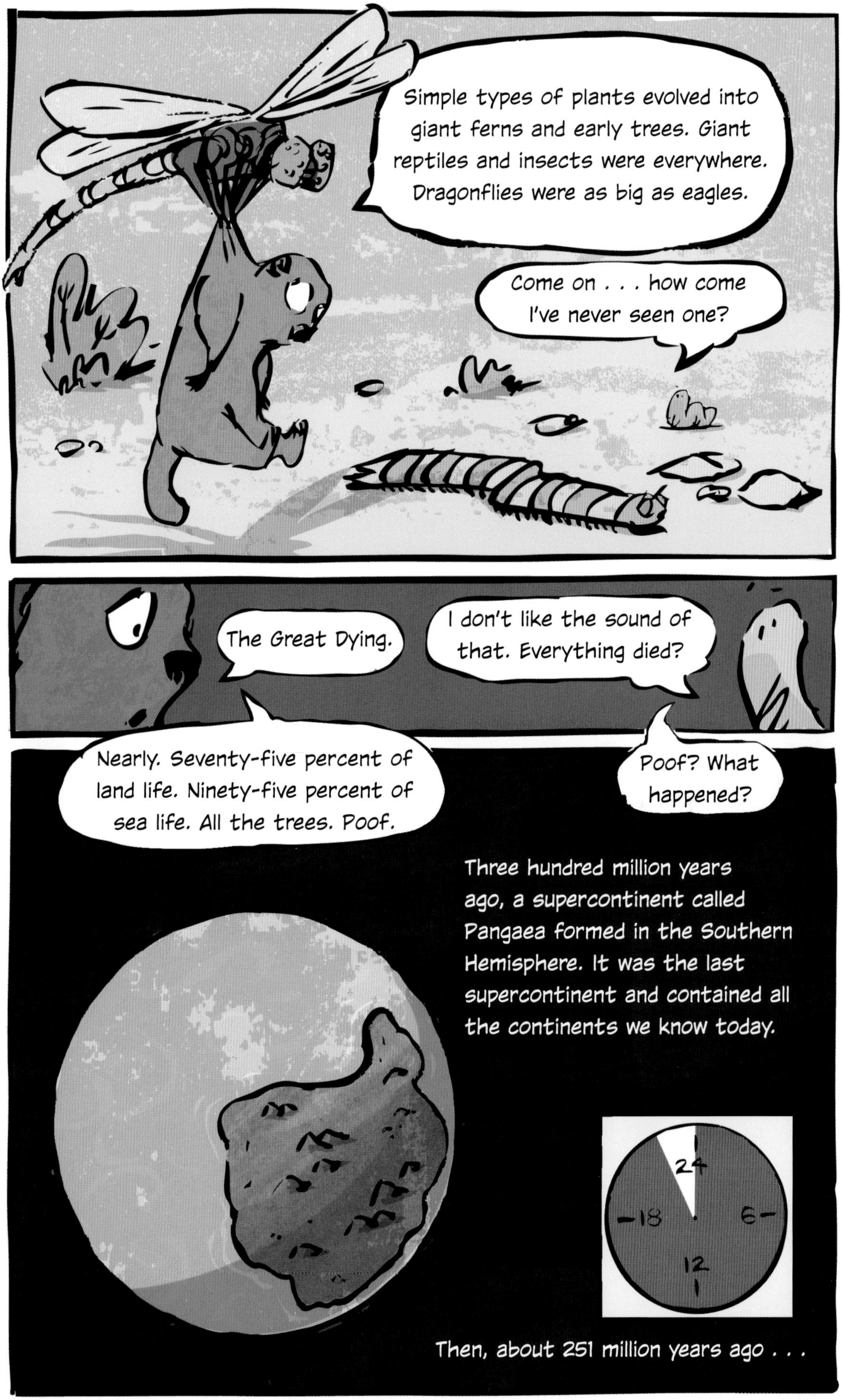
Simple types of plants evolved into giant ferns and early trees. Giant reptiles and insects were everywhere. Dragonflies were as big as eagles.
Come on . . . how come I've never seen one?
The Great Dying.
I don't like the sound of that. Everything died?
Nearly. Seventy-five percent of land life. Ninety-five percent of sea life. All the trees. Poof.
Poof? What happened?
Three hundred million years ago, a supercontinent called Pangaea formed in the Southern Hemisphere. It was the last supercontinent and contained all the continents we know today.
24
6
12
18
Then, about 251 million years ago . . .

. . . giant eruptions of lava sprouted everywhere.

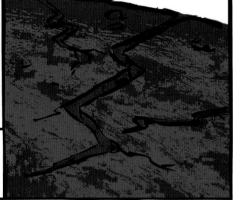

Uh-oh.

Lava spewed from cracks in Earth for a half a million years.

In places, two-and-a-half-mile-thick lava collected. The flows made a million cubic miles of basaltic rock.

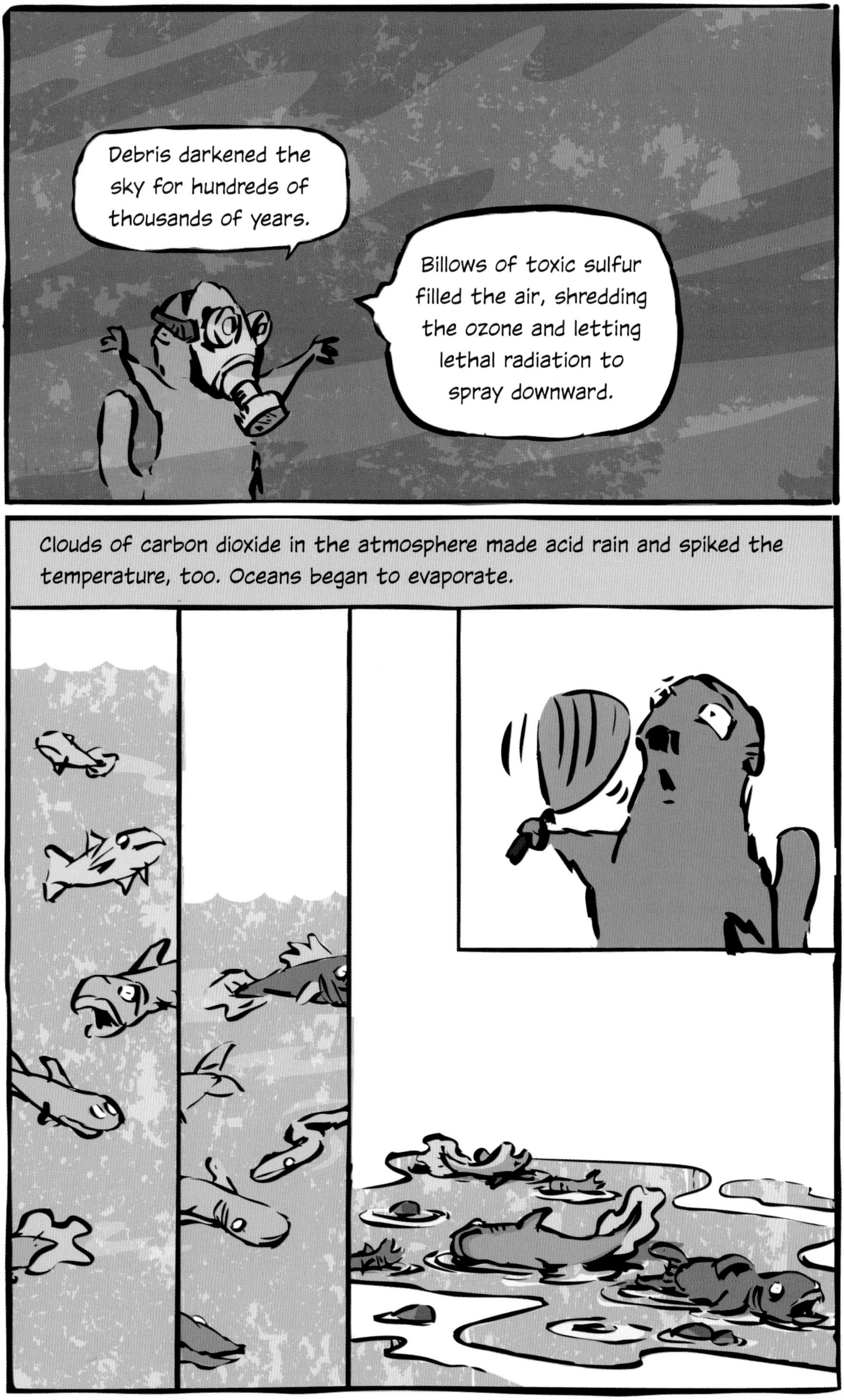
Debris darkened the sky for hundreds of thousands of years.
Billows of toxic sulfur filled the air, shredding the ozone and letting lethal radiation to spray downward.
Clouds of carbon dioxide in the atmosphere made acid rain and spiked the temperature, too. Oceans began to evaporate.

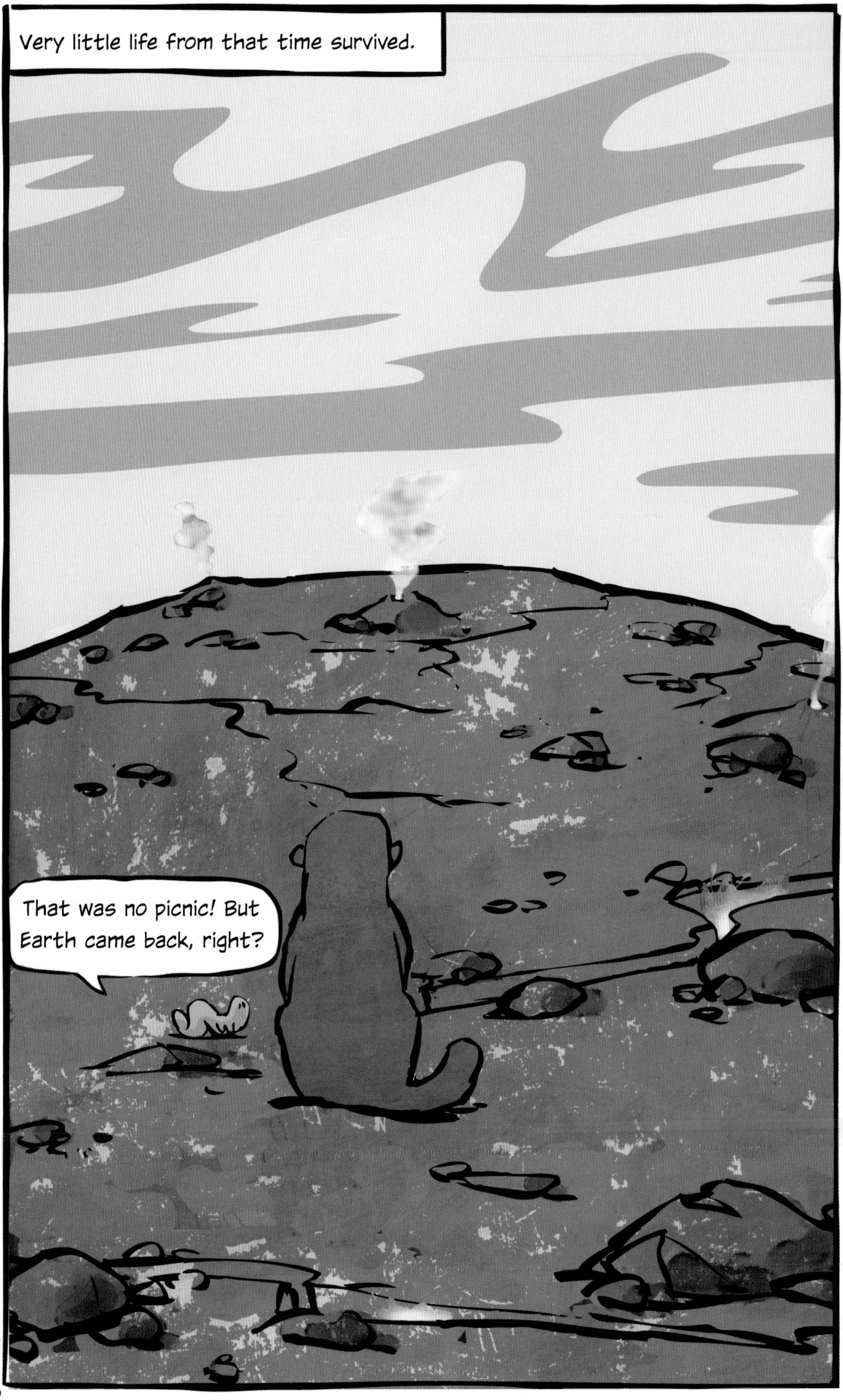
Very little life from that time survived.
That was no picnic! But Earth came back, right?

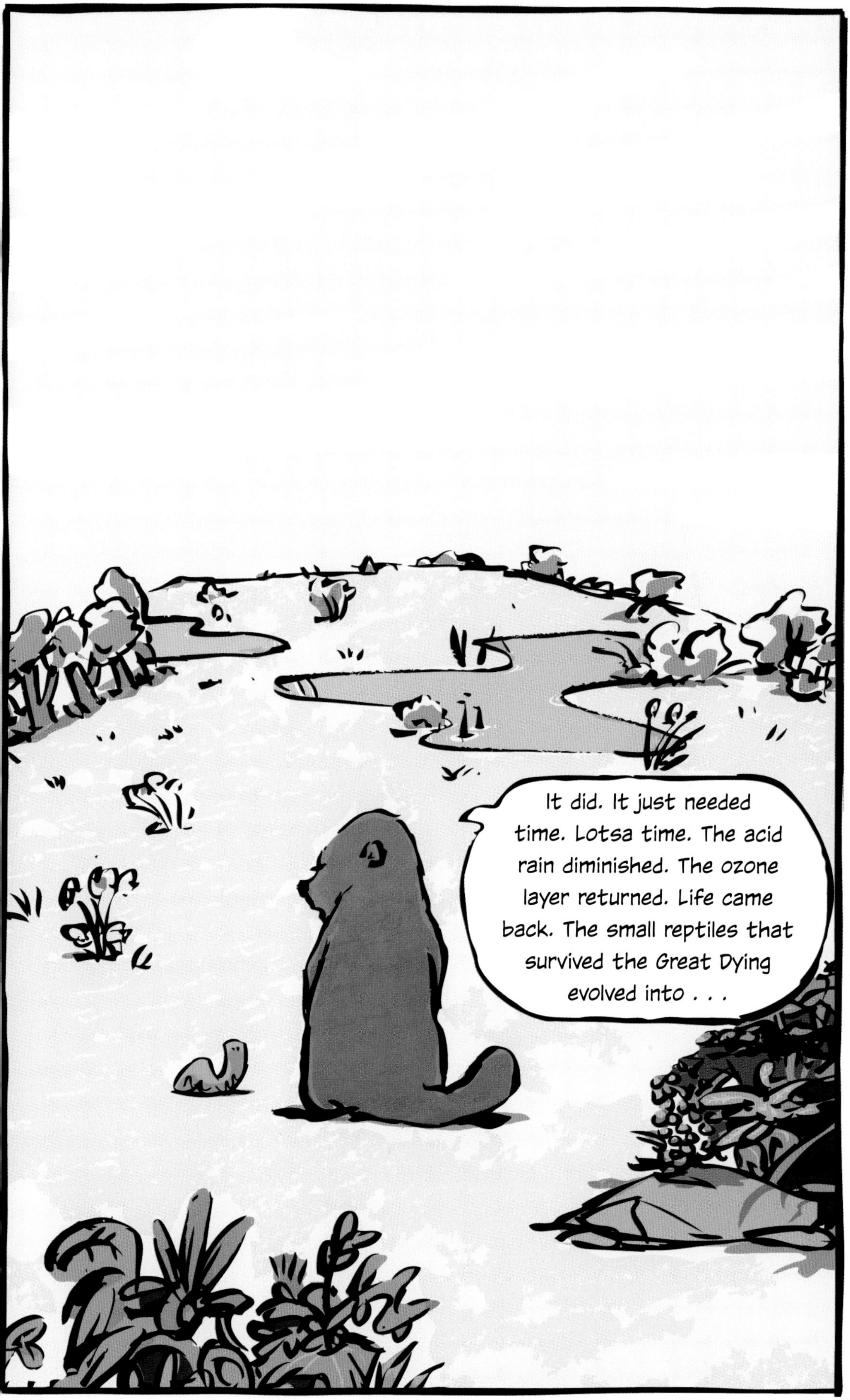
It did. It just needed time. Lotsa time. The acid rain diminished. The ozone layer returned. Life came back. The small reptiles that survived the Great Dying evolved into . . .

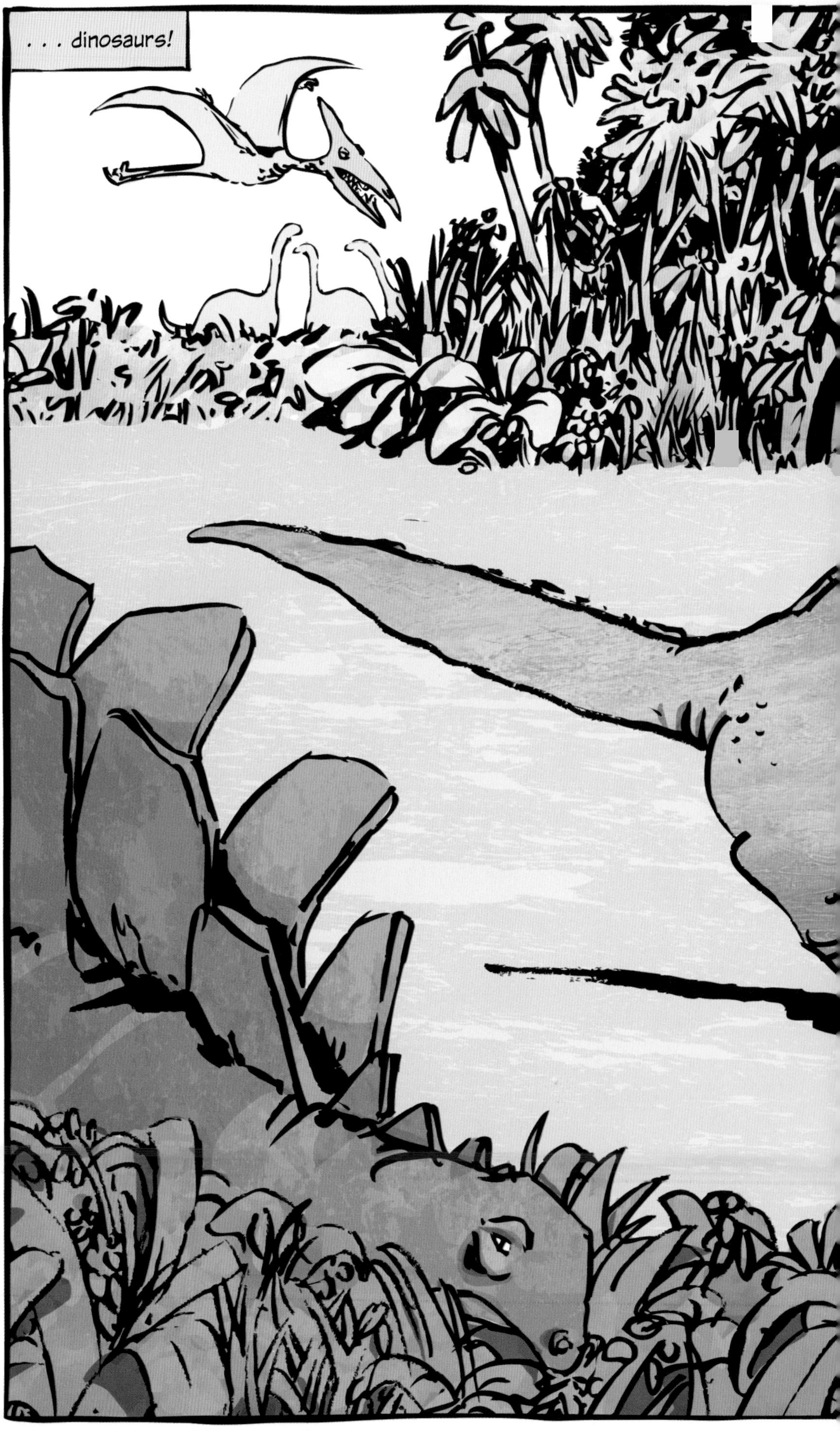
. . . dinosaurs!

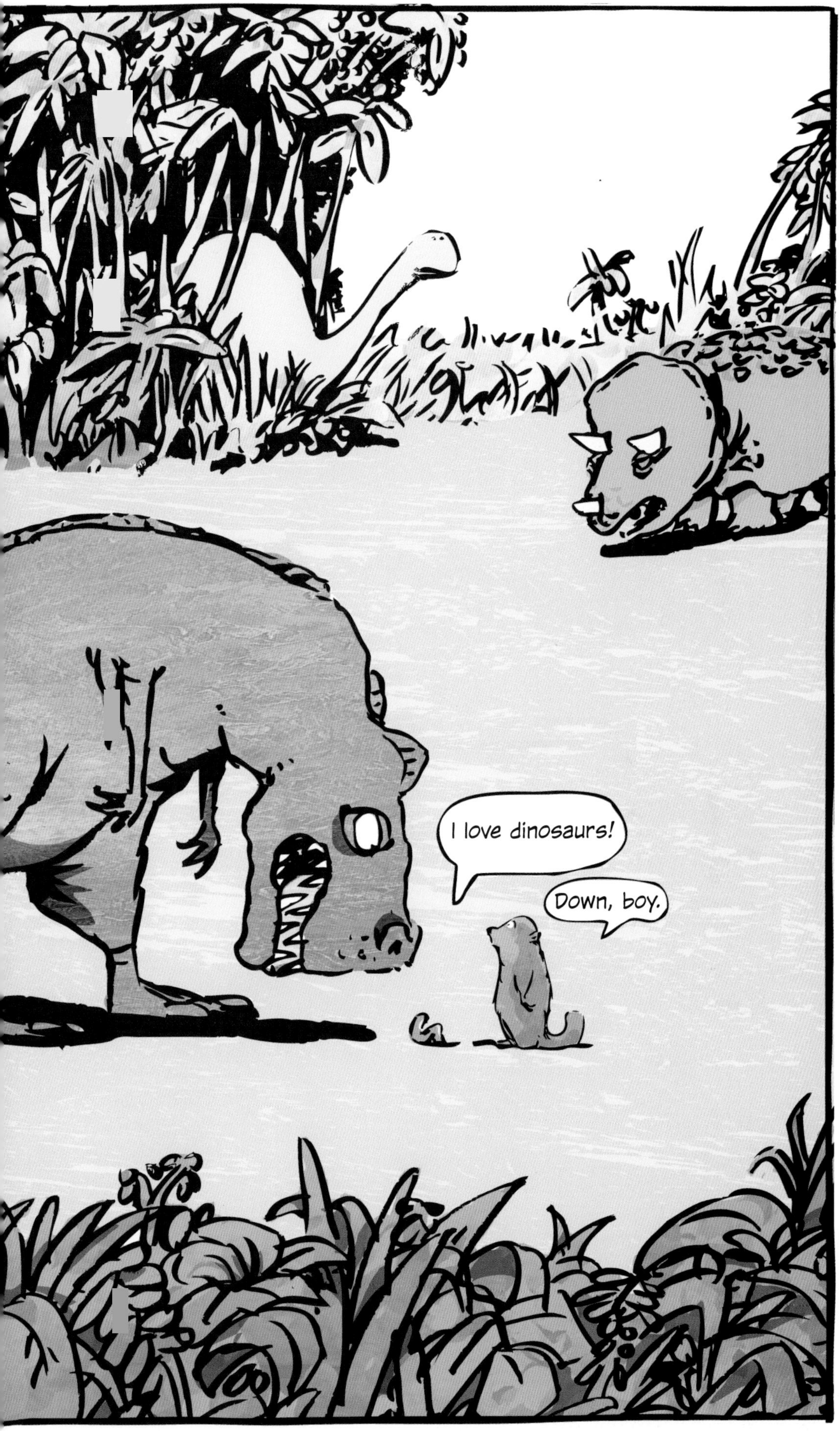
I love dinosaurs!
Down, boy.

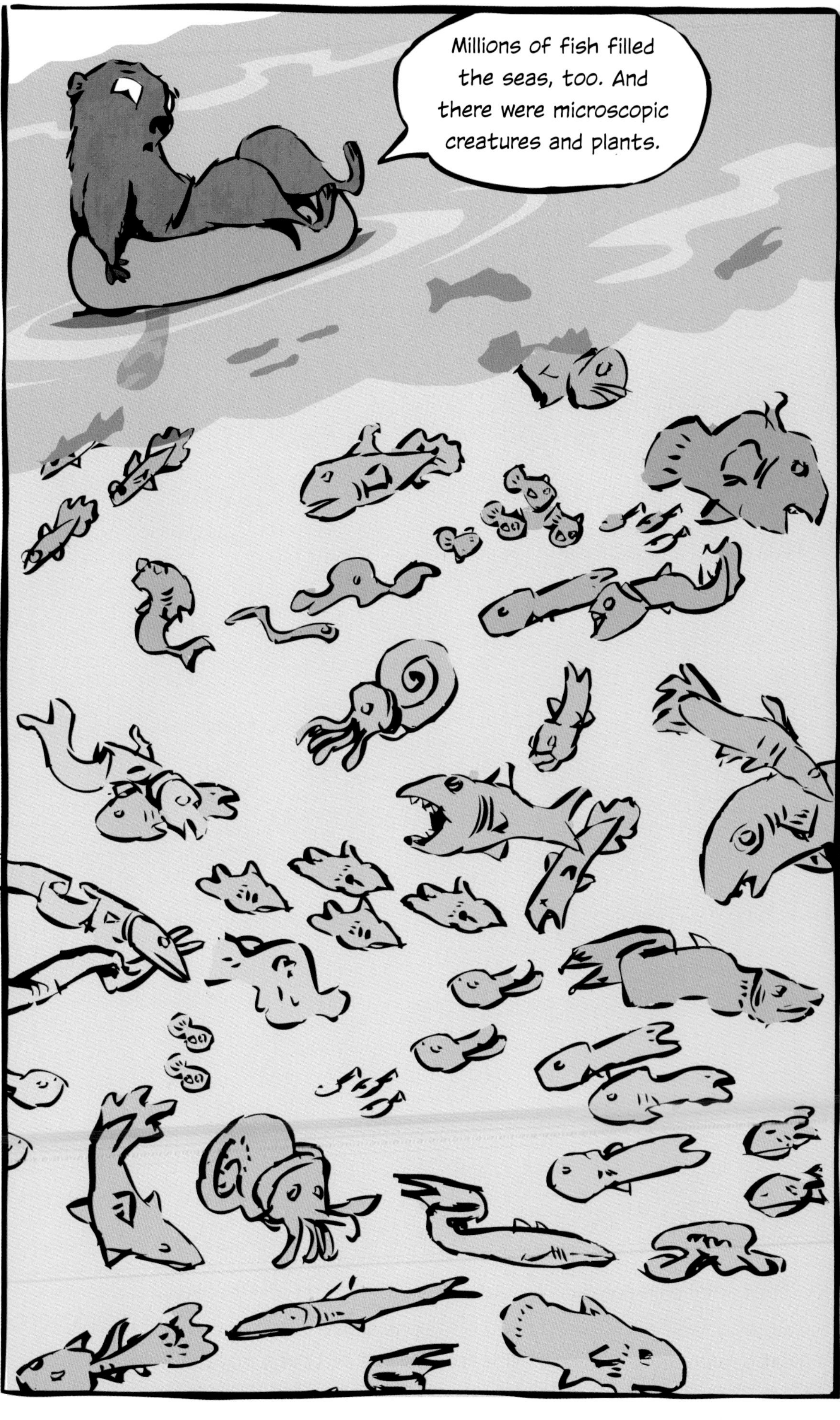
Millions of fish filled the seas, too. And there were microscopic creatures and plants.

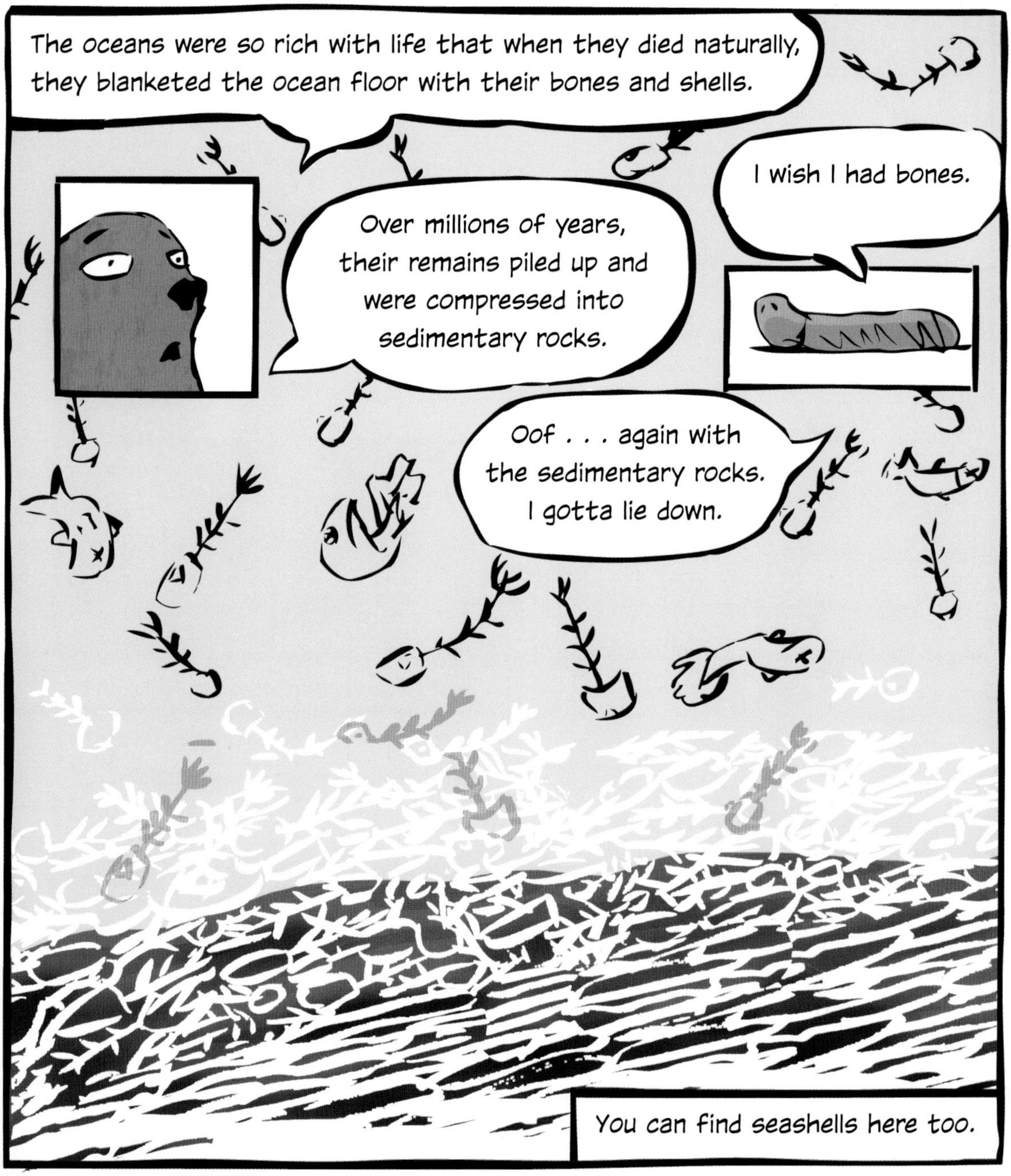
The oceans were so rich with life that when they died naturally, they blanketed the ocean floor with their bones and shells.
Over millions of years, their remains piled up and were compressed into sedimentary rocks.
I wish I had bones.
Oof . . . again with the sedimentary rocks. I gotta lie down.
You can find seashells here too.

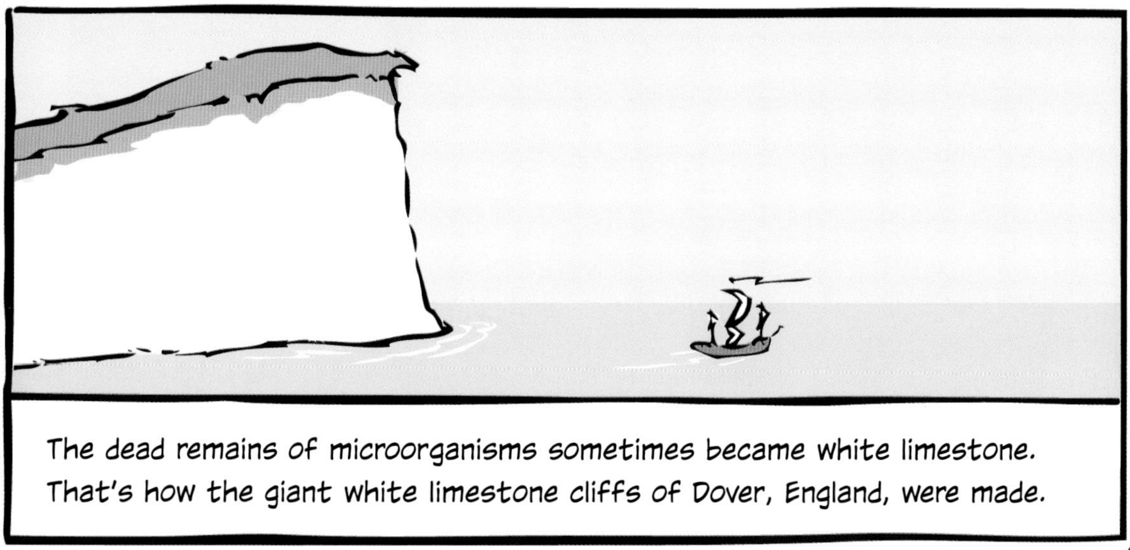
The dead remains of microorganisms sometimes became white limestone. That's how the giant white limestone cliffs of Dover, England, were made.

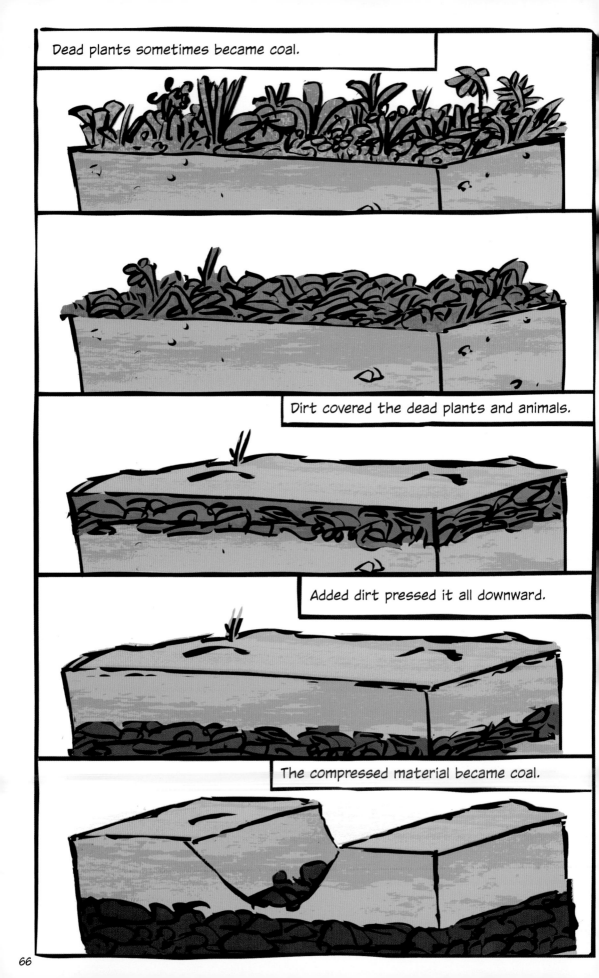

Dead plants sometimes became coal.

Dirt covered the dead plants and animals.

Added dirt pressed it all downward.

The compressed material became coal.

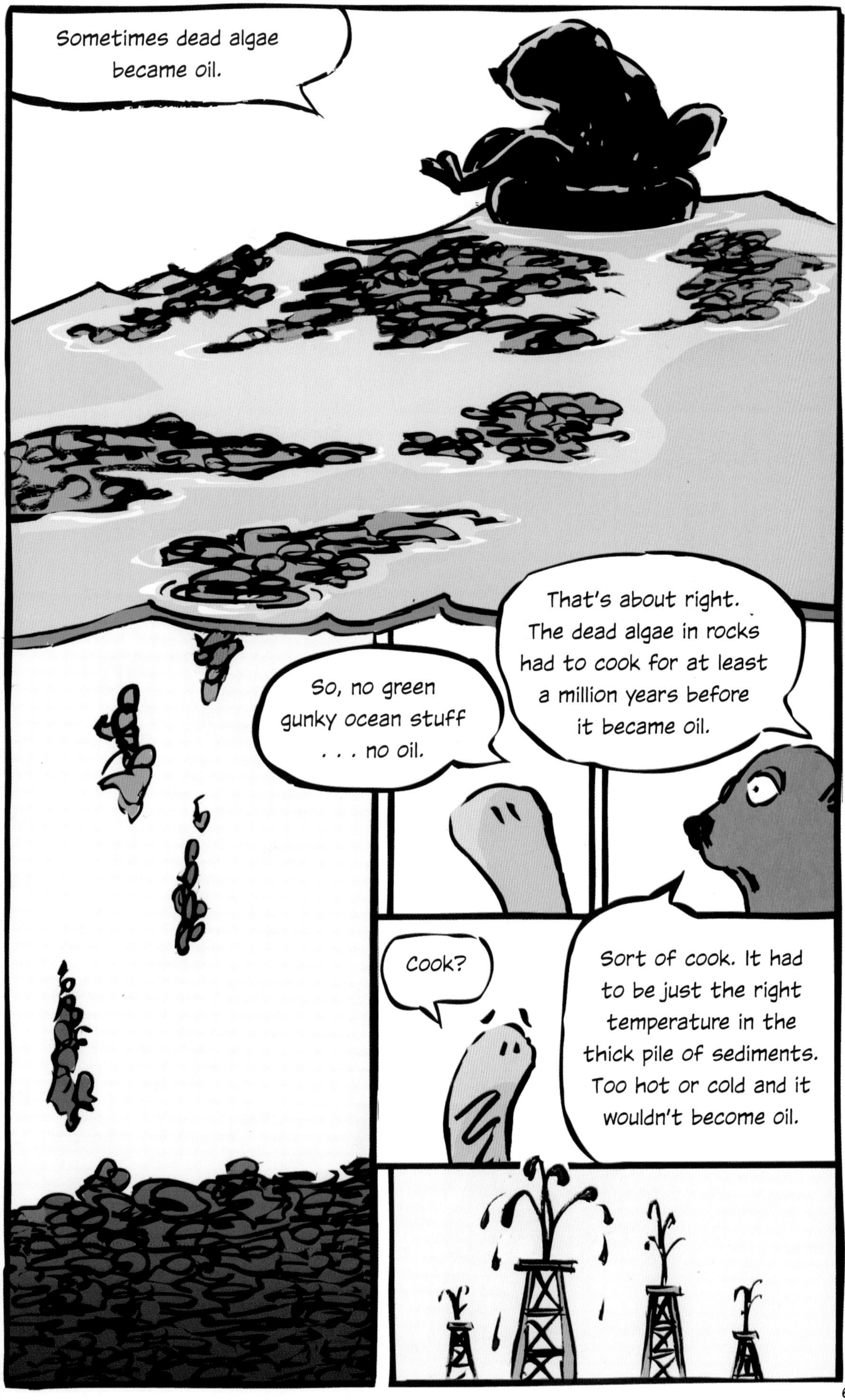

Sometimes dead algae became oil.
So, no green gunky ocean stuff . . . no oil.
That's about right. The dead algae in rocks had to cook for at least a million years before it became oil.
Cook?
Sort of cook. It had to be just the right temperature in the thick pile of sediments. Too hot or cold and it wouldn't become oil.

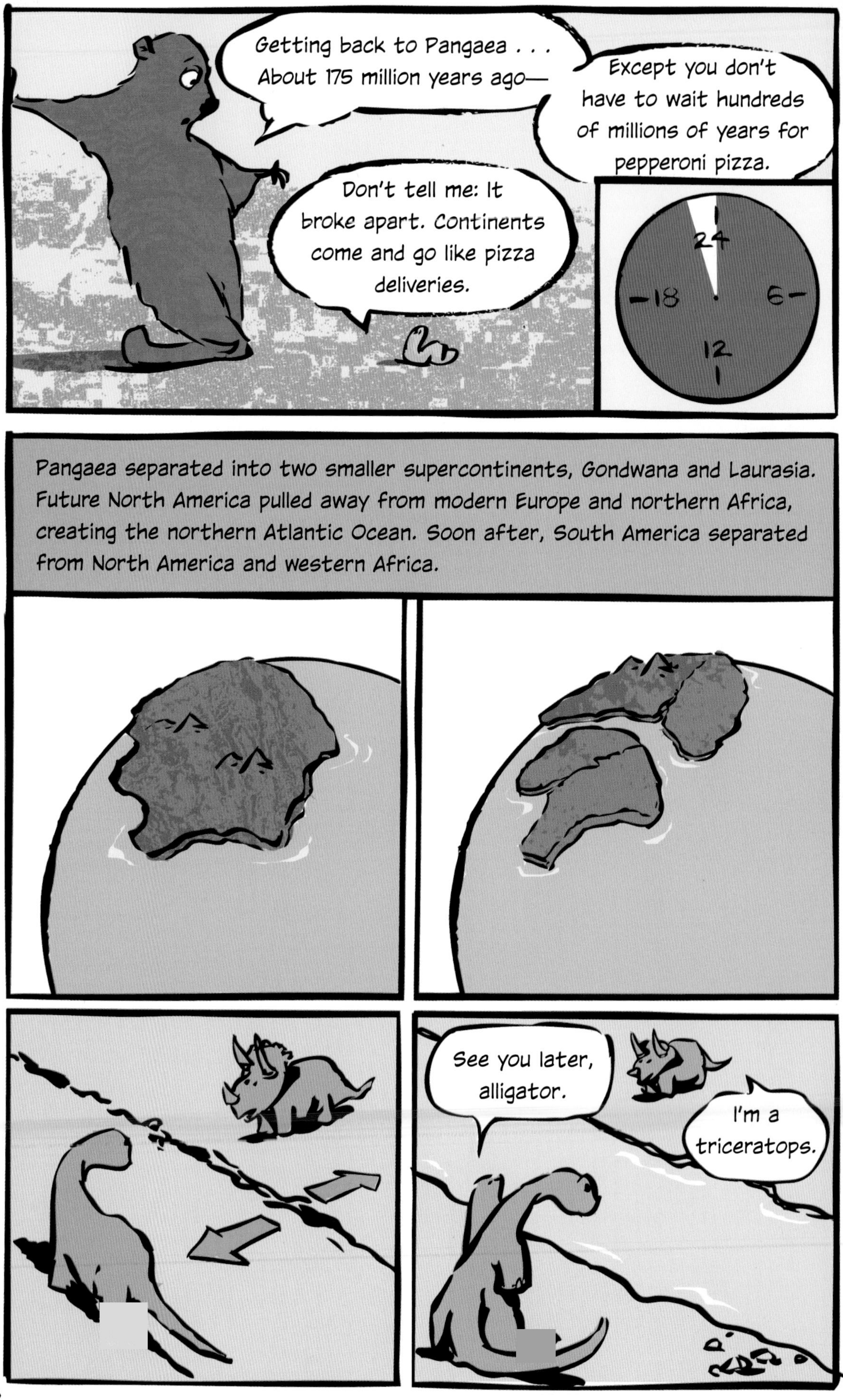

Getting back to Pangaea . . . About 175 million years ago—
Don't tell me: It broke apart. Continents come and go like pizza deliveries.
Except you don't have to wait hundreds of millions of years for pepperoni pizza.
24
6
12
18
Pangaea separated into two smaller supercontinents, Gondwana and Laurasia. Future North America pulled away from modern Europe and northern Africa, creating the northern Atlantic Ocean. Soon after, South America separated from North America and western Africa.
See you later, alligator.
I'm a triceratops.

The seam where the plates pulled apart made a scar of volcanoes that created underwater mountains.

Wow, that's amazing!

No one knew about it for a long time. It was deep beneath the sea and hidden from view. But a few people suspected something was going on.

Is it time for another episode of Deep Time Comix?

You've got a big brain, little guy.

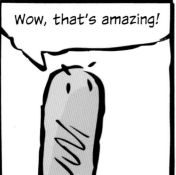

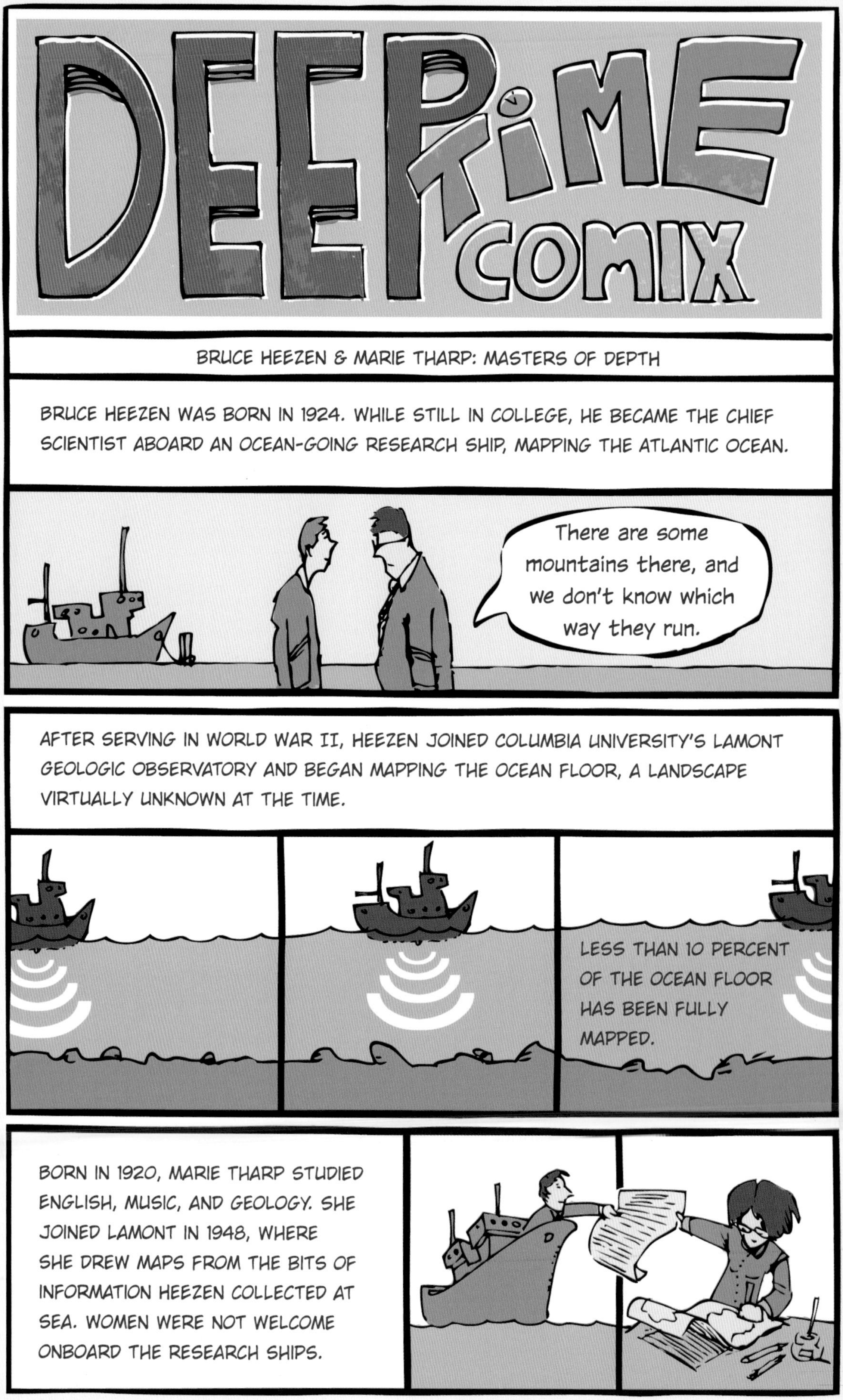
DEEP TIME COMIX
BRUCE HEEZEN & MARIE THARP: MASTERS OF DEPTH
BRUCE HEEZEN WAS BORN IN 1924. WHILE STILL IN COLLEGE, HE BECAME THE CHIEF SCIENTIST ABOARD AN OCEAN-GOING RESEARCH SHIP, MAPPING THE ATLANTIC OCEAN.
There are some mountains there, and we don't know which way they run.
AFTER SERVING IN WORLD WAR II, HEEZEN JOINED COLUMBIA UNIVERSITY'S LAMONT GEOLOGIC OBSERVATORY AND BEGAN MAPPING THE OCEAN FLOOR, A LANDSCAPE VIRTUALLY UNKNOWN AT THE TIME.
LESS THAN 10 PERCENT OF THE OCEAN FLOOR HAS BEEN FULLY MAPPED.
BORN IN 1920, MARIE THARP STUDIED ENGLISH, MUSIC, AND GEOLOGY. SHE JOINED LAMONT IN 1948, WHERE SHE DREW MAPS FROM THE BITS OF INFORMATION HEEZEN COLLECTED AT SEA. WOMEN WERE NOT WELCOME ONBOARD THE RESEARCH SHIPS.

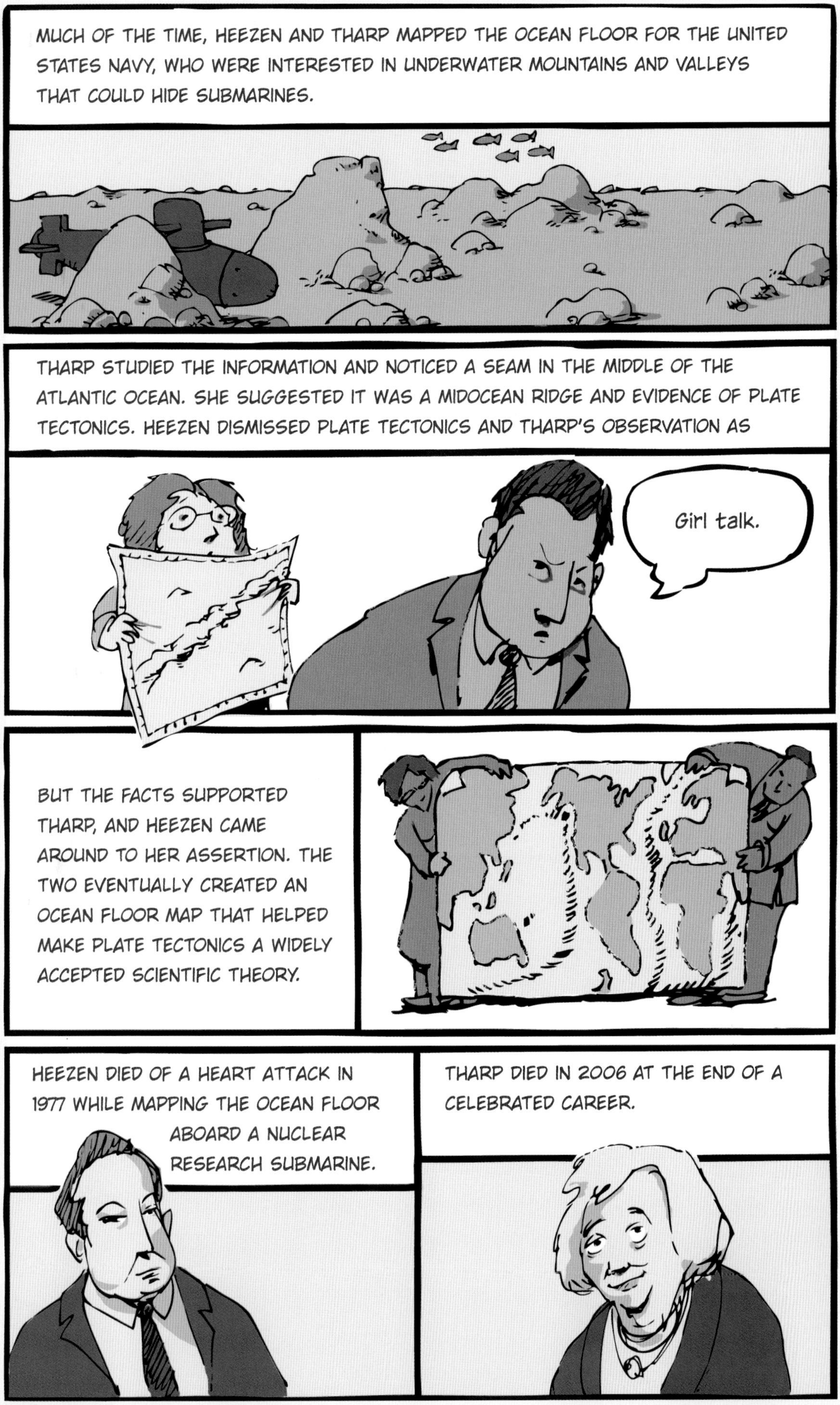
MUCH OF THE TIME, HEEZEN AND THARP MAPPED THE OCEAN FLOOR FOR THE UNITED STATES NAVY, WHO WERE INTERESTED IN UNDERWATER MOUNTAINS AND VALLEYS THAT COULD HIDE SUBMARINES.
THARP STUDIED THE INFORMATION AND NOTICED A SEAM IN THE MIDDLE OF THE ATLANTIC OCEAN. SHE SUGGESTED IT WAS A MIDOCEAN RIDGE AND EVIDENCE OF PLATE TECTONICS. HEEZEN DISMISSED PLATE TECTONICS AND THARP'S OBSERVATION AS
Girl talk.
BUT THE FACTS SUPPORTED THARP, AND HEEZEN CAME AROUND TO HER ASSERTION. THE TWO EVENTUALLY CREATED AN OCEAN FLOOR MAP THAT HELPED MAKE PLATE TECTONICS A WIDELY ACCEPTED SCIENTIFIC THEORY.
HEEZEN DIED OF A HEART ATTACK IN 1977 WHILE MAPPING THE OCEAN FLOOR ABOARD A NUCLEAR RESEARCH SUBMARINE.
THARP DIED IN 2006 AT THE END OF A CELEBRATED CAREER.

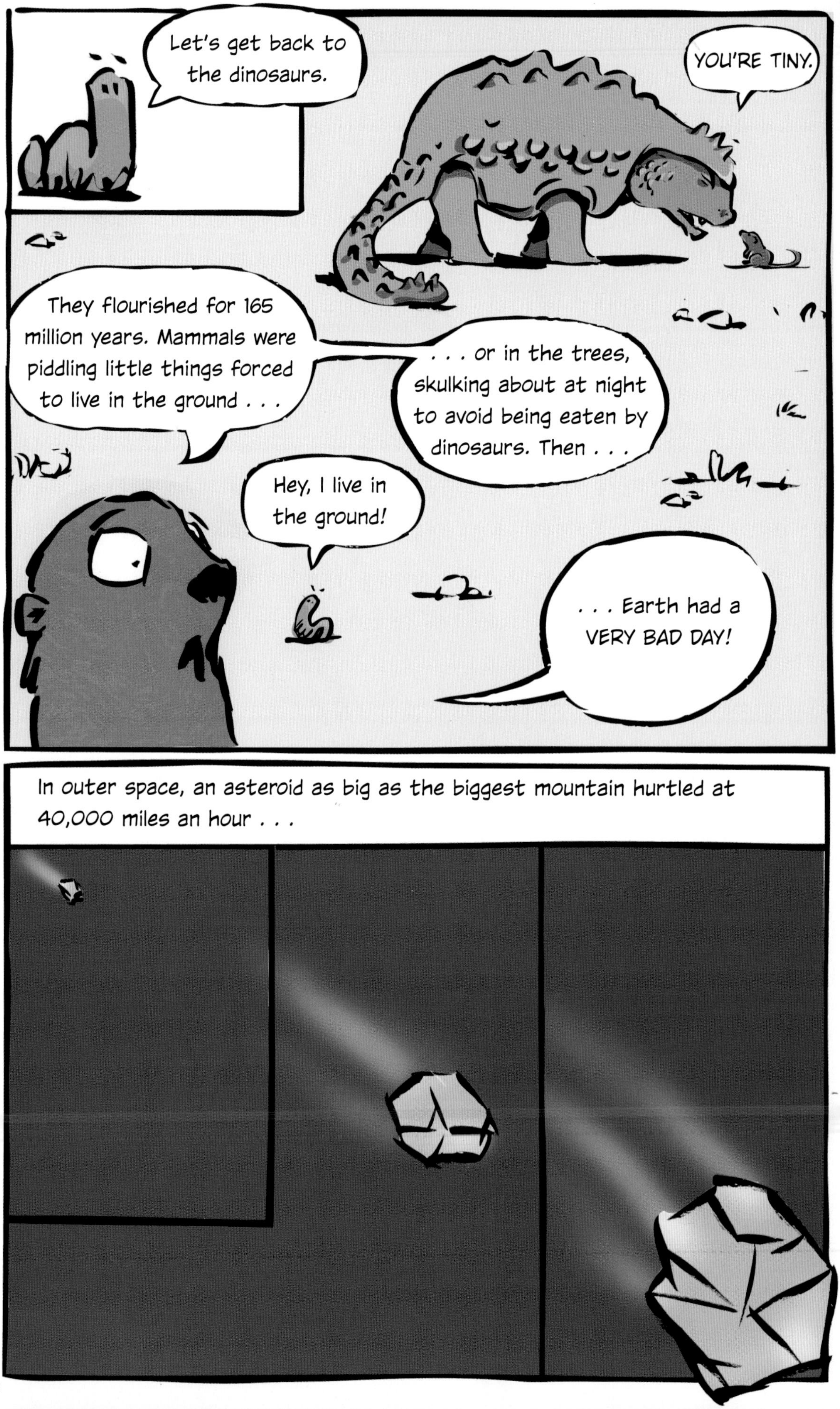
Let's get back to the dinosaurs.
YOU'RE TINY.
They flourished for 165 million years. Mammals were piddling little things forced to live in the ground . . .
. . . or in the trees, skulking about at night to avoid being eaten by dinosaurs. Then . . .
Hey, I live in the ground!
. . . Earth had a VERY BAD DAY!
In outer space, an asteroid as big as the biggest mountain hurtled at 40,000 miles an hour . . .

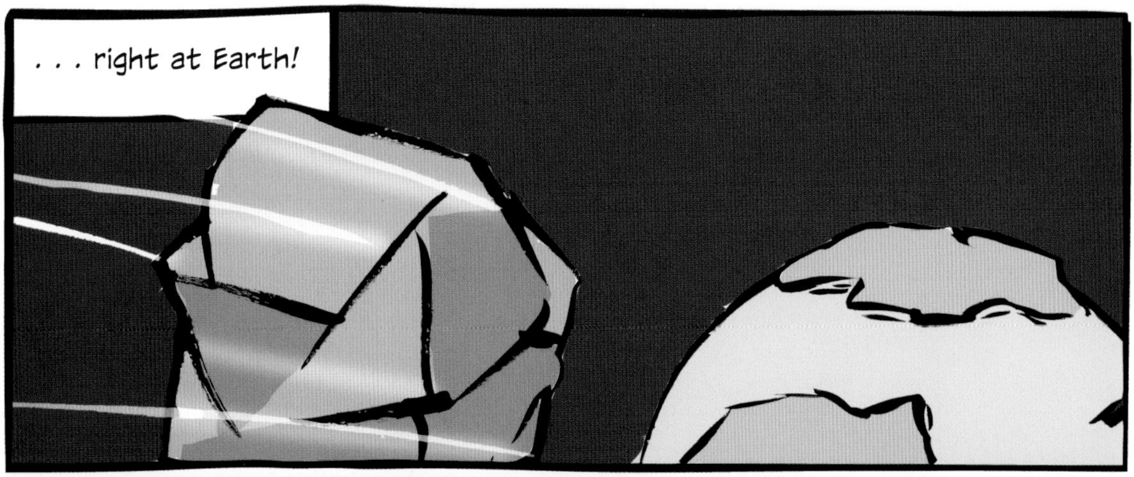
. . . right at Earth!

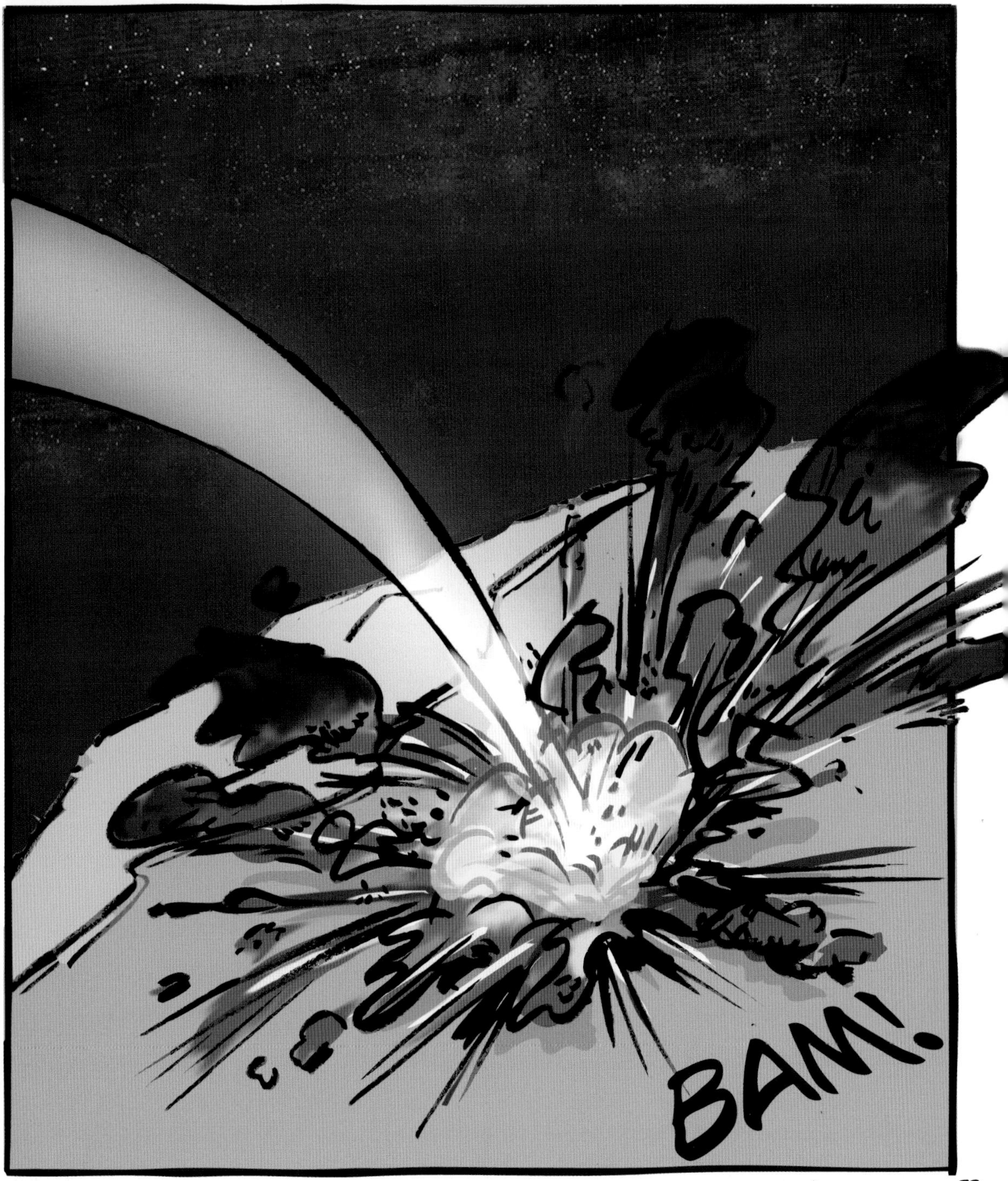
BAM!

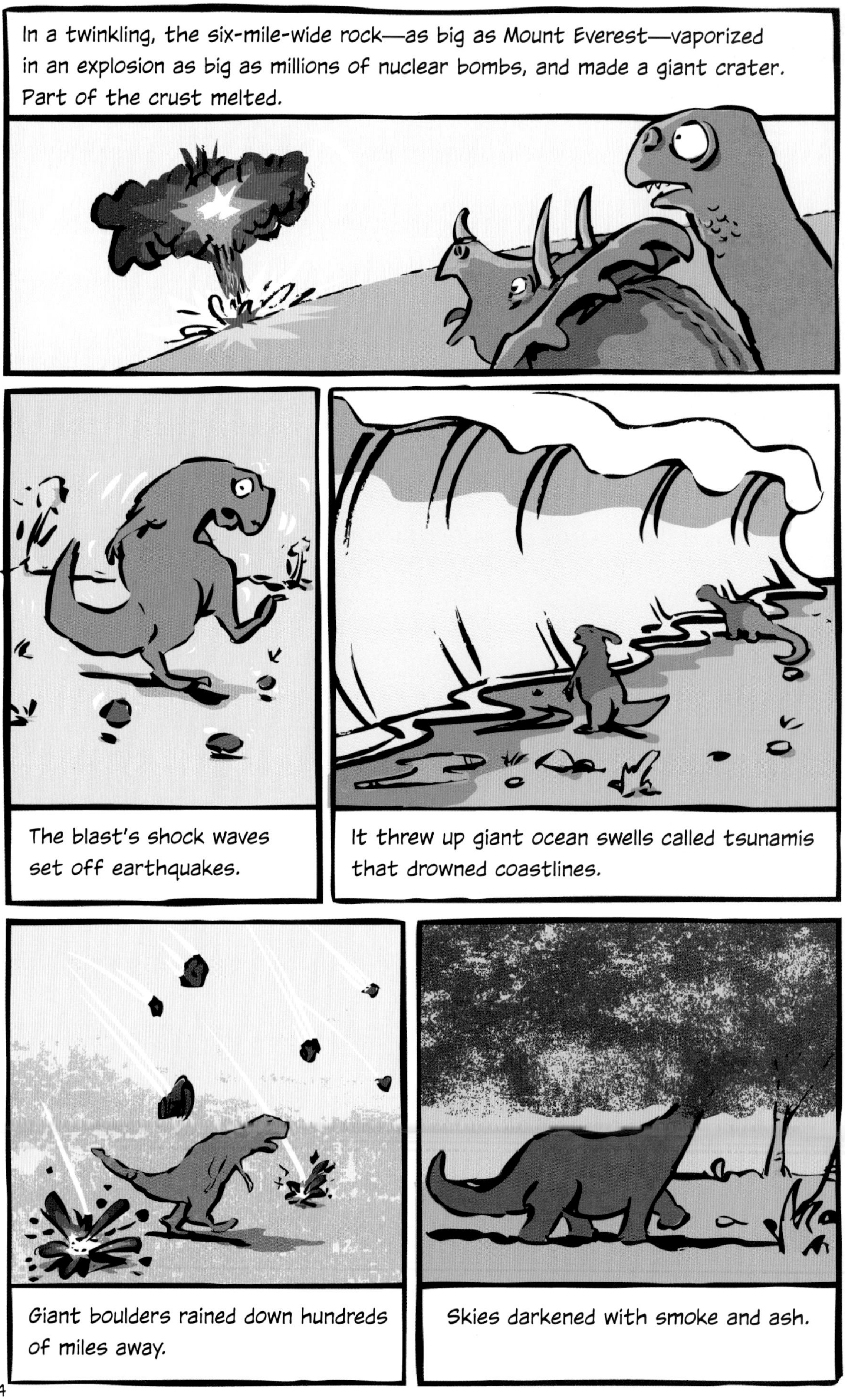
In a twinkling, the six-mile-wide rock—as big as Mount Everest—vaporized in an explosion as big as millions of nuclear bombs, and made a giant crater. Part of the crust melted.
The blast's shock waves set off earthquakes.
It threw up giant ocean swells called tsunamis that drowned coastlines.
Giant boulders rained down hundreds of miles away.
Skies darkened with smoke and ash.

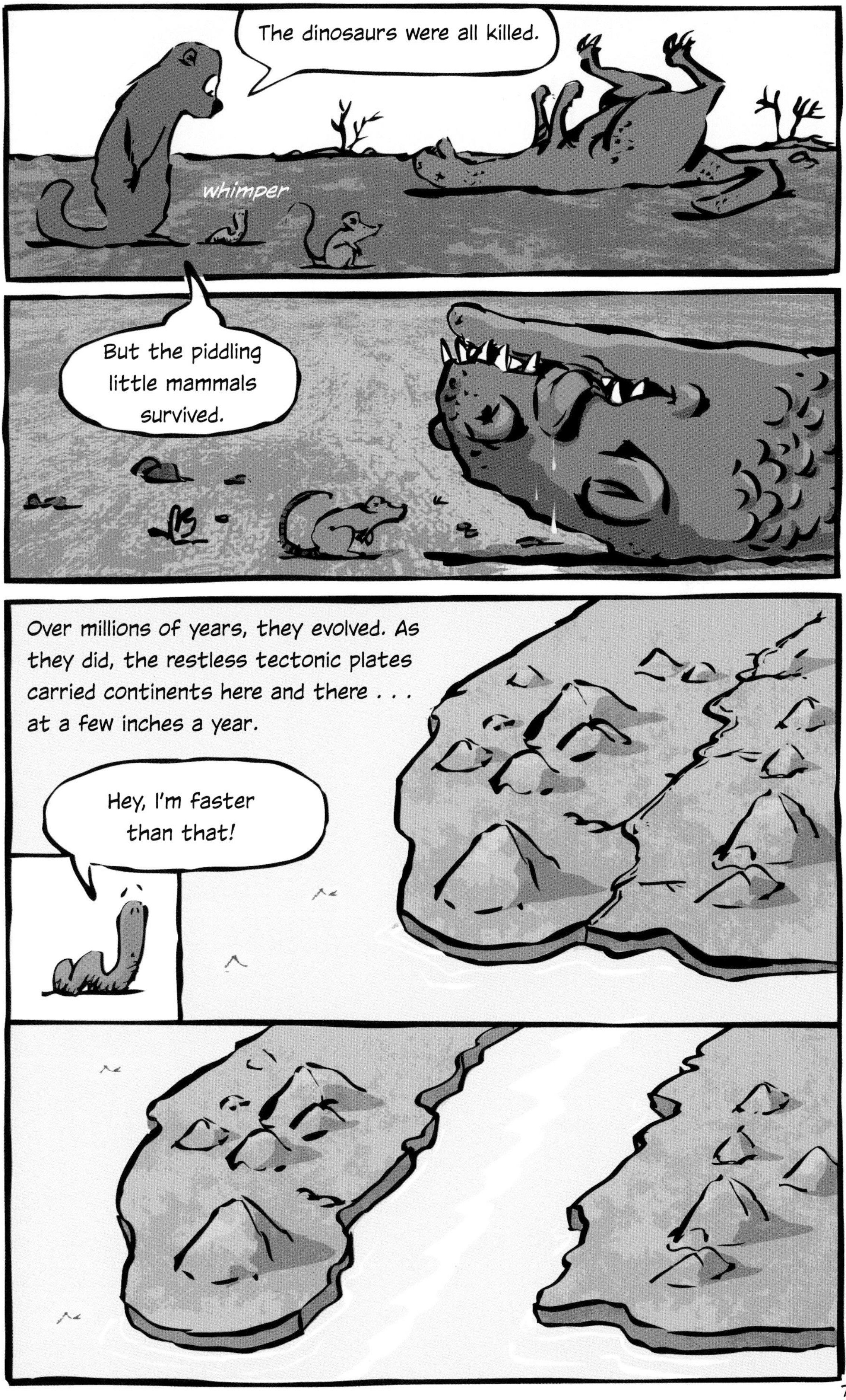
The dinosaurs were all killed.
whimper
But the piddling little mammals survived.
Over millions of years, they evolved. As they did, the restless tectonic plates carried continents here and there . . . at a few inches a year.
Hey, I'm faster than that!

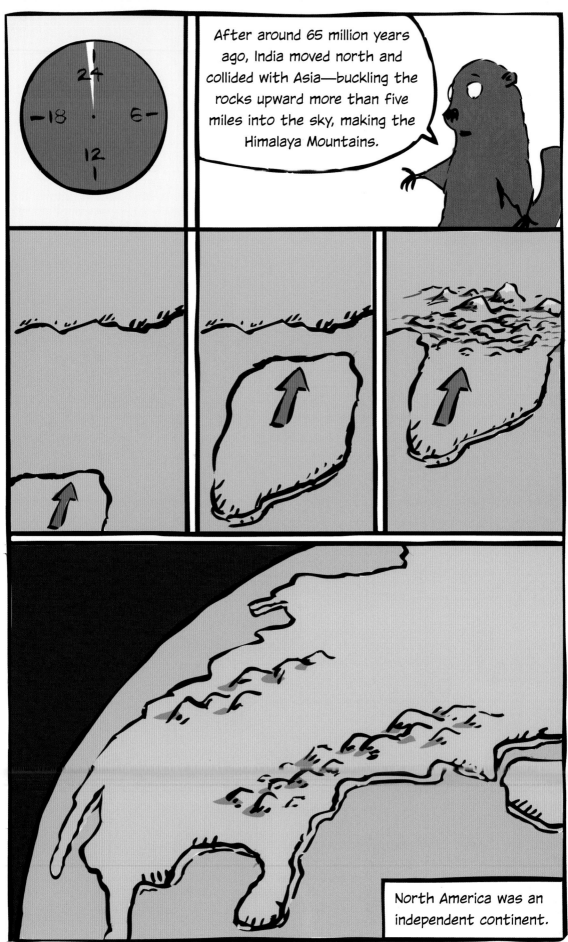

After around 65 million years ago, India moved north and collided with Asia—buckling the rocks upward more than five miles into the sky, making the Himalaya Mountains.

North America was an independent continent.

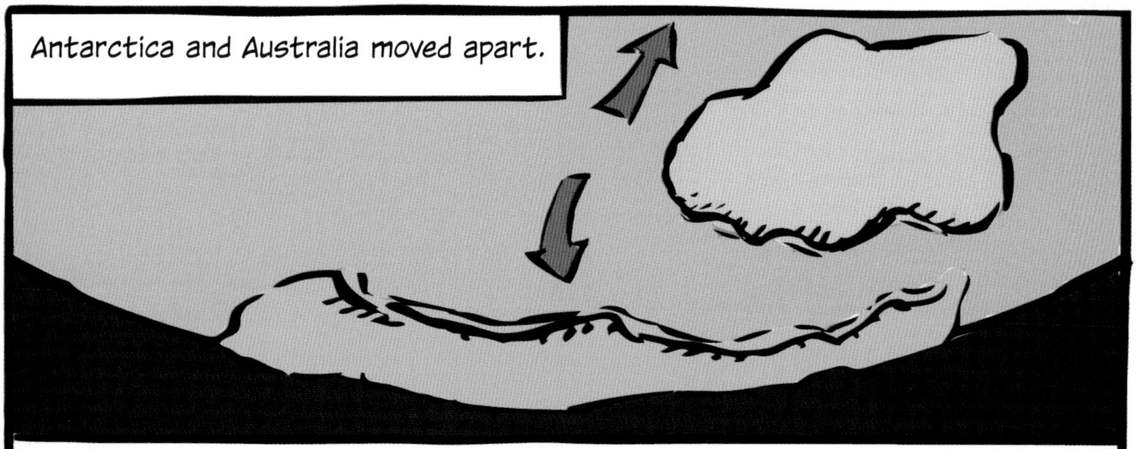
Antarctica and Australia moved apart.

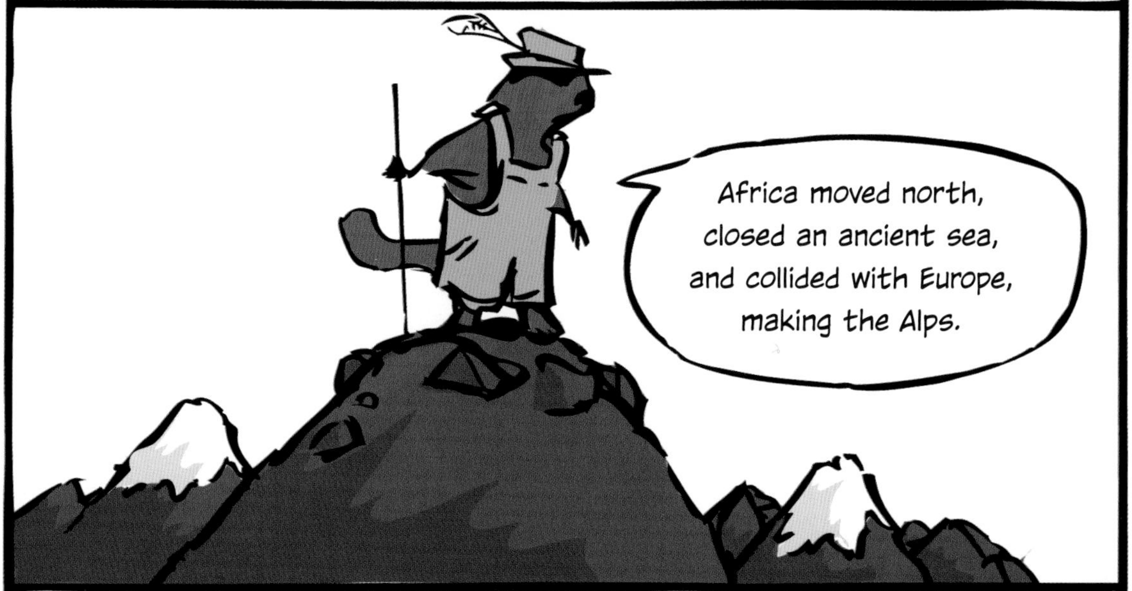
Africa moved north, closed an ancient sea, and collided with Europe, making the Alps.

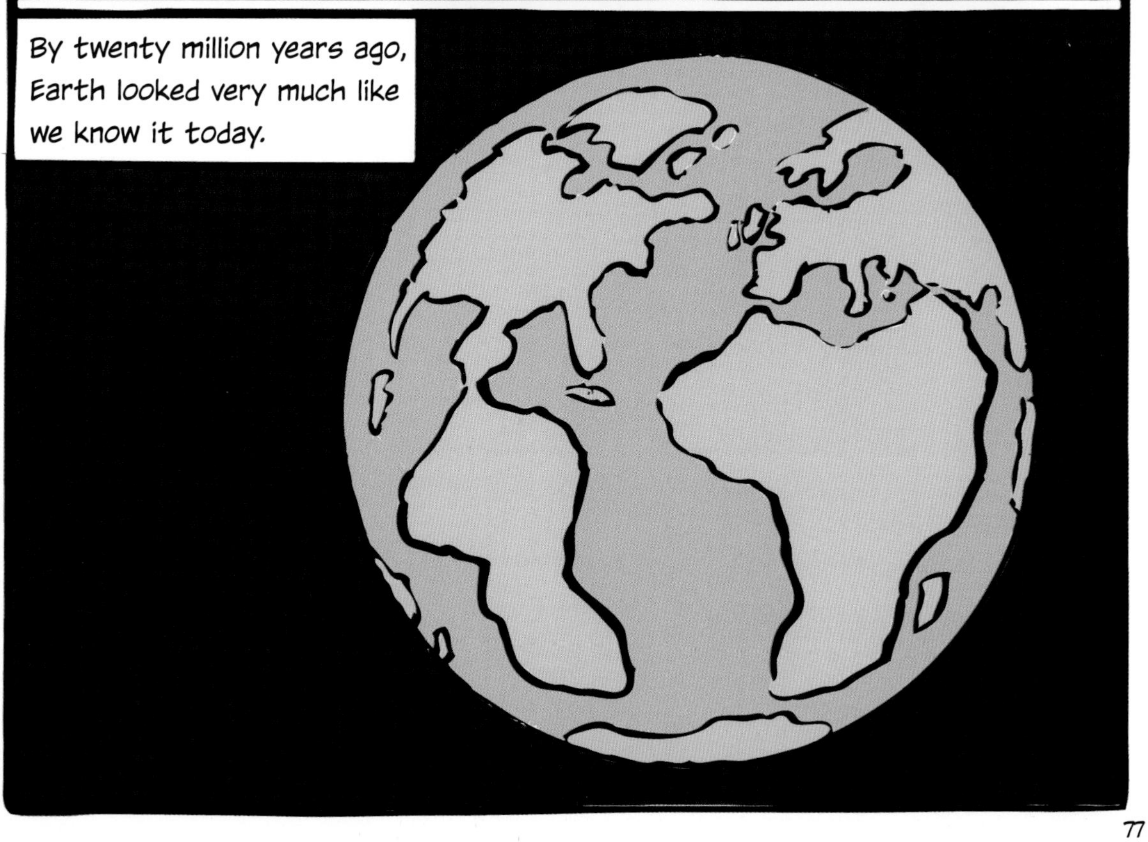
By twenty million years ago, Earth looked very much like we know it today.

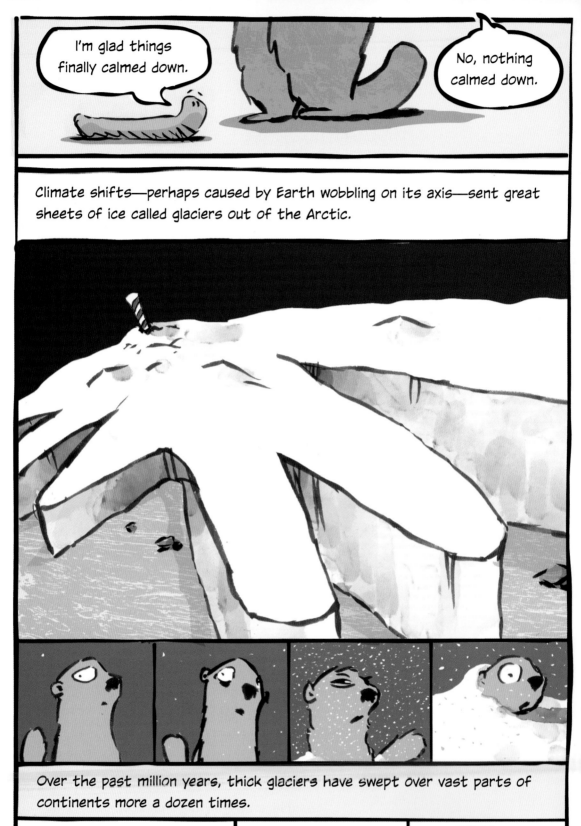

I'm glad things finally calmed down.

No, nothing calmed down.

Climate shifts—perhaps caused by Earth wobbling on its axis—sent great sheets of ice called glaciers out of the Arctic.

Over the past million years, thick glaciers have swept over vast parts of continents more a dozen times.

So much ice was formed that ocean levels may have dropped up to four hundred feet.

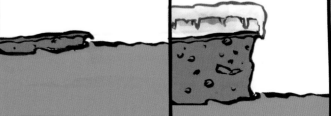

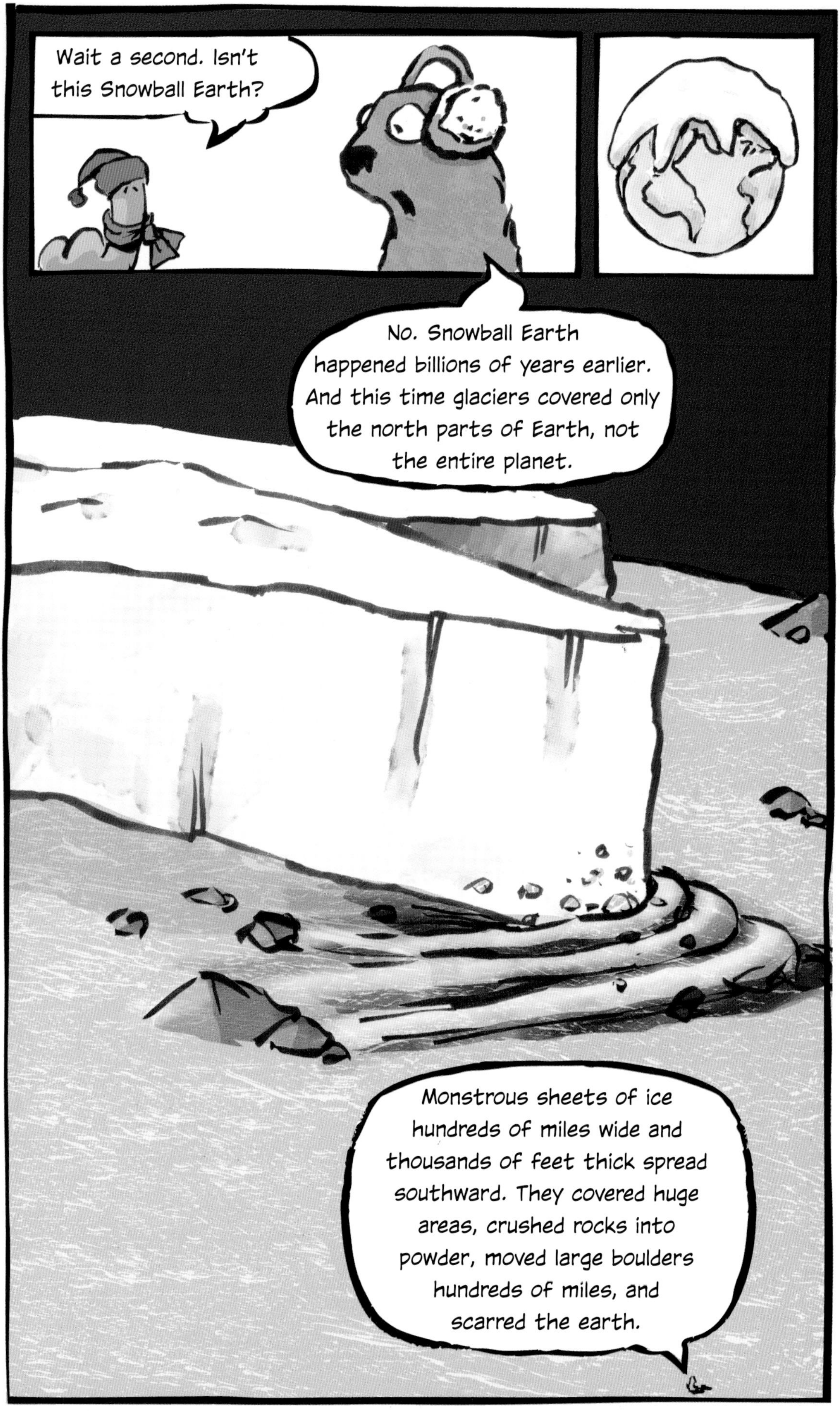
Wait a second. Isn't this Snowball Earth?
No. Snowball Earth happened billions of years earlier. And this time glaciers covered only the north parts of Earth, not the entire planet.
Monstrous sheets of ice hundreds of miles wide and thousands of feet thick spread southward. They covered huge areas, crushed rocks into powder, moved large boulders hundreds of miles, and scarred the earth.

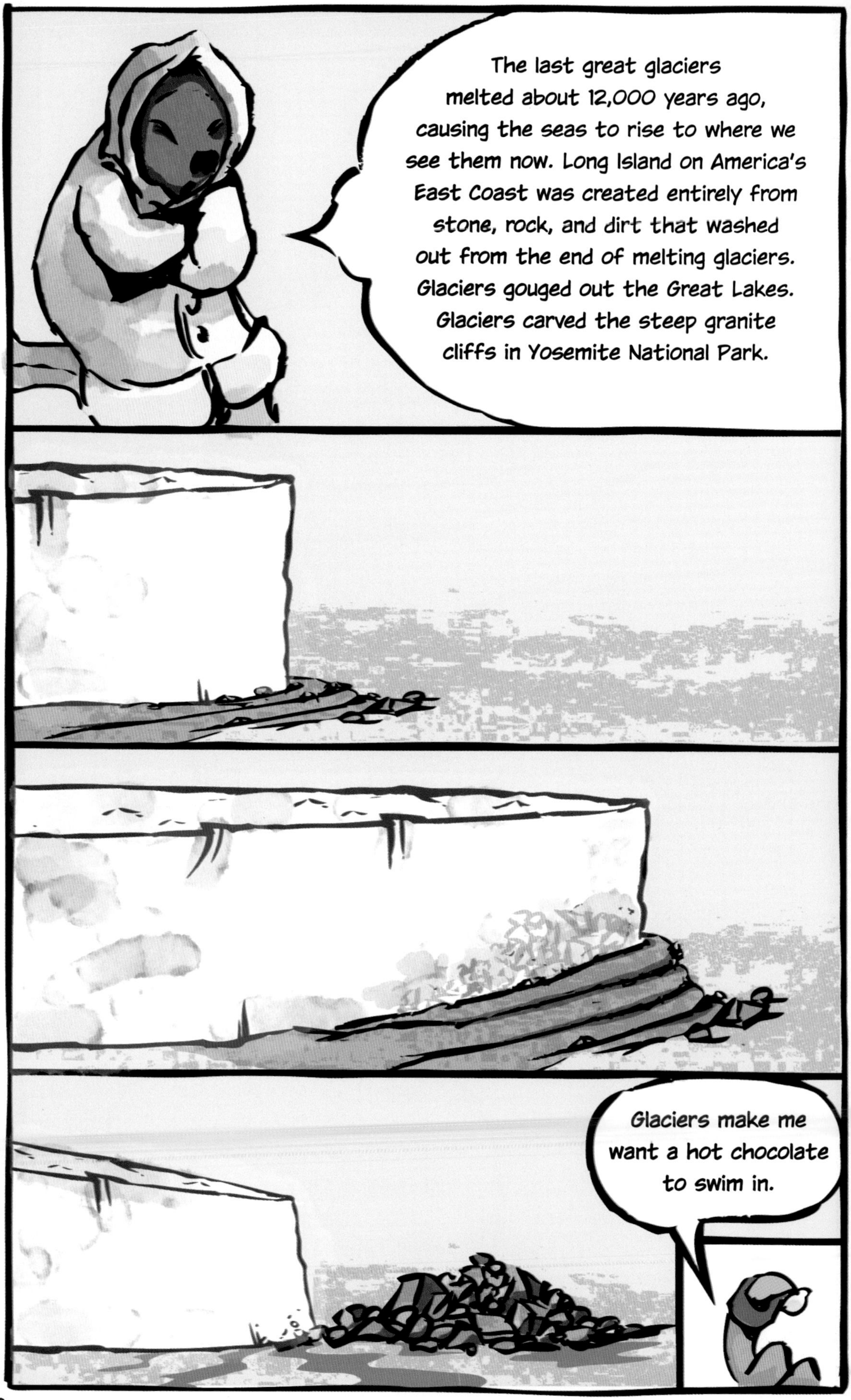
The last great glaciers melted about 12,000 years ago, causing the seas to rise to where we see them now. Long Island on America's East Coast was created entirely from stone, rock, and dirt that washed out from the end of melting glaciers. Glaciers gouged out the Great Lakes. Glaciers carved the steep granite cliffs in Yosemite National Park.
Glaciers make me want a hot chocolate to swim in.

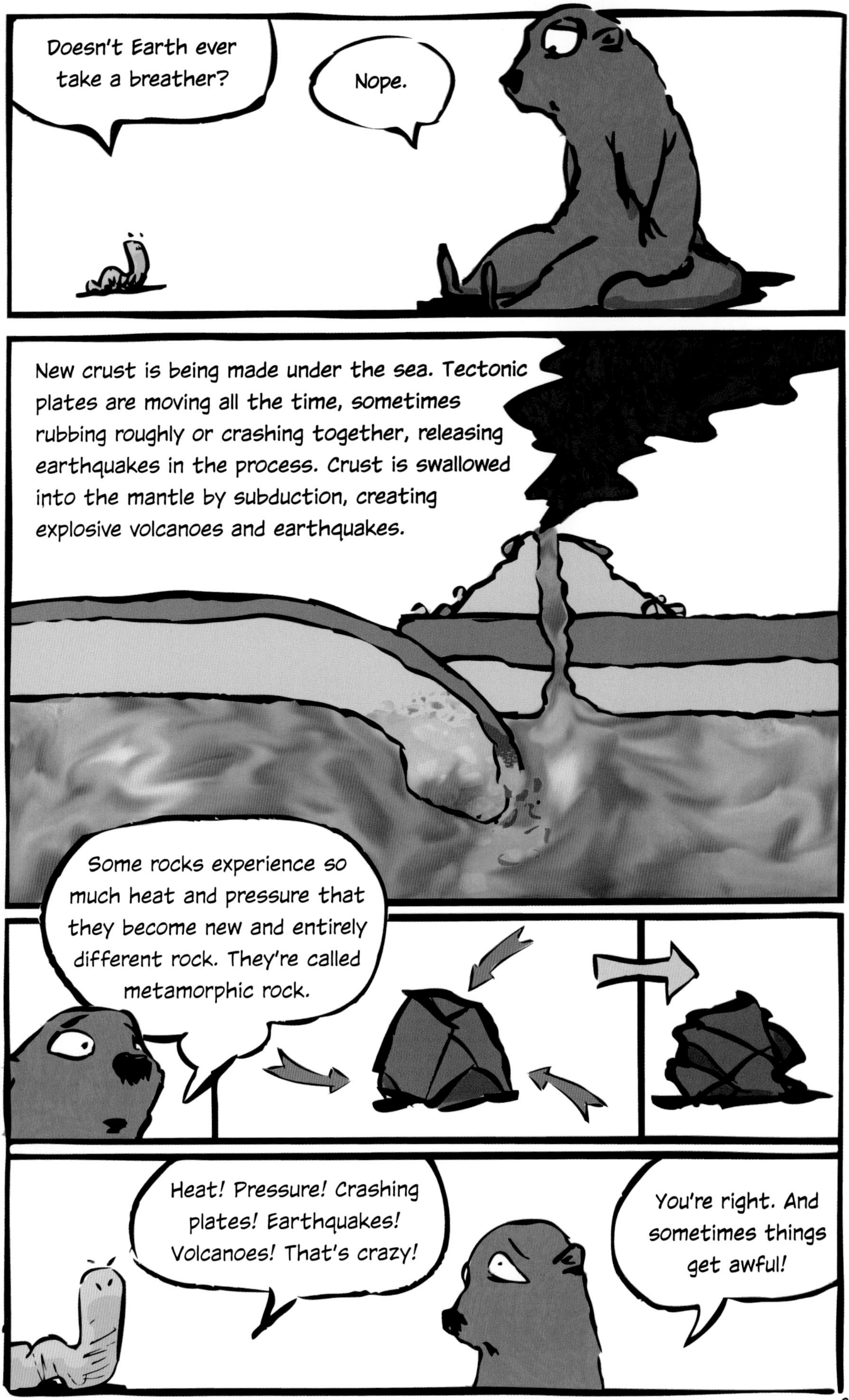
Doesn't Earth ever take a breather?
Nope.
New crust is being made under the sea. Tectonic plates are moving all the time, sometimes rubbing roughly or crashing together, releasing earthquakes in the process. Crust is swallowed into the mantle by subduction, creating explosive volcanoes and earthquakes.
Some rocks experience so much heat and pressure that they become new and entirely different rock. They're called metamorphic rock.
Heat! Pressure! Crashing plates! Earthquakes! Volcanoes! That's crazy!
You're right. And sometimes things get awful!

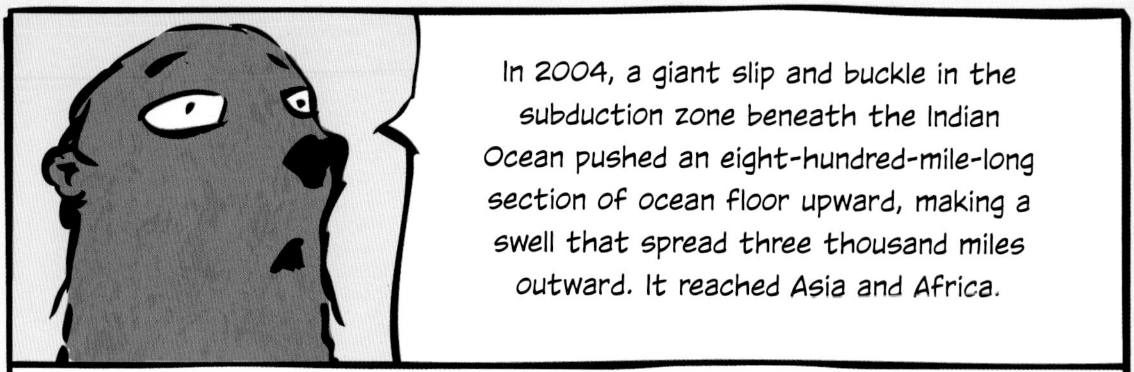
In 2004, a giant slip and buckle in the subduction zone beneath the Indian Ocean pushed an eight-hundred-mile-long section of ocean floor upward, making a swell that spread three thousand miles outward. It reached Asia and Africa.

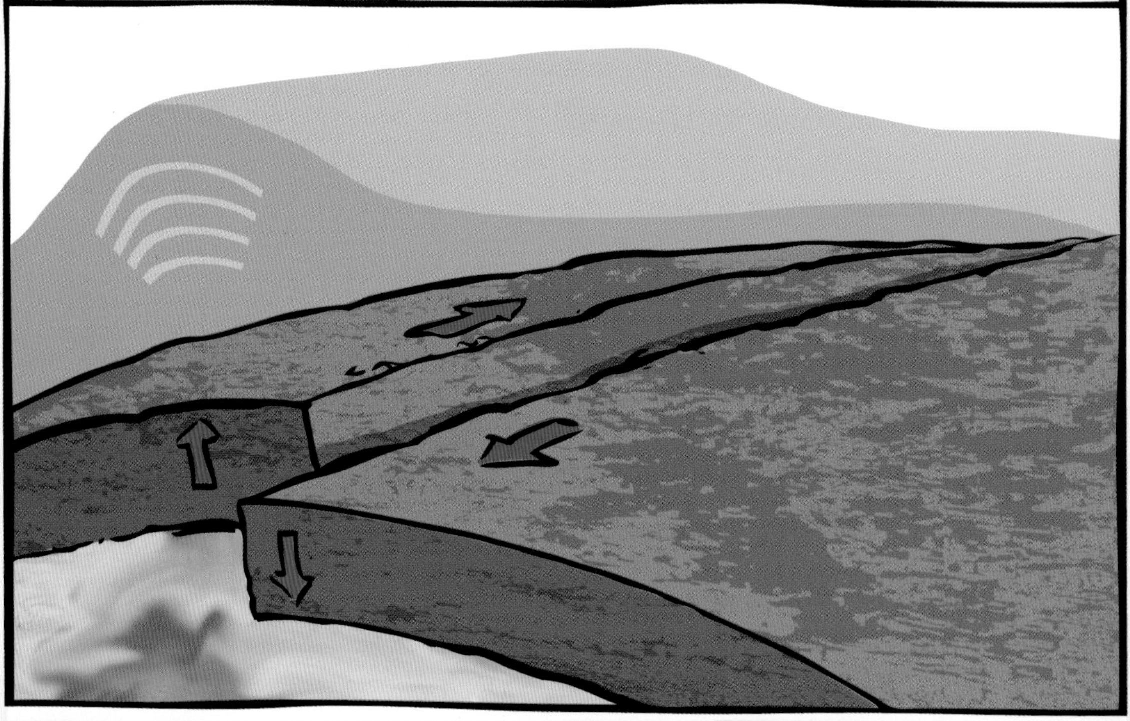

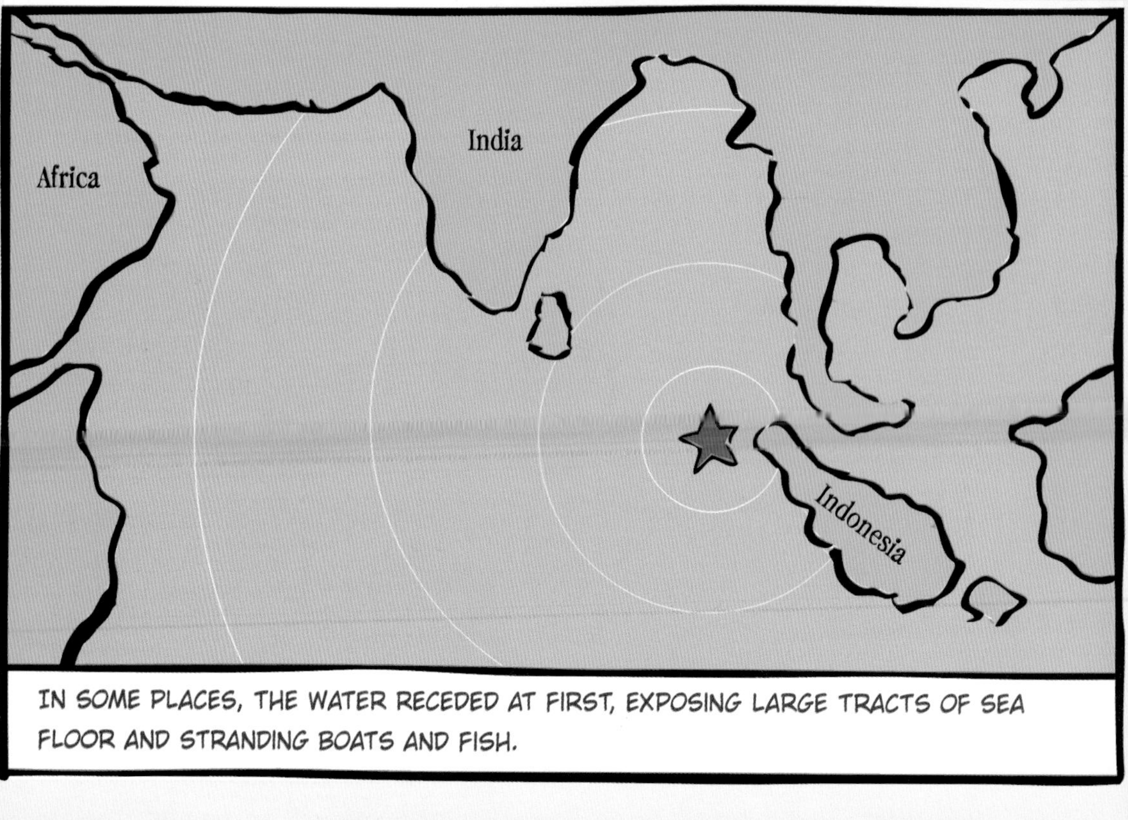
India
Africa
Indonesia
IN SOME PLACES, THE WATER RECEDED AT FIRST, EXPOSING LARGE TRACTS OF SEA FLOOR AND STRANDING BOATS AND FISH.

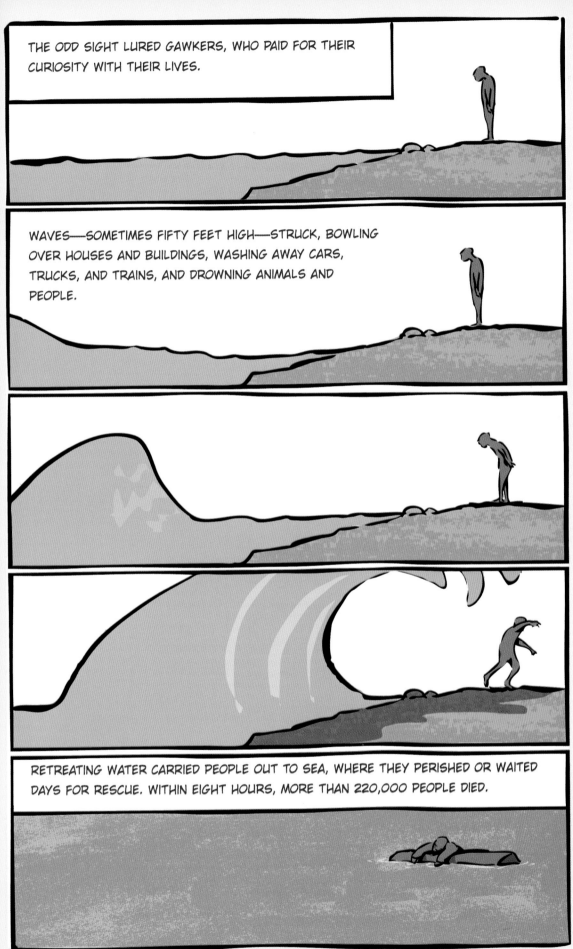

THE ODD SIGHT LURED GAWKERS, WHO PAID FOR THEIR CURIOSITY WITH THEIR LIVES.

WAVES—SOMETIMES FIFTY FEET HIGH—STRUCK, BOWLING OVER HOUSES AND BUILDINGS, WASHING AWAY CARS, TRUCKS, AND TRAINS, AND DROWNING ANIMALS AND PEOPLE.

RETREATING WATER CARRIED PEOPLE OUT TO SEA, WHERE THEY PERISHED OR WAITED DAYS FOR RESCUE. WITHIN EIGHT HOURS, MORE THAN 220,000 PEOPLE DIED.

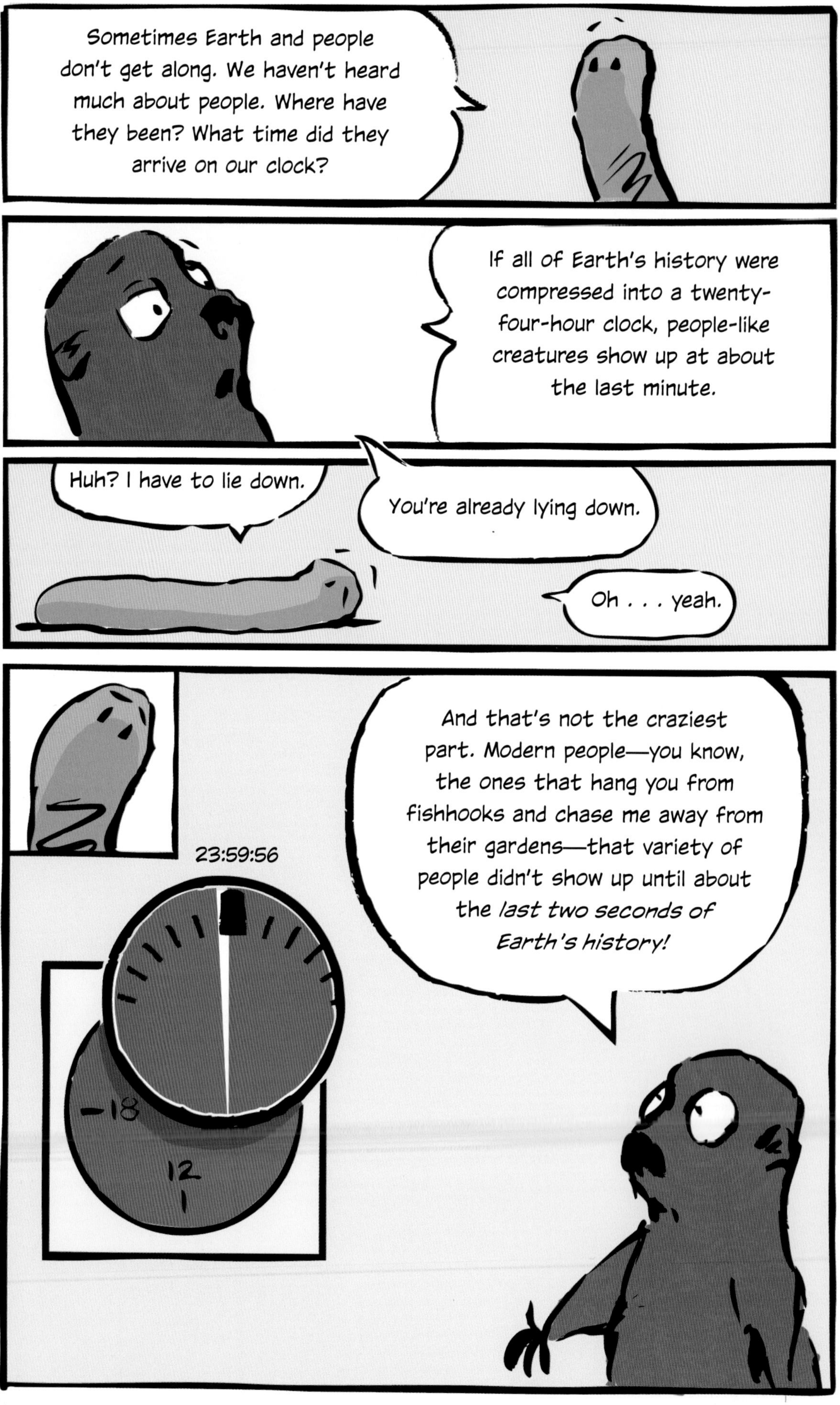
Sometimes Earth and people don't get along. We haven't heard much about people. Where have they been? What time did they arrive on our clock?
If all of Earth's history were compressed into a twenty-four-hour clock, people-like creatures show up at about the last minute.
Huh? I have to lie down.
You're already lying down.
Oh . . . yeah.
23:59:56
18
12
And that's not the craziest part. Modern people—you know, the ones that hang you from fishhooks and chase me away from their gardens—that variety of people didn't show up until about the *last two seconds of Earth's history!*

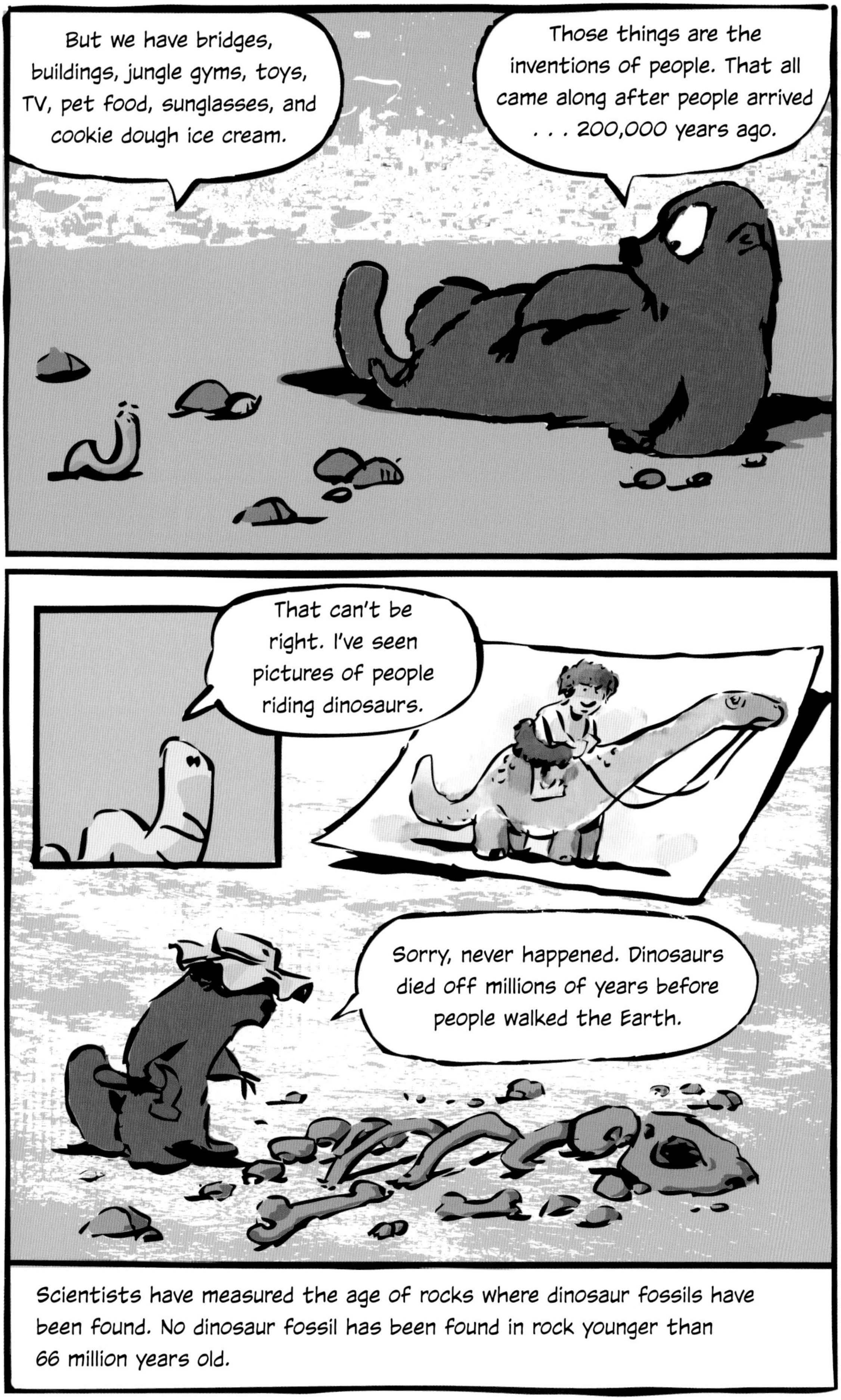
But we have bridges, buildings, jungle gyms, toys, TV, pet food, sunglasses, and cookie dough ice cream.
Those things are the inventions of people. That all came along after people arrived . . . 200,000 years ago.
That can't be right. I've seen pictures of people riding dinosaurs.
Sorry, never happened. Dinosaurs died off millions of years before people walked the Earth.
Scientists have measured the age of rocks where dinosaur fossils have been found. No dinosaur fossil has been found in rock younger than 66 million years old.

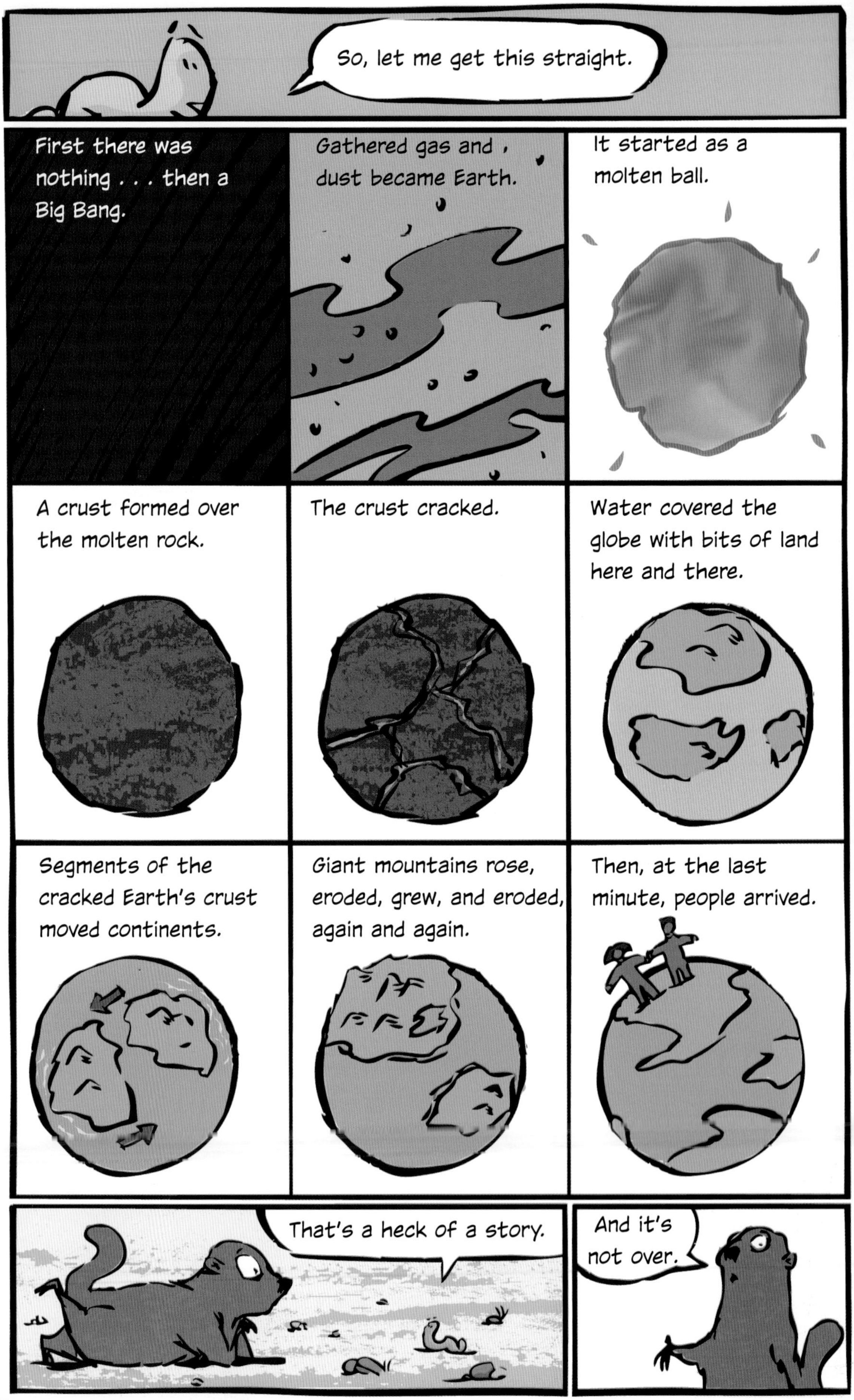
So, let me get this straight.
First there was nothing . . . then a Big Bang.
Gathered gas and dust became Earth.
It started as a molten ball.
A crust formed over the molten rock.
The crust cracked.
Water covered the globe with bits of land here and there.
Segments of the cracked Earth's crust moved continents.
Giant mountains rose, eroded, grew, and eroded, again and again.
Then, at the last minute, people arrived.
That's a heck of a story.
And it's not over.

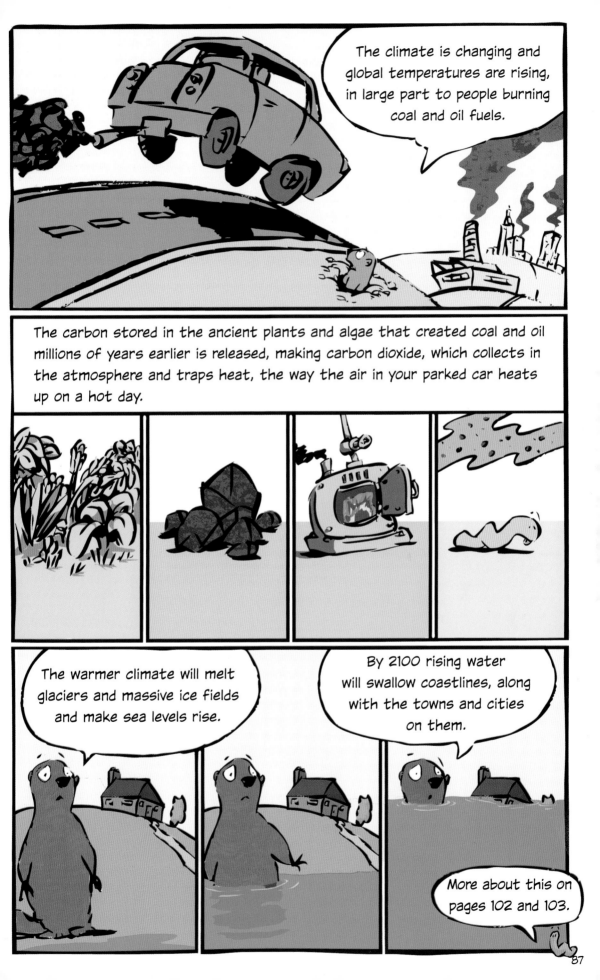

The climate is changing and global temperatures are rising, in large part to people burning coal and oil fuels.

The carbon stored in the ancient plants and algae that created coal and oil millions of years earlier is released, making carbon dioxide, which collects in the atmosphere and traps heat, the way the air in your parked car heats up on a hot day.

The warmer climate will melt glaciers and massive ice fields and make sea levels rise.

By 2100 rising water will swallow coastlines, along with the towns and cities on them.

More about this on pages 102 and 103.

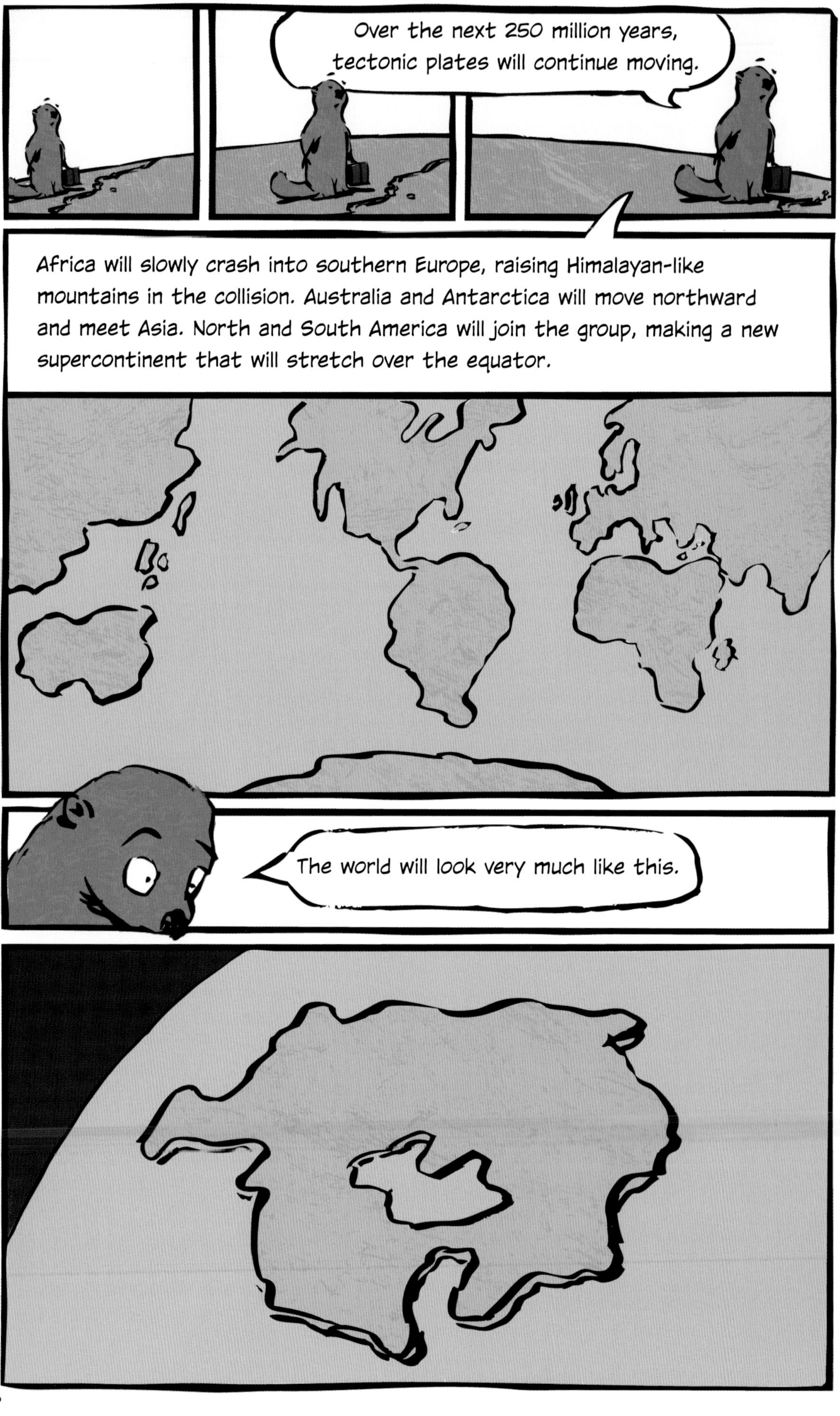
Over the next 250 million years, tectonic plates will continue moving.
Africa will slowly crash into southern Europe, raising Himalayan-like mountains in the collision. Australia and Antarctica will move northward and meet Asia. North and South America will join the group, making a new supercontinent that will stretch over the equator.
The world will look very much like this.

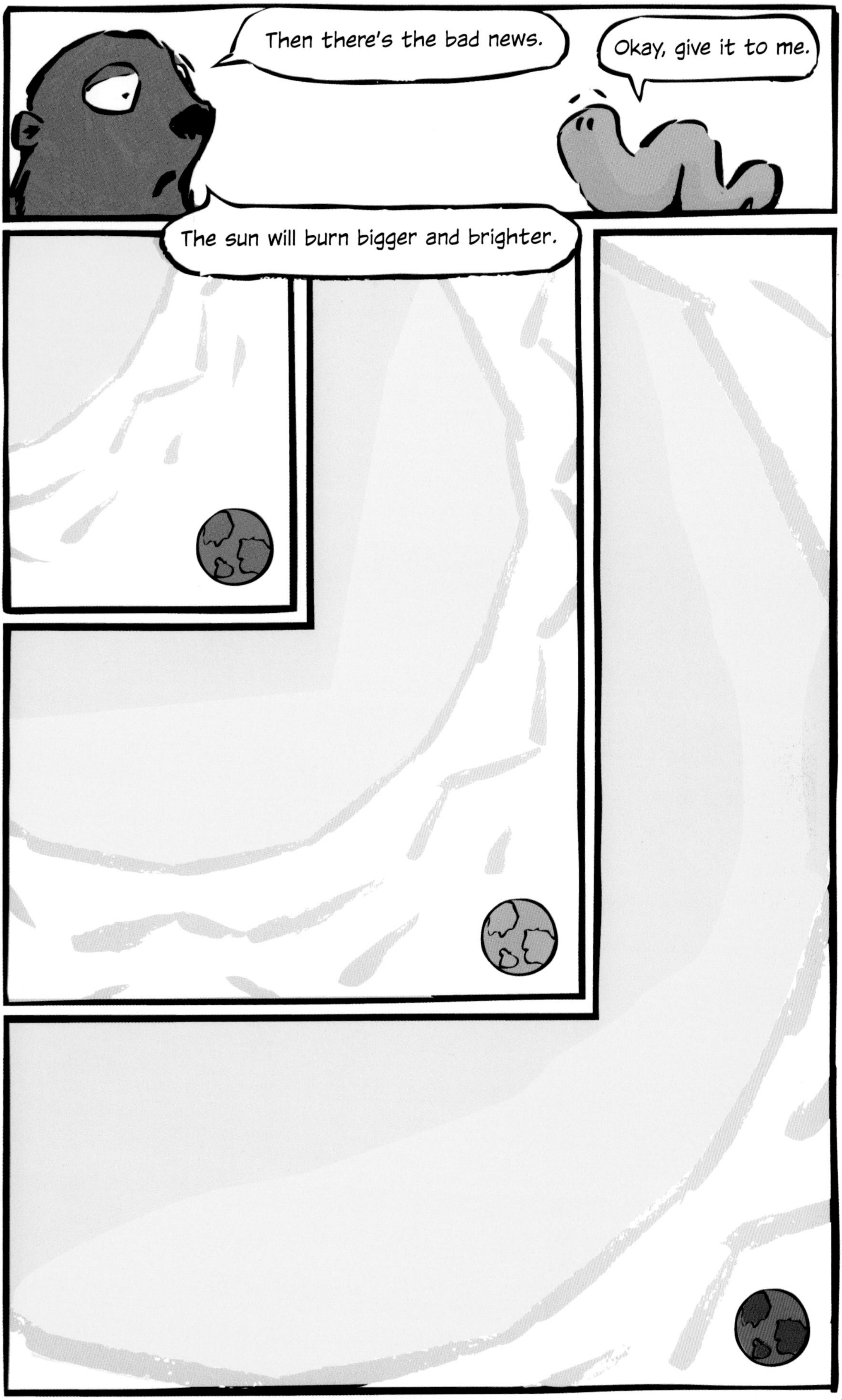
Then there's the bad news.
Okay, give it to me.
The sun will burn bigger and brighter.

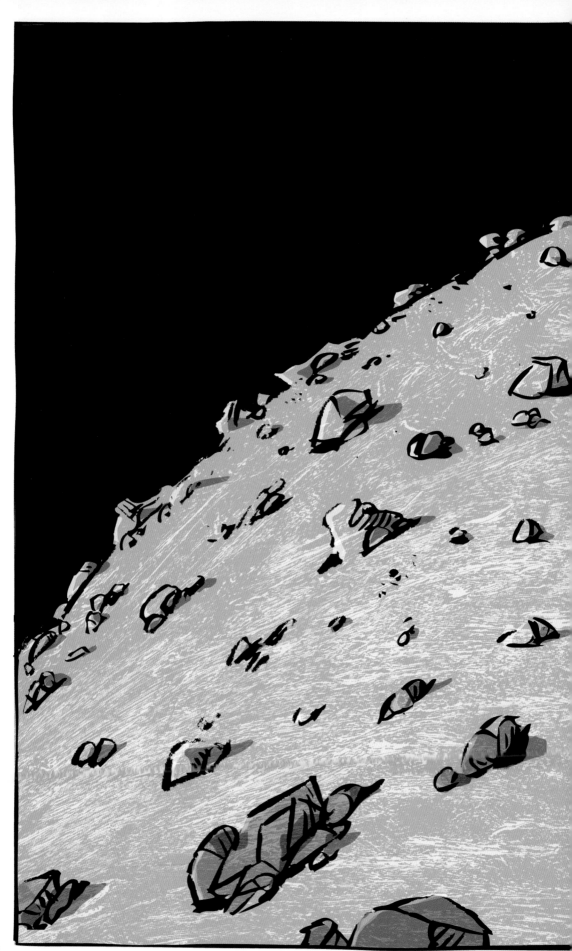

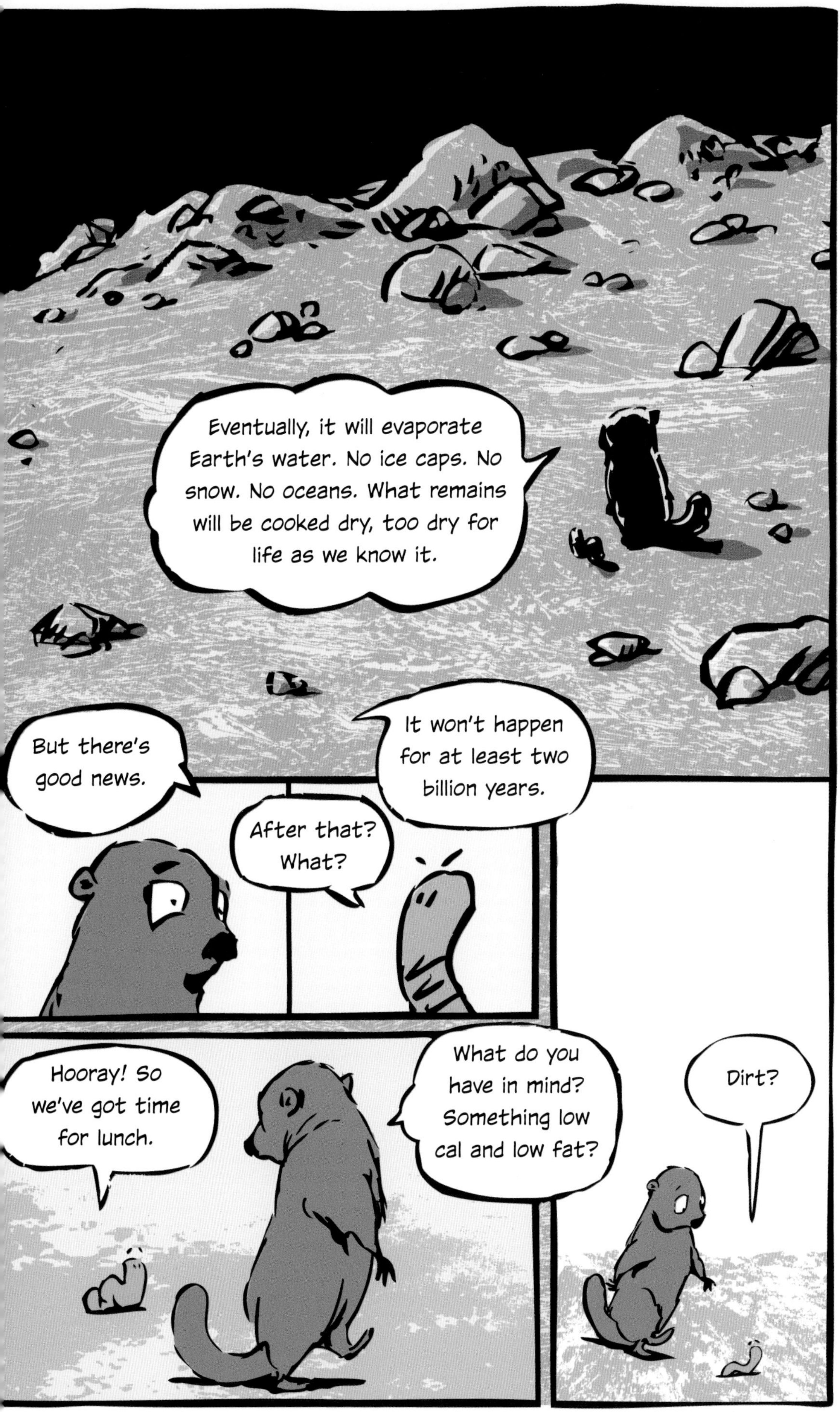
Eventually, it will evaporate Earth's water. No ice caps. No snow. No oceans. What remains will be cooked dry, too dry for life as we know it.
But there's good news.
It won't happen for at least two billion years.
After that? What?
Hooray! So we've got time for lunch.
What do you have in mind? Something low cal and low fat?
Dirt?

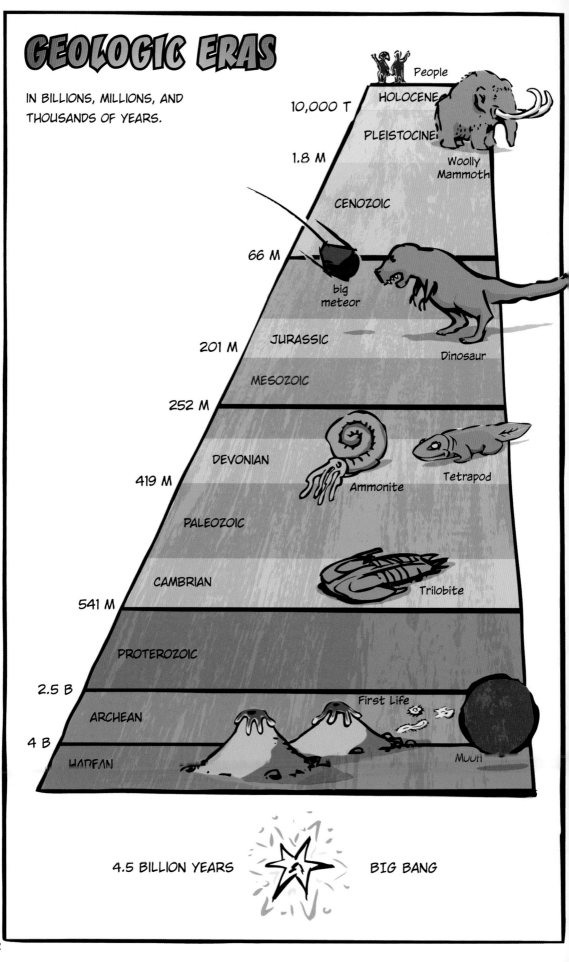

GEOLOGIC ERAS

IN BILLIONS, MILLIONS, AND
THOUSANDS OF YEARS.

People

HOLOCENE

10,000 T

PLEISTOCINE

1.8 M

Woolly
Mammoth

CENOZOIC

66 M

big
meteor

Dinosaur

201 M

JURASSIC

MESOZOIC

252 M

DEVONIAN

Ammonite

Tetrapod

419 M

PALEOZOIC

CAMBRIAN

Trilobite

541 M

PROTEROZOIC

2.5 B

ARCHEAN

First Life

4 B

HADEAN

Moon

4.5 BILLION YEARS

BIG BANG

24-HOUR EARTH CLOCK

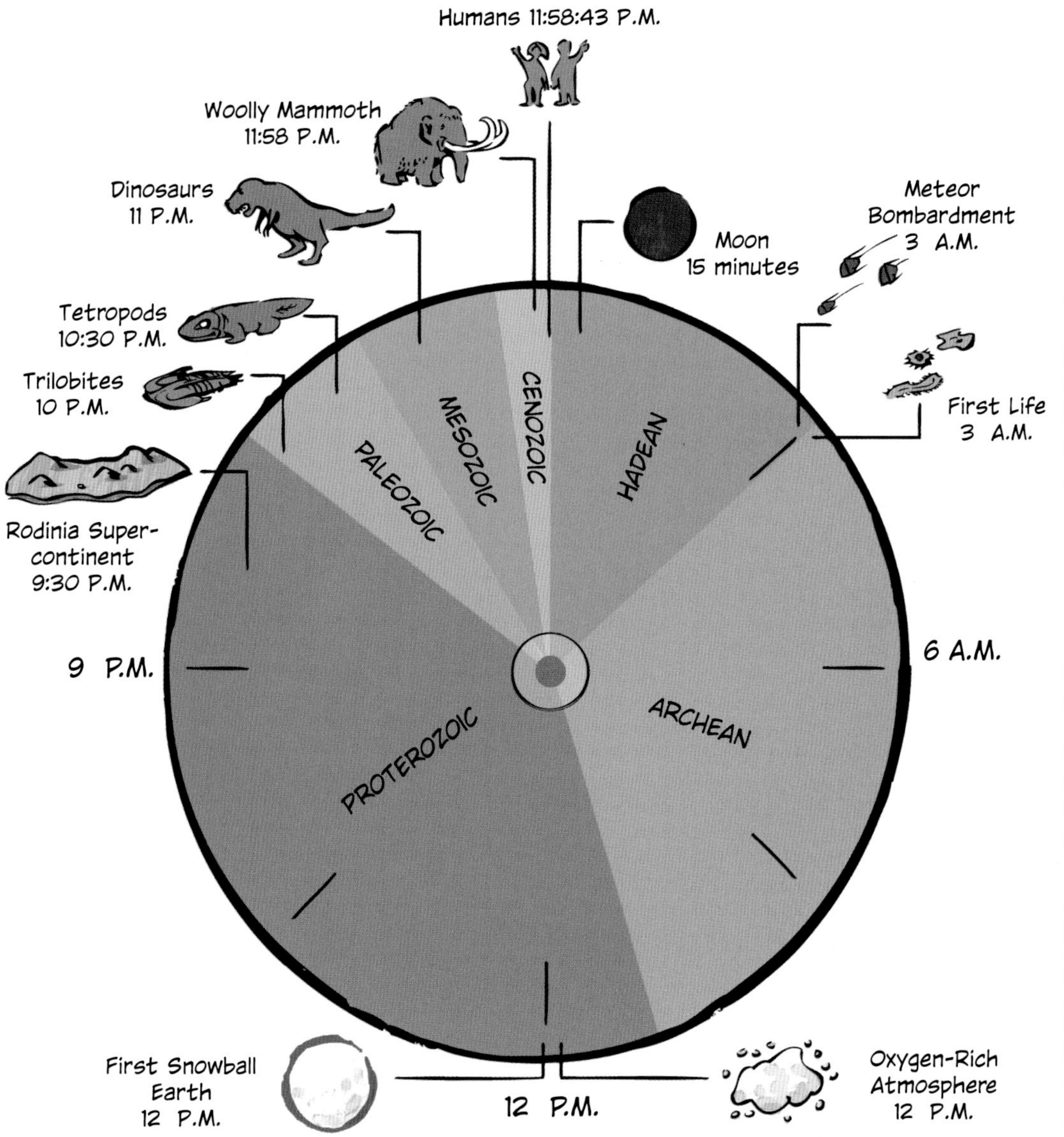

Humans 11:58:43 P.M.
Woolly Mammoth 11:58 P.M.
Dinosaurs 11 P.M.
Meteor Bombardment 3 A.M.
Moon 15 minutes
Tetropods 10:30 P.M.
Trilobites 10 P.M.
First Life 3 A.M.
Rodinia Super-continent 9:30 P.M.
CENOZOIC
MESOZOIC
PALEOZOIC
HADEAN
9 P.M.
6 A.M.
ARCHEAN
PROTEROZOIC
First Snowball Earth 12 P.M.
12 P.M.
Oxygen-Rich Atmosphere 12 P.M.

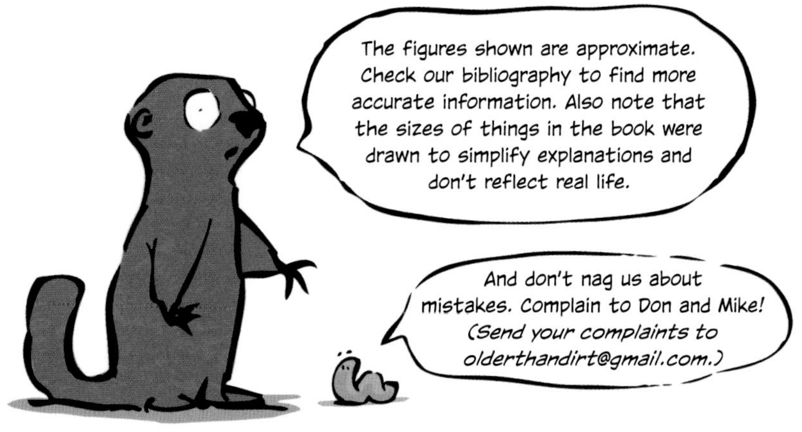

The figures shown are approximate. Check our bibliography to find more accurate information. Also note that the sizes of things in the book were drawn to simplify explanations and don't reflect real life.
And don't nag us about mistakes. Complain to Don and Mike! (Send your complaints to olderthandirt@gmail.com.)

EARTH'S TECTONIC PLATES

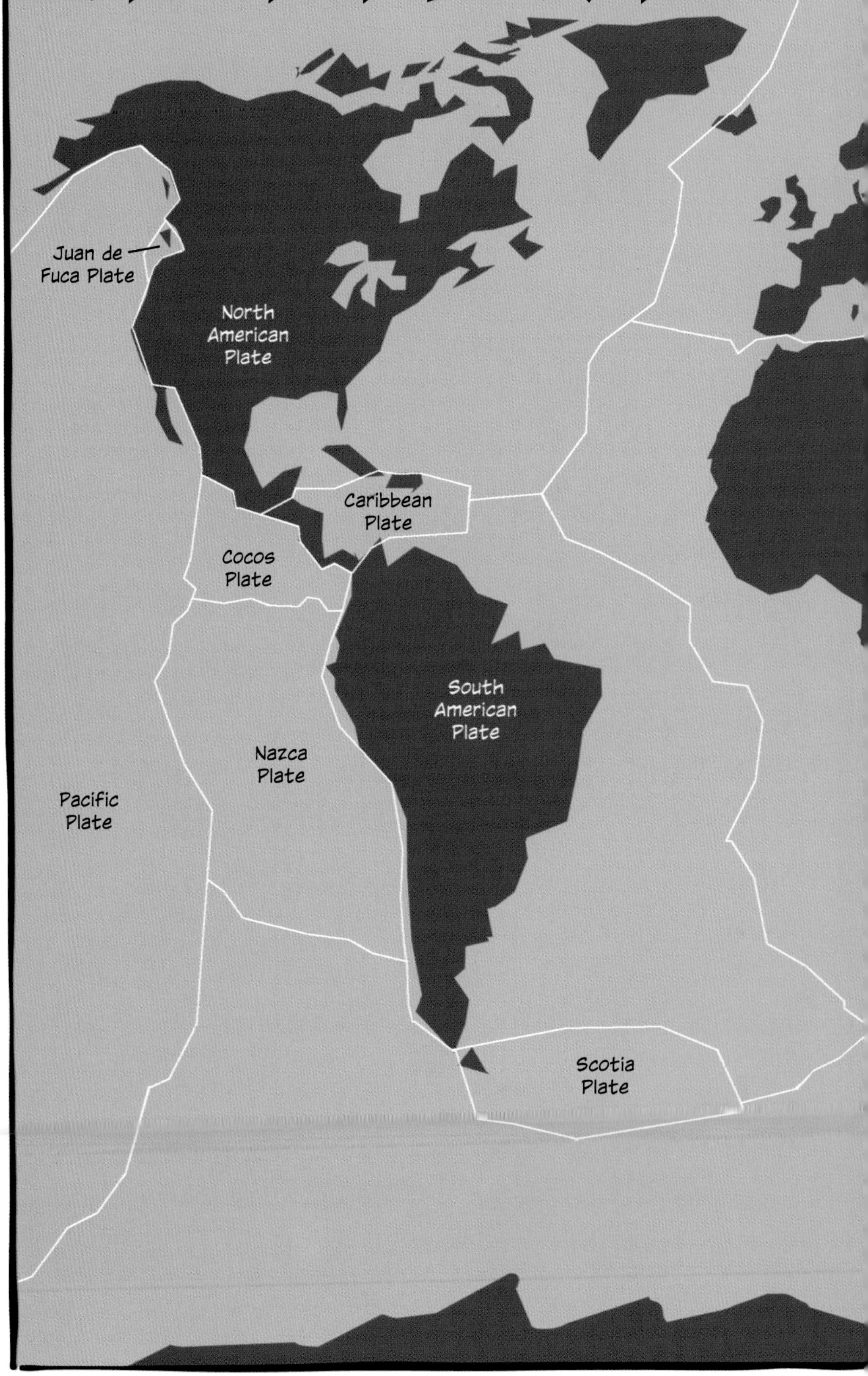
Juan de Fuca Plate
North American Plate
Caribbean Plate
Cocos Plate
South American Plate
Nazca Plate
Pacific Plate
Scotia Plate

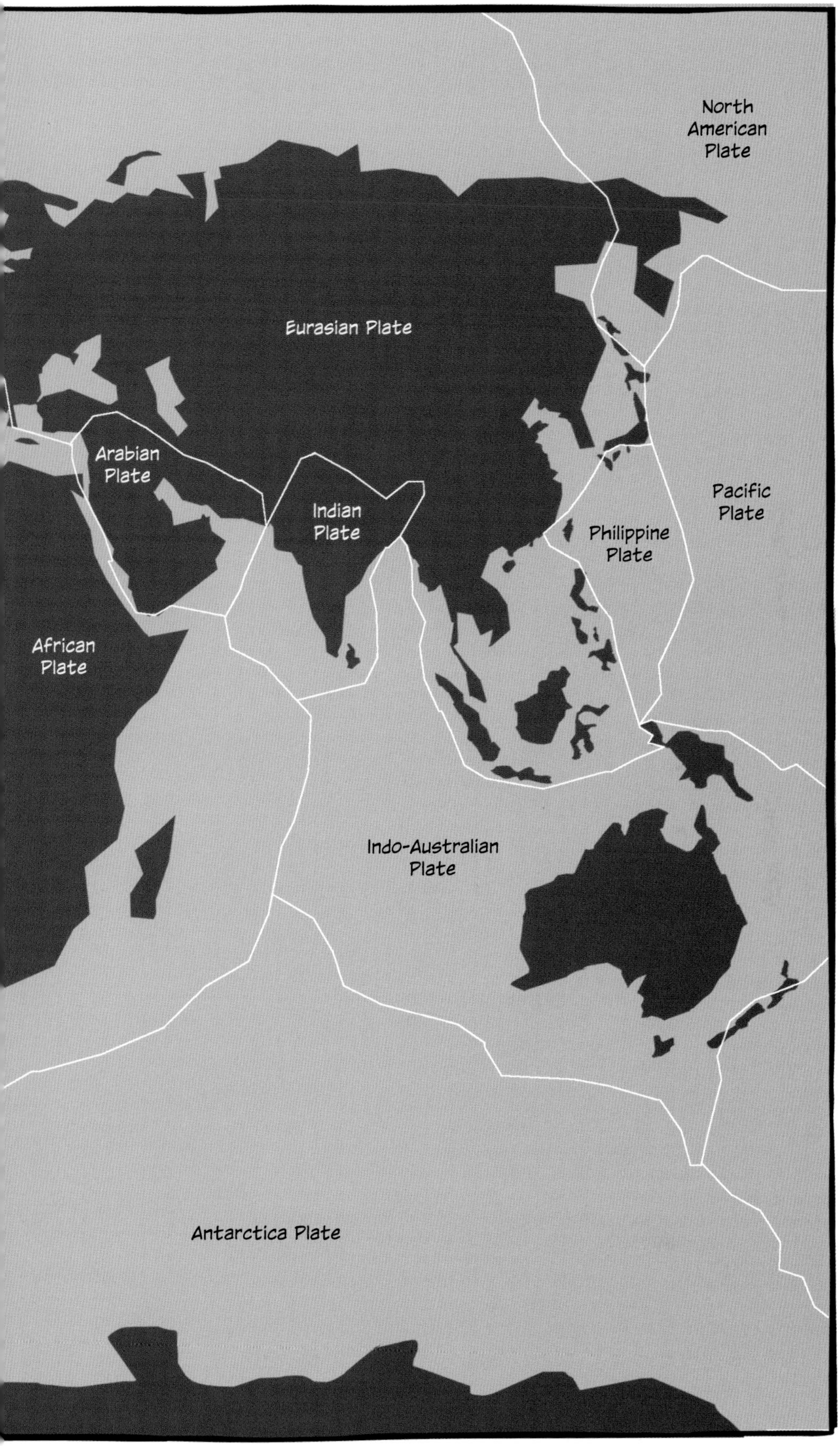
North American Plate
Eurasian Plate
Arabian Plate
Indian Plate
Pacific Plate
Philippine Plate
African Plate
Indo-Australian Plate
Antarctica Plate

SOURCE NOTES

6 *The universe exploded into existence*: Lutgens and Tarbuck, *Essentials of Geology*, 19.

The rock and dust collided to make clumps: Hazen, *The Story of Earth*, 19.

7 *About 4.5 billion years ago*: Ibid., 25.

9 *Poisonous gas spewed upward*: National Geographic, *The Story of Earth*.

Meteors streaking across the solar system: Valley, "Early Earth," 201.

10 *It's rock that is so hot*: Personal interview with Professor Michael Perfit, distinguished professor of geology, University of Florida, January 15, 2016.

11 *The topmost layer is the crust*: Lutgens and Tarbuck, *Essentials of Geology*, 21-23.

14 *The crash tilted Earth*: Press, Siever, Grotzinger, and Thomas, *Understanding Earth*, 6-7.

15 *The modern moon's gravitational*: Hazen, *The Story of Earth*, 49-50.

16 *All sorts of rubble left over*: Ibid., 51-54.

17 *Still, about one hundred tons of rocks*: MacDougall, *Why Geology Matters*, 21.

The meteors that survive the crash: Lutgens and Tarbuck, *Essentials of Geology*, 176.

The odds of being struck: Howard, "What Are the Odds."

18 *Eventually, the lava*: Press, Siever, Grotzinger, and Thomas,

Understanding Earth, 93.

19 *After hundreds of millions of years*: Powell, "How Earth Was Watered."

20 *Then the steam cooled*: Hazen, *The Story of Earth*, 94.

22 *Scientists can measure the amount*: Ibid., 97; Understanding Evolution, "The Nitty Gritty on Radioisotopic Dating."

23 *Many volcanoes formed on the ocean floor*: National Geographic, *The Story of Earth*.

24 *"A black and dreadful cloud"*: British Museum, *Life and Death: Pompeii and Herculaneum*.

25 *Fleeing residents were buried*: Auld, "Pompeii Exhibition."

They were filled with plaster: History .com staff, "Deconstructing History."

26 *Earth's basalt crust is very thin*: MacDougall, *Why Geology Matters*, 30.

28 *Like an iceberg*: Press, Siever, Grotzinger, and Thomas, *Understanding Earth*, 83.

29 *Massive collections of plutons*: Hazen, *The Story of Earth*, 186.

31 *Hutton's theories of rock destruction*: Bressan, "James Hutton."

"In our measurement of time": Thompson, "Vestiges of James Hutton."

To be truthful: O'Connor and Robertson, "James Hutton."

Scientists eventually called it Deep Time: Mathez, "James Hutton."

32 *The heated water, chemicals, and minerals*: National Geographic, *The Story of Earth*.

34 *Oxygen bubbled into the ocean*: PBS, *Making of North America: Life*; National Geographic, *The Story of Earth*; Hazen, *The Story of Earth*, 173.

35 *Steel bridges, buildings, automobiles*: National Geographic, *The Story of Earth*.

37 *Mount Everest and the Himalaya*: Bilham, "Birth of the Himalaya."

Because of plate tectonics: National Geographic Society, "Plate Tectonics."

39 *He perished in a snowstorm*: Alfred Wegener Institute, "Alfred Wegener."

42 *A huge earthquake in Alaska*: Sokolowski, "The Great Alaskan Earthquake."

43 *Sliding or shearing one piece*: United States Geological Survey, "Faults FAQs."

44 *Twenty-eight thousand homes were destroyed*: United States Geological Survey, "Casualties and Damage After the 1906 Earthquake."

45 *Among the smoking ruins*: Head, "One Boy's Experience."

46 *It broke apart and was replaced*: Hazen, *The Story of Earth*, 195.

47 *Water, air, and organic material*: United States Department of Agriculture, "What Is Soil?"

51 *It happened three times*: Hoffman et al., "What Caused the Snowball Earths?"; Hazen, *The Story of Earth*, 212-14; Feulner, Hallman, and Kiernert, "Snowball Cooling."

53 *There weren't land animals yet*: PBS, *Making of North America: Life*; Hazen, *The Story of Earth*, 235-38.

54 *You already have one*: Hazen, *The Story of Earth*, 236.

57 *Seventy-five percent of land life*: Ibid., 250-52.

59 *Clouds of carbon dioxide*: National Geographic, *The Story of Earth*; Hoffman, "The Permian Extinction."

61 *The small reptiles that survived*: Hazen, *The Story of Earth*, 252-54.

65 *That's how the giant white limestone*: Dover Museum, "White Cliffs of Dover."

67 *Too hot or cold and it wouldn't become oil*: Press, Siever, Grotzinger, and Thomas, *Understanding Earth*, 174-75; BBC, "Chemistry: How Crude Oil Was Formed."

68 *Soon after, South America separated*: Hazen, *The Story of Earth*, 234.

69 *The seam where the plates*: Lutgens and Tarbuck, *Essentials of Geology*, 353.

71 *Heezen died*: Longden, "Bruce Heezen."

75 *The dinosaurs were all killed.* PBS, *Making of North America: Life*; National Geographic, *The Story of Earth*; Hazen, The Story of Earth, 253.

80 *Glaciers carved the steep granite cliffs*: PBS, *The Making of North America: Origins*.

83 *More than 220,000 people died*:
National Geographic News, "The
Deadliest Tsunami in History?";
Taylor, "Ten Years Since."

84 *Modern people*:
Northern Arizona University,
"History of Life on Earth";
Brightmore, "Deep Time."

85 *No dinosaur fossil has been found*: Yale
University, "Last Dinosaur."

88 *North and South America will join*:
Hazen, *The Story of Earth*, 261.

91 *What remains will be cooked dry*: Ibid.,
258-59.

BIBLIOGRAPHY

Virtually all the information in *Older Than Dirt* can be obtained in an introductory college geology textbook. Nevertheless, we've done our best to point to more casual, reader-friendly sources, most of which can be accessed online at reputable sites.

Alfred Wegener Insititute. "Alfred Wegener." (www.awi.de/en/about-us/organisation/alfred-wegener.html; accessed December 5, 2016)

Auld, Tim. "Pompeii Exhibition: The Eruption of the Volcano." *Telegraph* Online. March 3, 2013. (www.telegraph.co.uk/history/pompeii/9850103/Pompeii-exhibition-the-eruption-of-the-volcano.html; accessed December 5, 2016)

BBC. "Chemistry: How Crude Oil Was Formed." BBC Online's Standard Grade Bitesize. May 24, 2014. (www.bbc.co.uk/bitesize/standard/chemistry/materialsfromoil/how_crude_oil_was_formed/revision/1; accessed December 5, 2016)

Bilham, Roger. "Birth of the Himalaya." PBS Online. (www.pbs.org/wgbh/nova/everest/earth/birth.html; accessed December 5, 2016)

Bressan, David. "James Hutton (3 June 1726-26 March 1797): We Find No Vestige of a Beginning, no Prospect of an End." Field of Science: A Science Blog Network. June 5, 2010. (historyofgeology.fieldofscience.com/2010/06/james-hutton-3-june-1726-26-march-1797.html; accessed December 5, 2016)

Brightmore, Jamie. "Deep Time: A History of the Earth—Interactive Infographic." (deeptime.info; accessed December 5, 2016)

British Museum. *Life and Death: Pompeii and Herculaneum* exhibit. March 28-September 29, 2013. (www.britishmuseum.org/whats_on/exhibitions/pompeii_and_herculaneum/pompeii_live/eruption_timeline.aspx; accessed December 5, 2016)

Columbia News. "Remembered: Marie Tharp, Pioneering Mapmaker of the Ocean Floor." November 14, 2007. (www.columbia.edu/cu/news/06/08/tharp.html; accessed December 5, 2016)

Cutler, Alan. *The Seashell on the Mountaintop*. New York: Dutton, 2003.

Dover Museum. "White Cliffs of Dover." (www.dovermuseum.co.uk/Information-Resources /Articles–Factsheets/White-Cliffs-of-Dover.aspx; accessed December 5, 2016)

Ellsworth, W. L. "Earthquake History, 1769-1989," chapter 6 of "The San Andreas Fault System, California," edited by R. E. Wallace (U.S. Geological Survey Professional Paper 1515, pp. 152-87), excerpted as "The Great 1906 San Francisco Earthquake" by United States Geological Survey. (earthquake.usgs.gov/regional/nca/1906/18april; accessed December 5, 2016)

Feulner, George, Christian Hallmann, and Hendrik Kienert. "Snowball Cooling After Algal Rise." *Nature Geoscience* 8, no. 9 (2015): 659-62.

Fischman, Josh. "Best View Ever of Hidden Seafloor Revealed in New Images [Slide Show]: Scientists Use Satellites to Produce Astoundingly Detailed Pictures of Unmapped Terrain." *Scientific American* online. October 3, 2014. (www.scientificamerican.com /article/best-view-ever-of-hidden-seafloor-revealed-in-new-images-slide-show; accessed December 5, 2016)

Hazen, Robert M. *The Story of Earth*. New York: Viking, 2012.

Head, Lloyd. "One Boy's Experience: A Member of the Roosevelt Boys' Club Writes of His Experience During and After the Great Earthquake." Virtual Museum of the City of San Francisco. (www.sfmuseum.net/1906/ew7.html; accessed December 5, 2016)

History.com staff. "Deconstructing History: Pompeii." A+E Networks. 2010. (www.history .com/topics/ancient-history/pompeii; accessed December 5, 2016)

Hoffman, Hillel J. "The Permian Extinction–When Life Nearly Came to an End." *National Geographic* online. (science.nationalgeographic.com/science/prehistoric-world /permian-extinction/#page=3; accessed December 5, 2016)

Hoffman, Paul F., et al. "What Caused the Snowball Earths?" Snowball Earth, 2006-9. (www .snowballearth.org/cause.html; accessed December 5, 2016)

Howard, Brian Clark. "What Are the Odds a Meteorite Could Kill You?" *National Geographic* online. February 9, 2016. (news.nationalgeographic.com/2016/02/160209-meteorite -death-india-probability-odds; accessed December 5, 2016)

Longden, Tom. "Bruce Heezen." *Des Moines Register* online. (data.desmoinesregister.com /famous-iowans/bruce-heezen; accessed December 5, 2016)

Lutgens, Frederick K., and Edward J. Tarbuck. *Essentials of Geology*. Upper Saddle River, N.J.: Pearson Prentice Hall, 2009.

MacDougall, Doug. *Why Geology Matters: Decoding the Past, Anticipating the Future*. Berkeley: University of California Press, 2001.

Mathez, Edmond A. "James Hutton: The Founder of Modern Geology." Excerpted from *Earth: Inside and Out* (New York: New Press, 2000). American Museum of Natural History. (www.amnh.org/explore/resource-collections/earth-inside-and-out/james-hutton-the -founder-of-modern-geology; accessed December 5, 2016)

McPhee, John. *Annals of the Former World.* New York: Farrar, Straus and Giroux, 1998.

Mervine, Evelyn. "A Famous Ocean Floor Map." American Geophysical Union. December 24, 2010. (blogs.agu.org/georneys/2010/12/24/a-famous-ocean-floor-map; accessed December 2, 2016)

National Geographic. *The Story of Earth.* 2011. Television movie available on YouTube. (www .youtube.com/watch?v=SYOarZKipnU; accessed December 5, 2016)

National Geographic News. "The Deadliest Tsunami in History?" January 7, 2005. (news .nationalgeographic.com/news/2004/12/1227_041226_tsunami.html; accessed December 5, 2016)

National Geographic Society. "Plate Tectonics: The Changing Shape of the Earth." 2013. (nationalgeographic.org/media/plate-tectonics; accessed December 5, 2016)

Northern Arizona University. "History of Life on Earth." (jan.ucc.nau.edu/~lrm22/lessons /timeline/24_hours.html; accessed December 5, 2016)

NOVA Evolution Library. "The Cambrian Explosion." PBS. 2001. (www.pbs.org/wgbh /evolution/library/03/4/l_034_02.html; accessed December 5, 2016)

——. "What Killed the Dinosaurs?" PBS. 2001. (www.pbs.org/wgbh/evolution/extinction /dinosaurs/asteroid.html; accessed December 5, 2016)

O'Connor, J. J., and E. F. Robertson. "James Hutton." January 2004. School of Mathematics and Statistics, University of St. Andrews, Scotland. (www-history.mcs.st-and.ac.uk /Biographies/Hutton_James.html; accessed December 5, 2016)

PBS. *Making of North America: Life.* A NOVA production by WGBH Boston/2015 WGBH Educational Foundation. (www.pbs.org/video/2365603832; accessed December 5, 2016)

——. *Making of North America: Origins.* A NOVA production by WGBH Boston/2015 WGBH Educational Foundation. (www.pbs.org/video/2365598165; accessed December 5, 2016)

Pogge von Strandmann, Philip A. E., et al. "Selenium Isotope Evidence for Progressive Oxidation of the Neoproterozoic Biosphere." *Nature Communications* 6, no. 10157 (2015). (www.nature.com/ncomms/2015/151218/ncomms10157/full/ncomms10157 .html#auth-1; accessed December 5, 2016)

Powell, Alvin. "How Earth Was Watered." Phys.org. February 28, 2014. (phys.org/news/2014 -02-earth.html#jCp; accessed December 5, 2016)

Press, Frank. Raymond Siever, John Grotzinger, and Jordan H. Thomas. *Understanding Earth.* New York: W. H. Freeman and Company, 2004.

Simpson, Ernest S. "The Wisdom of the Dogs." Virtual Museum of the City of San Francisco. Originally published in the *San Francisco Chronicle.* May 6, 1906. (www.sfmuseum.net /1906/ew6.html; accessed December 5, 2016.)

Sokolowski, Thomas J. "The Great Alaskan Earthquake and Tsunamis of 1964." National Oceanographic and Atmospheric Administration. (wcatwc.arh.noaa.gov/about/64quake .htm; accessed December 5, 2016)

Taylor, Alan. "Ten Years Since the 2004 Indian Ocean Tsunami." *Atlantic*. December 26, 2014. (www.theatlantic.com/photo/2014/12/ten-years-since-the-2004-indian-ocean -tsunami/100878; accessed December 5, 2016)

Thompson, Keith. "Vestiges of James Hutton." *American Scientist* 89, no. 3 (2001): 212. (www.americanscientist.org/issues/pub/vestiges-of-james-hutton; accessed December 5, 2016)

Understanding Evolution. "The Origins of Tetrapods." University of California Museum of Paleontology. (evolution.berkeley.edu/evolibrary/article/evograms_04; accessed December 5, 2016)

———. "The Nitty Gritty on Radioisotopic Dating." University of California Museum of Paleontology. (evolution.berkeley.edu/evolibrary/article/radioisotopic_dating; accessed December 5, 2016)

United States Geological Survey. "Faults FAQs." (www2.usgs.gov/faq/categories/9838/3312; accessed December 5, 2016)

———. "Casualties and Damage After the 1906 Earthquake." April 7, 2016. (earthquake.usgs .gov/regional/nca/1906/18april/casualties.php; accessed December 5, 2016)

University of California Museum of Paleontology. "Alfred Wegener (1880-1930)." (www .ucmp.berkeley.edu/history/wegener.html; accessed December 5, 2016)

University of Maryland College of Computer, Mathematical, and Natural Sciences. "New Study Zeros in on Plate Tectonics' Start Date." January 21, 2016. (cmns.umd.edu/news -events/features/3404; accessed December 5, 2016)

USDA Natural Resources Conservation Service. "What Is Soil?" (www.nrcs.usda.gov/wps /portal/nrcs/detail/soils/edu/?cid=nrcs142p2_054280; accessed September 16, 2016)

Valley, John W. "Early Earth." *Elements* 2, no. 4 (2006): 201-4.

Woods Hole Oceanographic Institution. "Marie Tharp Bio." December 12, 2006. (www.whoi .edu/sbl/liteSite.do?litesiteid=9092&articleId=13407; accessed December 5, 2016)

Yale University. "Last Dinosaur Before Mass Extinction Discovered." *Science Daily*. July 13, 2011. (www.sciencedaily.com/releases/2011/07/110712211016.htm; accessed December 5, 2016)

IS CLIMATE CHANGE A REAL THING?

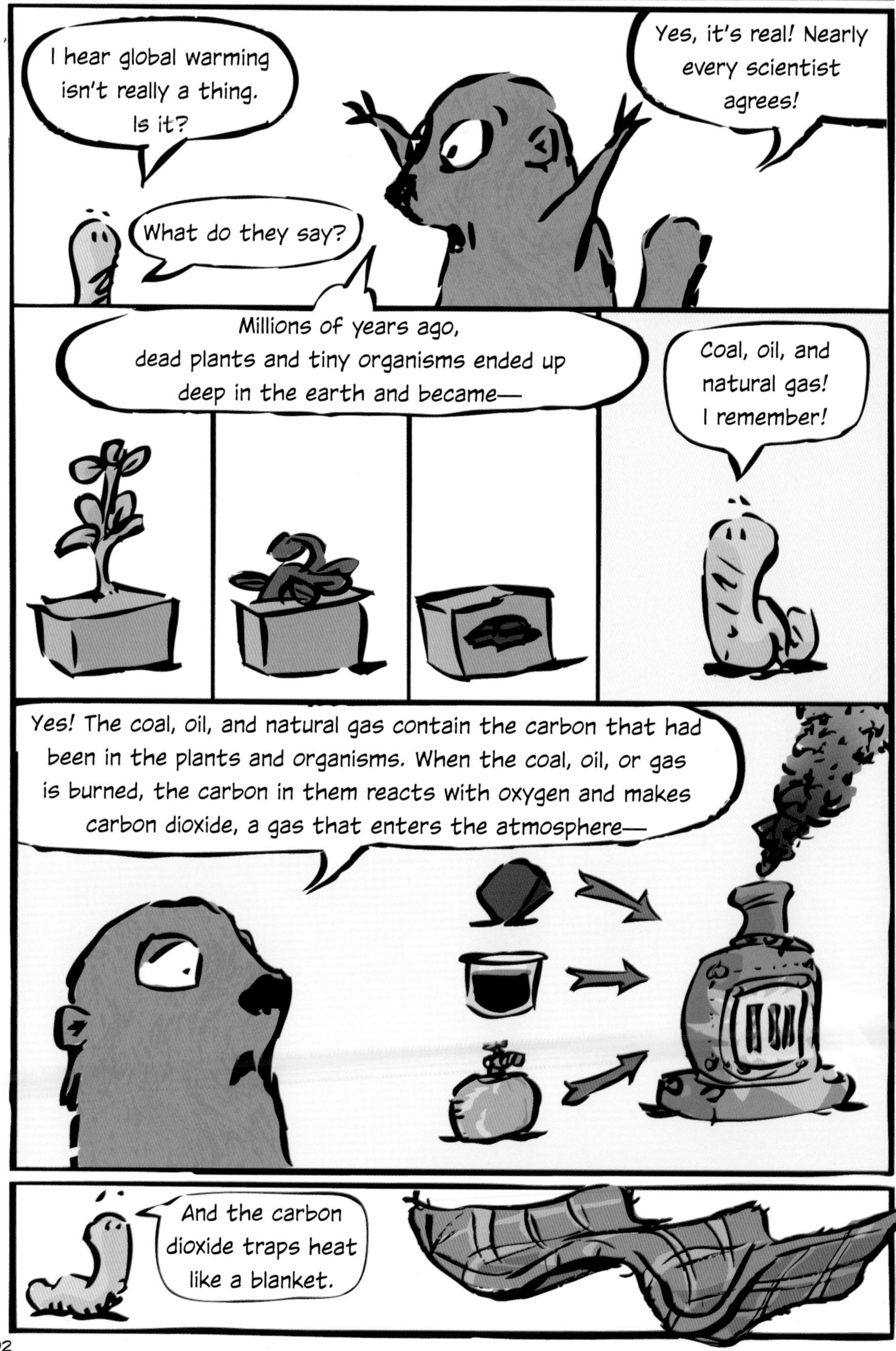

I hear global warming isn't really a thing. Is it?
Yes, it's real! Nearly every scientist agrees!
What do they say?
Millions of years ago, dead plants and tiny organisms ended up deep in the earth and became—
Coal, oil, and natural gas! I remember!
Yes! The coal, oil, and natural gas contain the carbon that had been in the plants and organisms. When the coal, oil, or gas is burned, the carbon in them reacts with oxygen and makes carbon dioxide, a gas that enters the atmosphere—
And the carbon dioxide traps heat like a blanket.

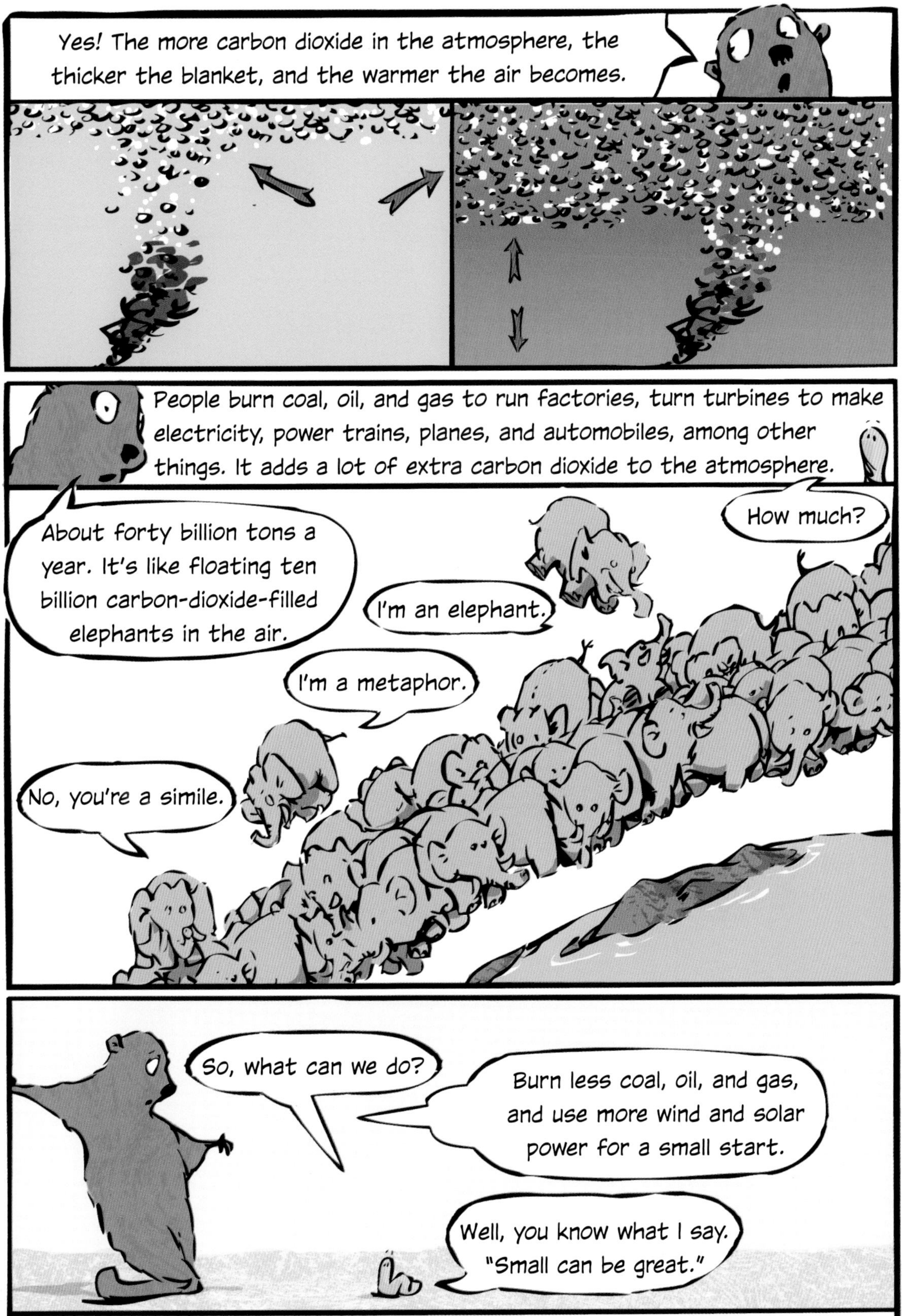
Yes! The more carbon dioxide in the atmosphere, the thicker the blanket, and the warmer the air becomes.
People burn coal, oil, and gas to run factories, turn turbines to make electricity, power trains, planes, and automobiles, among other things. It adds a lot of extra carbon dioxide to the atmosphere.
How much?
About forty billion tons a year. It's like floating ten billion carbon-dioxide-filled elephants in the air.
I'm an elephant.
I'm a metaphor.
No, you're a simile.
So, what can we do?
Burn less coal, oil, and gas, and use more wind and solar power for a small start.
Well, you know what I say. "Small can be great."

LEARN MORE HERE: → ScienceStraightTalk.com

For Deborah, my touchstone
—D.B.

For Ryan, Melissa, and Renee
—M.P.

The illustrations in this book were hand drawn and scanned;
color and texture were added digitally.

The text type was set in CC Wild Words Lower.
The display type was set in Road Art.

Library of Congress Cataloging-in-Publication Data
Names: Brown, Don, 1949- author. I. Perfit, Michael R., 1949- author.
Title: Older than dirt / by Don Brown & Dr. Mike Perfit.
Description: Boston ; New York : Houghton Mifflin Harcourt, [2017]
Identifiers: LCCN 2016018643 I ISBN 9780544805033 (hardcover)
Subjects: LCSH: Historical geology–Juvenile literature. I Earth sciences–
Juvenile literature. I Earth (Planet)–Origin–Juvenile literature.
Classification: LCC QE28.3 .B76 2017 T DDC 551.7–dc23
LC record available at https://lccn.loc.gov/2016018643

Manufactured in China
SCP 10 9 8 7 6 5 4 3 2 1
4500654533